Debating Immigration in the Age of Terrorism, Polarization, and Trump

Debating Immigration in the Age of Terrorism, Polarization, and Trump

Joshua Woods

C. Damien Arthur

LEXINGTON BOOKS
Lanham • Boulder • New York • London

Published by Lexington Books
An imprint of The Rowman & Littlefield Publishing Group, Inc.
4501 Forbes Boulevard, Suite 200, Lanham, Maryland 20706
www.rowman.com

Unit A, Whitacre Mews, 26-34 Stannary Street, London SE11 4AB

Copyright © 2017 by Lexington Books

All rights reserved. No part of this book may be reproduced in any form or by any electronic or mechanical means, including information storage and retrieval systems, without written permission from the publisher, except by a reviewer who may quote passages in a review.

British Library Cataloguing in Publication Information Available

Library of Congress Cataloging-in-Publication Data Available

LCCN 2017947139 | ISBN 978-1-4985-3521-2 (hardback : alk. paper) | ISBN 978-1-4985-3522-9 (ebook)

♾ ™ The paper used in this publication meets the minimum requirements of American National Standard for Information Sciences—Permanence of Paper for Printed Library Materials, ANSI/NISO Z39.48-1992.

Printed in the United States of America

Contents

Acknowledgments	vii
Introduction	ix
1 Grand Contradictions	1
2 The Perceived Threat of Terrorism and the Authoritarian Turn in Attitudes toward Immigration	27
3 The News Media, Terrorism, and the Immigration Threat Nexus	47
4 The President Goes Negative	71
5 Congressional Hearings: Immigration Frames in Expert Testimonies	97
6 The Partisan Fear of Terrorism, the Polarization of Immigration Attitudes, and the 2016 Presidential Campaign	119
Conclusion	147
References	157
Index	189
About the Authors	195

Acknowledgments

We would like to convey gratitude to several students from West Virginia University for their help in coding newspaper articles, including Katherine Burns, Tyler Burroughs, Lynnsie Doty, Allison Fleming, Kimberly Hash, Casey Layne, Chelsea Morphis, Matt Nichols, Madelaine Richards, Danielle Steel, Jonathan Vanscoy, and Ashley Zultanky. We also thank Richard Anderson, Sophia Mills, Jordyn Reed, and Derek Taylor for their contributions to the research and coding for the chapter on congressional hearings. Special thanks to Jill Woods for creating the index for this book, and her editorial work. Finally, we thank *Presidential Studies Quarterly* and *Sociological Spectrum* for allowing us to republish parts of two journal articles, including "The Threat of Terrorism and the Changing Public Discourse on Immigration after September 11" (*Sociological Spectrum*) and "The Contextual Presidency: The Negative Shift in Presidential Immigration Rhetoric" (*Presidential Studies Quarterly*).

Introduction

Much of the immigration debate in the United States rests on the issue of openness. Two questions in particular—How open should the door be? and What type of immigrant should walk through it?—have characterized policy disputes for well over a century (Beasley, 2006). In the current debate, expansionists want to see more legal immigrants in the United States and greater tolerance and respect for the estimated 11 million unauthorized immigrants in the country (Frum & Friedersdorf, 2017; Hunt, 2002; Democratic Party Platform, 2016). Restrictionists favor lower levels of immigration stronger borders, and tighter law enforcement measures to stop unauthorized migration (Frum & Friedersdorf, 2017; Hunt, 2002; Republican Party Platform, 2016). The first aim of this book is to describe how these opposing views materialized in public opinion, the news media, political rhetoric, and, ultimately, in immigration policy at the start of the twenty-first century. Our second and more formidable task is to explain how and why the restrictionists rose to prominence during this period.

Much of our argument rests on the idea that history matters, that the dominant narrative about immigration is in constant flux, and that the "winner" of the immigration debate is determined by the joint effects of current events, enduring traditions, and political-economic forces. Although this book has a wide historical scope that begins with President William Jefferson Clinton's first election campaign and concludes with the presidential election of 2016, much of our analysis focuses on the first decade following the terrorist attacks on September 11, 2001 (9/11). This was a period of national insecurity, an anxious decade when the threat of terrorism loomed higher in the public mind-set than during any prior period in U.S. history (Woods, 2012). The nation also experienced its worst economic crisis since the Great Depression (Arthur, 2014; Arthur & Woods, 2013). For many Americans, financial worries lingered throughout much of this period. While imagining job loss and violence on a grand scale, Americans also learned about record increases in the unauthorized immigrant population (D'Appollonia, 2012). Numerous policymakers and media pundits fueled the securitization of the immigration debate, often linking immigration policy to the threat of terrorism and arguing that increased border security and immigration law enforcement were necessary tools in the war on terror (Alexseev, 2006). Meanwhile the internet and social media solidified its position as a dominant media outlet, decentralized the debate over immigration, and gave extreme anti-immigrant organizations the opportunity to build their networks, make inroads to the mainstream debate, and voice their opinions directly to a growing number of Americans (Woods, Manning & Matz, 2015).

In the first post-9/11 decade, these conditions helped the restrictionists reactivate certain long-standing beliefs and cultural orientations and gain several victories in the realms of media, public opinion, politics, and policy (Arthur & Woods, 2017). These conditions also set the stage for one of the most contentious presidential campaigns in U.S. history, during which the immigration debate took center stage and people's attitudes toward immigration, as well as their concerns about terrorism, became deeply polarized.

Our approach to the immigration debate avoids deterministic claims and grand-scale projections. Although we argue with conviction that the climate of fear surrounding terrorist attacks has played an important role in shaping the debate, the fear itself and its effects on social attitudes and public policy were neither inevitable nor necessarily long lasting. There is no single resounding force that pushes the debate in one direction or another. There is no straightforward theory of human nature or psychology that properly explains the rise or fall of either side. The debate is rooted in history, but it also responds to the moving pieces of everyday politics, propaganda, and current events. Given its ideological complexity, we can see both similarities and differences between today's debate and those of the distant past.

Consider, for instance, the public discussion of immigration at the beginning of our Republic, just after we fought a revolution for independence, when we constructed a series of legislation called the *Alien and Sedition Acts*, which enabled the United States to restrict the number of immigrants granted access to the new country. In these acts, we made it harder for foreigners to become citizens of the United States, and more difficult for immigrants to vote. Lastly, the legislation empowered the new U.S. government to forcefully remove immigrants who were considered to be a threat, both culturally and bodily, from the geographical boundaries of the country.

Our immigration policy is riddled with an "us versus them" undergirding that has manifested itself time and again. For instance, more recently, Franklin Delano Roosevelt used an Executive Order to round up and force

Introduction

Americans with nationalities from "hostile" countries to live in internme
camps, as the government assessed their loyalties and trustworthiness. Ro
sevelt's *Executive Order 9066,* in 1942, was a response to the Decemb
1941 Pearl Harbor attack. He claimed the military response and detention
American citizens was to protect "against espionage and against sabotage to
national-defense" (National Archives, 2017). The Order was used to displace
more than 100,000 Japanese-Americans, holding them in internment camps
as their loyalty was questioned and many of their lives destroyed. They were
singled out because their race was the same race as those who perpetrated the
atrocious acts of terror at Pearl Harbor.

In our 1954 *Operation Wetback* approach we instituted a program that fundamentally defined what we meant, culturally, by Americans and non-Americans—the dominant in-group defined the out-group. Hyman and Iskander (2016) argued that "Operation Wetback's enforcement approach—assuming those who were not white had dubious citizenship—" showed how we used fear, violence, and racial hatred to remove immigrants without their input or due process. The prevailing idea is still embraced by contemporary restrictionists. In November 2016, for instance, Trump said,

> "I like Ike," right? The expression. "I like Ike." Moved a million-and-a-half illegal immigrants out of this country, moved them just beyond the border. They came back. Moved them again beyond the border, they came back. Didn't like it. Moved them way south. They never came back. (Hyman & Iskander, 2016)

In a reversal of sorts, the 1965 *Hart-Celler Act* focused on familial relationships and connections rather than country quotas (Hunt, 2002). One scholar argued that "Congress opened the door to redefining 'immigrant' and the problem of immigration" with this legislation, offering credence to the notion that America is a country of immigrants and welcomes their participation and contributions to our civic life (Hunt, 2002, p. 82).

The expansionist approach continued to define immigration policy in the United States for years—focusing on the problems and solutions to refugees in the *1976 Immigration Act,* the *1980 Refugee Act,* and the *1986 Immigration Reform and Control Act* (Hunt, 2002). Since the *Hart-Celler Act,* "most of the legislative changes have generally been in the direction of liberalizing immigration policy measures" (Hunt, 2002, p. 84). Recently, however, particularly after 9/11, in the *Enhanced Border Security and Visa Entry Reform Act of 2002,* "there has been strong and consistent support for a restrictionist approach to limit the number of immigrants and control the diversity of the composition of immigrant streams" (Hunt, 2002, p. 84).

Variations of these approaches to immigration policy have existed from the *Alien and Sedition Acts* to President Trump's current attempt to "ban"

Muslims from entering the United States, because they are allegedly "members or sympathizers of terrorist groups" and they have "hostile attitudes to our principles" (Park, 2016). Just as the *1798 Alien and Sedition Acts* emboldened the United States to restrict immigration or deport dangerous immigrants posing threats or coming from hostile nations, Trump has argued that "We must suspend immigration from regions linked with terrorism until a proven vetting method is in place" (Park, 2016). To some extent, we have come full circle with Trump's attempted Muslim Ban through an Executive Order in 2017. Despite the administration's failure to successfully write an Executive Order that could withstand judicial review, it showed that authoritarian sentiment pervades our immigration policy now just as it did during the early years of the Republic.

Another important historical parallel to the theme of this book was the immigration debate of the late nineteenth century. The social and economic conditions of the day—the turmoil of post–Civil War race relations, rapid industrialization, urbanization, and the continued Westward expansion—were no doubt unique. The communication systems that mediated the debate were far removed from today's fast-moving information technology. There was no radio or television, no twenty-four-hour news cycle, no websites, no blogs, no online social networks, no internet, no presidential Tweets. Unlike its current position, the federal government played a limited role in regulating immigration (Hunt, 2002). The federal government did not take control of immigration until 1890 when it developed the nation's first federal immigration station on Ellis Island. California, which is now home to more foreign-born residents than any other state, had only recently joined the union. The immigrant groups that were most feared by the non-immigrant public, denounced in the press, and targeted for prohibition did not look or sound like today's primary targets (Dorsey, 2007).

However, despite these obvious differences, the politics of exclusion of the late nineteenth century were similar to the contemporary context of exclusion (Beasley, 2004). Back then the debate reached a poignant climax when the Congress put forward the *Chinese Exclusion Act* in 1882. Upheld by the Supreme Court in 1889, the law restricted immigration from China by placing heavy fines and the threat of jail time on ship captains carrying Chinese immigrants to the United States. A single immigrant group dominated the discussion during this period, particularly in the American West where Chinese immigrants had initially been recruited to work as laborers in the minerals and railroad industries.

The central argument against Chinese immigration rested on a vivid immigrant threat narrative involving a mix of social and economic hazards. These risks were dramatized and widely disseminated in news reports, editorials, and political speeches. The Chinese would steal jobs from Americans rather

Introduction

than contribute to economic growth. They would alter mainstream traditions culture, and values rather than embrace them. Chinese immigrants would add to the nation's problems of drug abuse, crime, and neighborhood disorde rather than promote hard work, innovation, and democracy. At the end of th day, the Chinese would remain loyal to the old country and undermine th new one.

Future commentators and scholars would demonstrate that most of these worries were unfounded. But at the time, fears of Chinese immigration had a profound influence on voting patterns and served as a storehouse of political capital for those who used it to push for legislative changes. The *Chinese Exclusion Act* itself states in its opening line that newcomers from China "endanger the good order of certain localities within the territory."

The current debate is dominated by similar pessimistic prognostications and appeals to fear, uncertainty, and risk. As in the past, restrictionists have identified a single immigrant group—this time Latinos—as the main source of the danger. Perceived threats to the economy, culture, and national security are still deeply woven in the social consciousness and political atmosphere surrounding the debate (Hunt, 2002).[1] Ominous claims about Latinos and Mexicans are being voiced louder and with greater regularity in news media and politics than careful reasoning and scientific assessments, as evidenced by Donald Trump's 2015–2016 presidential campaign during which, among other disparaging comments, he likened Mexican immigrants to criminals, drug dealers, and rapists.

Most non-Hispanic Americans harbor negative attitudes toward the influx of immigrants from Mexico (Bell, 2014). Several prominent politicians and other officials have gained popularity for their fiery support of restrictionist policies, such as reducing legal immigration, tightening border security, and creating harsher law enforcement measures for dealing with undocumented immigrants. The reality has created a difficult "relationship between borders and citizenship" which, as Cisneros (2014) argues, "breeds perpetual anxiety over the purported sanctity of the border, the security of a nation, and the integrity of civic identity." The laws governing immigration, particularly at the state level, have reflected a similar authoritarian tendency, while expansionist projects have been quashed or put on hold, especially at the federal level (Cisneros, 2011).

The politics of exclusion of the past, notwithstanding its anachronistic components, represents the cultural backbone of the current debate (Hunt, 2002). The idea that immigrants negatively affect the country comes to mind so easily today partly because it came to mind so often in the past. Put differently, the worries and concerns about immigration at the start of the twenty-first century were not new (Hunt, 2002). They were built upon a foundation of stereotypical beliefs, errors in attribution, and prejudice that formed far

xiv *Introduction*

before the events of 9/11 or the financial crisis of 2007–2008. The specific characteristics of this cognitive framework in the early twenty-first century, though unique in many respects, were anchored in a "dominant symbolic repertoire" (Maney, Woehrle & Coy, 2005; Williams, 2002) that has existed for decades.

At the same time, the expansionists' messaging and framing of immigration also has a cultural backbone (Hunt, 2002). Few countries have celebrated the immigrant experience with the same amount of enthusiasm and consistency as the United States. As Franklin Roosevelt declared, "Remember, remember always, that all of us, and you and I especially, are descended from immigrants and revolutionists" (Caty, 2004). References to the United States as a "nation of immigrants" in news and popular culture are as old as they are clichéd. Praise for immigrants, or at least acknowledgment of immigration's important role in U.S. history, can even be found in the statements of restrictionist pundits and politicians (Beasley, 2006). Immigration has long been perceived by many Americans as a source of strength, vitality, and innovation, and as a proving ground for the American dream. Immigrants certainly suffer under the force of several negative stereotypes, but they also benefit, in some respects, from the popular belief that newcomers are hardworking and creative (Beasley, 2006).

The question, of course, is which of immigration's cultural backbones is carrying the current debate? To begin answering this question, we now turn to our theoretical framework for explaining how restrictionists prevailed in the early 2000s.

THE SOCIAL AMPLIFICATION OF IMMIGRATION THREAT

Our theoretical approach to the immigration debate draws on a conceptual framework developed by Kasperson et al. (1988) called the "social amplification of risk." Their work builds on multiple academic traditions to explain how hazardous situations or "risk events" affect society. The amplification framework is most commonly applied to people's perceptions of emerging environmental hazards, such as a massive chemical spill, or public health risks like mad cow disease. The underlying assumption of the theory is that only a small number of people have direct experiences with risk events. Almost all the images, interpretations, and information about risk events travel through intermediaries before reaching an audience or "receiver." As the information passes through intermediaries, it is filtered and transformed in a way that either amplifies or attenuates the audience's perceptions of the threat (Pidgeon, Kasperson & Slovic, 2003).

These assumptions fit the case of 9/11 quite well. Although thousands of people tragically experienced the attacks firsthand, almost all Americans learned about 9/11 through intermediaries. Broadcast news networks were among the most influential intermediaries in the first days after 9/11. But over the years, a variety of other individuals, groups, and organizations, from teachers, activist groups, and scientists to government agencies, political parties, and presidents, disseminated information about 9/11 and subsequent terrorist attacks. As argued by several social researchers, the most dominant American intermediaries of the day amplified the perceived threat of terrorism among a large portion of the U.S. population, which elevated public support for the "war on terror" and several harsh counterterrorism measures (Woods, 2012).

Intermediaries have also filtered information about risk events involving immigration. In fact, the debate itself is a contest between intermediaries who wish to either amplify or attenuate public concerns about immigration for the sake of shaping public policy. After 9/11, the most powerful intermediaries in American society developed a link between the risk events of immigration and terrorism, which amplified public worries and risk perceptions of both issues and bolstered support for new laws and government measures with far-reaching consequences for immigrants.

But who are the most influential intermediaries of the immigration debate? And what explains their willingness and ability to influence people's thoughts and feelings about immigration? Under what conditions does information about immigration amplify or attenuate perceptions of threat? How are the public's perceptions of threat related to actual policies and government actions?

Whether a risk event produces an increase or decrease in risk perceptions depends on a range of factors. First, intermediaries are not independent actors, randomly dispersed through a social system, who have an equal likelihood of mass producing information about immigration. Rather, they occupy social positions in a hierarchy and carry out roles that are dictated by cultural and institutional structures. The way intermediaries filter and transform information about immigration depends on their cultural and cognitive biases, organizational values, and material interests. Their ability to spread information depends on their social position. Actors of all types—friends, family members, coworkers—can play the role of intermediary, but some intermediaries have far more access to receivers than others.

Intermediaries in privileged positions control information about immigration on a large scale through mass media. These intermediaries systematically select and repeat certain words, phrases, ideas and images, and shape messages using rhetorical devices and evocative imagery. Although there is always a struggle between intermediaries with conflicting organizational interests and ideological positions, a prevailing discourse on both immigration and terrorism emerged after 9/11 (Woods, 2012). This "dominant symbolic repertoire" (Maney, Woehrle & Coy, 2005; Williams, 2002) provided a structure for people and policymakers to interpret immigration threat, and thereby constrained their attitudes and actions toward immigration policies. As discussed below, this book investigates this process by analyzing the filtered messages and frames created and dispersed by three important intermediaries, including print and broadcast news organizations, presidents, and members of Congress.

Moving beyond the messages of important intermediaries, we also examine the individual psychological processes that take place as individuals process these messages. As suggested by the social amplification framework, a person's perception of danger depends not only on the social and cultural context, but also on individual-level cognitive and affective processes (Woods & Marciniak, 2017). Sociological and cultural perspectives explain the content of the dominant symbolic repertoire on immigration, but they cannot explain how any of the repertoire's specific messages, symbols, or imagery become meaningful to individuals. An overly social perspective also fails to explain the relationship between an individual's concerns about terrorism and his or her attitudes toward immigration. Therefore, the overarching goal of this book is to combine sociological, psychological, and political approaches to explain important changes in the immigration debate after 9/11—one of the most spectacular and tragic risk events in U.S. history.

This book offers a broad interdisciplinary approach to the recent changes in the U.S. immigration debate. Our story accounts for multiple factors, including history, culture and politics, power, organizations, social psychological processes, and political change. The relationship between immigration law, human emotion, social cognition, organizational behavior, political economy, and fateful historical events is as complex as it is abstract. Examining this relationship in the contemporary context requires a lengthy voyage across academic disciplines, a synthesis of seemingly contradictory assumptions about human thought and behavior, and a grasp of research traditions so vast and confusing that an accurate rendering may seem implausible. And yet, to tell the story of the contemporary immigration debate in any other way is to tell it in part. Our goals may be ambitious, but they are also supported by a growing interdisciplinary tradition in the social sciences. A nation's reaction to foreigners has as much to do with sociology as it does with political science, economics, and psychology. Without drawing on knowledge from each of these disciplines, our understanding of the immigration debate will remain mundane, partial, and imperfect. There are many books that address one aspect of our argument, through various institutions, but fail to comprehensively address this multifaceted topical issue. Therefore, we maintain that there is no *other* book that does what this book seeks to accomplish.

Introduction xvii

CHAPTER SUMMARY

Our plan for realizing this goal begins with chapter 1, "Grand Contradictions." One of the most interesting facets of the ongoing contest over immigration policy resides in the fact that many of the nation's most powerful social actors promote the expansionist position, and yet restrictionists have still found a strong voice in American politics, media, and public opinion. This contradiction only becomes more surprising when we scrutinize the four most common restrictionist claims about the effects of immigration on American society. Although much has been written and spoken about the negative influence of immigrants on the economy, crime rate, national security, and culture, we find these claims wanting when tested against the findings of peer-reviewed studies and scientific investigation.

Even though anti-immigrant rhetoric is based more on myth than on empirical observation, the restrictionists' positions became more attractive to many Americans and played a greater role in politics after the devastating terrorist attacks of 9/11. Chapter 2, "The Perceived Threat of Terrorism and the Authoritarian Turn in Attitudes toward Immigration," begins to explain these changes by examining how and why people's concerns about the terrorist threat increased and remained elevated for more than a decade after 9/11. The events of 9/11 provoked a deeply felt, widely shared, long-term understanding of terrorism that encouraged a range of authoritarian values, attitudes, and beliefs, including immigration policy preferences. Drawing on four diverse research traditions, we focus on how the perceived threat of terrorism has reinforced restrictionist views on immigration at the individual level.

In chapter 3, "The News Media, Terrorism, and the Immigration Threat Nexus," we analyze the news media's portrayal of terrorism and immigration issues. This chapter uses articles from the opinion-leading press to investigate how the news media's repertoire of negative portrayals changed after 9/11. We find that the percentage of negative frames involving not only terrorism but also other non-terrorist threats increased significantly in the post-9/11 period. The elevated frequency of negative frames in press coverage of immigrants was found in two leading newspapers, the *New York Times* and the *Wall Street Journal*, but the increase was significantly greater in the latter periodical.

In chapter 4, "The President Goes Negative," we study presidential immigration rhetoric before and after 9/11, and highlight the disconnect between the positivity about immigration in Party Platforms and the negativity in presidential rhetoric, including the speeches of presidents Clinton, Bush, and Obama. We use the platforms as a baseline for each president's stance on immigration, which reveals how presidents sometimes deviate from their expected positions as the social context changes. This analysis offers a descriptive and explanatory understanding of how contextual factors, particularly terrorism, are associated with the use of negative frames in presidential immigration rhetoric. We argue that the content of presidential rhetoric is typically determined by the context in which it is given rather than an autonomous entrepreneurial policy exposition.

Chapter 5, "Congressional Hearings: Immigration Frames in Expert Testimonies," seeks to determine if the context of congressional hearings can predict how members of Congress and immigration experts use negative immigration narratives. In building a comprehensive database on the discussion of immigration, we coded remarks from every congressional hearing from the 103rd Congress (1993–1994) through the 109th Congress (2005–2007), and mapped trends in the framing of immigration in congressional debates. Rather than determining if congressional attention to immigration is capable of effecting change in the policy narrative, as an entrepreneurial mechanism of power, this chapter provides a discussion on the importance of context in congressional leadership, which offers a more enriching analysis of the immigration discussion.

In chapter 6, "The Partisan Fear of Terrorism, the Polarization of Immigration Attitudes, and the 2016 Presidential Campaign" we extend the ideas discussed in chapters 2–5 to the most recent period. The presidential campaign of 2015–2016 included one of the fiercest and most polarized debates on immigration in decades. New concerns about terrorism rose high in the public mind-set as a handful of high-profile attacks took place in Europe and the United States, and pundits and politicians politicized the resettlement of Syrian refugees. By examining public opinion polls, news coverage, presidential rhetoric, and congressional discourse, this chapter explains how the authoritarian political culture that crystalized after 9/11 was reinforced and amplified by contemporary intermediaries, who used it to win the immigration debate during the run-up to the presidential election in 2016, and take the White House in 2017.

NOTE

1. See Carol Winkler (2006) who argues that each threat, although similar, is framed as new and shapes future behavior, as many "out-groups" resist the label of "terrorist." Moreover, she argues that this framework of each leader wherein every threat is labeled a new threat and requires a new response has fundamentally altered our political culture.

Chapter 1

Grand Contradictions

In the first years of the twenty-first century, several indicators of public opinion revealed growing animosity toward immigrants in the United States. Nativist groups attracted greater attention from mainstream media. Tougher border security and immigration law enforcement initiatives were born (Cisneros, 2014). American intelligence agencies became more focused on the immigrant population. The number of undocumented immigrants locked up each year was on the rise. Efforts to reform federal immigration laws stalled (Edwards & Herder, 2012). The idea that immigration threatens U.S. interests, a persistent belief in the past, became even more plausible to many Americans. In sum, the immigration debate in the early twenty-first century was marked by the dominance of restrictionist ideas.

It goes without saying that a rise in public concerns about immigration and an increase in restrictionist policies should correspond to a similar elevation in immigration's negative effects on the nation. If, for instance, a growth in violent crime could be linked to immigration, growing worries about a migrant influx would be understandable. However, based on a review of scientific studies, it appears that much of the fear about immigration is misplaced. The main goal of this chapter is to carefully summarize peer-reviewed research on several contentious issues in the American immigration debate of the early twenty-first century. Although some studies represent interesting exceptions, a substantial literature squarely contradicts what many restrictionists claim and what many Americans believe.

A comprehensive examination of research on the effects of immigration goes beyond the aims of this chapter. Aspiring to strategic abbreviation, the analysis here focuses on five assertions about immigration that have received the most attention in the news media. As discussed in chapter 3, anti-immigration rhetoric in news and political commentary takes many forms,

1

2 *Chapter 1*

but the great majority of claims involve at least one of five threats. First in popularity are references to "illegal immigration" and to the flow of unauthorized immigrants being out of control or increasing rapidly. The second most common claim involves the supposedly high rate of criminal behavior among immigrants compared to people born in the United States. Third in popularity are suggestions that immigration increases the threat of terrorism. Fourth are the negative frames associated with immigrant culture. Although xenophobic pronouncements of all sorts can be found in the public discussion of immigration, the most common *cultural* complaints appearing in the mainstream news media involve the supposed resistance of contemporary immigrants to assimilate to the dominant culture in the United States, and adopt the English language. And the fifth most common claim is that immigration harms various aspects of the U.S. economy.

THE NUMBER OF UNAUTHORIZED IMMIGRANTS

The unauthorized immigrant community in the United States has been the focal point of several different policy debates. Essential to the logic of these discussions is, of course, the number of unauthorized immigrants who reside in the country. Disagreements about the size of this population have existed for years, but the disparity between estimates increased substantially when the G.O.P.'s 2016 presidential hopefuls began campaigning with greater intensity in the summer of 2015. At the time, Donald Trump, the clear front-runner in the Republican primary race, had taken a harsh tone on immigration and repeatedly identified "illegal immigrants" as the source of major societal ills. Perhaps to accentuate the intensity of the problems, Trump publicized an estimate of the unauthorized immigrant population that far exceeded previous estimates. In July 2015, during a phone interview with MSNBC's *Morning Joe,* Trump stated that the number was 30 million to 34 million. When asked for the source of this information, Trump said, "I am hearing it from other people, and I have seen it written in various newspapers" (MSNBC, July 24, 2015).

As discussed below, the high end of Trump's estimate was three times greater than almost any serious approximation that was being made at the time (Baker & Rytina, 2012; Passel et al., 2014). Nevertheless, with the help of Trump, the estimate of "30 million" undocumented immigrants echoed through television news media for several months. In many cases, the figure emerged not in the context of live interviews, but rather when a news program read a Trump quote or aired a video clip from one of his speeches or press conferences. For instance, on July 3, 2015, CNN's *The Situation Room* played a clip of Trump defending his statement on the number of

Grand Contradictions 3

unauthorized immigrants and referring once again to the newspapers as his source: "All you have to do is read the newspapers. You have 20 million, 30 million, nobody knows what it is. It used to be 11 million. Now, today, I hear it's 11, but I don't think it's 11. I actually heard you probably have 30 million" (CNN, July 3, 2015, 6:00 PM EST).

Days later, Fox News host Geraldo Rivera used Trump's estimate of 30 million undocumented immigrants during a debate on the Fox News show *Hannity*; in response to Rivera's statement, conservative commentator Ann Coulter, who appeared as a guest during the same segment, said: "Right. Well, first of all, I want it on the record Geraldo and everyone else is now admitting there are a minimum of 30 million illegals in the country" (Fox News, July 9, 2015, 10:00 PM EST). Trump's talk of "30 million" was also aired or quoted, sans criticism, by Republican political consultant Karl Rove on *The O'Reilly Factor* (Fox News Network, July 13, 2015, 8:00 PM EST), by NBC News National Correspondent Peter Alexander on the *Today Show* (NBC News, July 24, 2015, 7:00 AM EST), and by CNN news host Don Lemon on *CNN Tonight* (CNN, October 30, 2015, 9:00 PM EST).

Even during otherwise confrontational interviews, Trump could reference the highly inflated "30 million" without being pressed to back up his claim with evidence. For instance, during a frosty interview with George Stephanopoulos on the Sunday morning program *This Week,* Trump made his case in this way:

> You have so many illegals. We don't even know how many illegals. I hear 11 million. I hear 30 million. The government has no idea. We have lost control of our country. We've lost control of our borders. The government has no idea how many illegals there are. I've been hearing 11 million for five years. Then the other day, I heard 30. (ABC News, August 23, 2015, 10:35 AM EST)

In a similar fashion, Trump inserted his estimate during an interview with Jake Tapper on CNN's *State of the Union* (CNN, October 25, 2015, 9:00 AM EST).

Although Trump may have been the loudest voice in this echo chamber, he was not alone. Before the ball dropped in Times Square at the end of 2015, several other authors, commentators, and talk show guests had reinforced the estimate of "30 million." Lisa Boothe, a Republican political consultant (Fox News Network, September 7, 2015, 4:42 PM EST), Fox News analyst Howard Kurtz (Fox News Network, August 2, 2015, 11:00 AM EST), conservative television personality Eric Bolling (Fox News Network, July 28, 2015, 5:00 PM EST), Geoffrey Lord, the former political director for Ronald Reagan (CNN, September 3, 2015, 7:00 AM EST), and Pax Hart, a 45-year-old software engineer and Trump supporter (CNN, August 21, 2015, 6.30

AM EST) each referenced the 30 million on a national television news show without attributing the estimate to Trump. Ann Coulter, in addition to the case mentioned above, made three other appearances on Fox News in August 2015 where she used this estimate. In fact, in one instance, Coulter upped the number to 50 million: "There are an absolute bare minimum of 30 million illegal immigrants, mostly from Central America coming across Mexico, mostly from Mexico. There are probably more like 50 million here" (Fox News Network, August 26, 2015, 9:00 PM EST).

The *30 million* was a myth, manufactured with intent by political partisans, which ignored decades of careful thinking and research on the topic. If, in the early 1970s, Trump had claimed that the government did not know the size of the unauthorized population, he would have been right. In 1972, the Immigration and Naturalization Service (INS), pressured to demonstrate its understanding of what some saw as a growing problem, offered the guess of roughly one million, but serious efforts to develop an accurate count did not begin until the mid-1970s (Kelly, 1977), and almost all the early attempts at constructing an estimate received heavy criticism from professional demographers. One of the only solid data points available at that time was the number of border apprehensions. During this period, immigrants were being apprehended at an increasing rate on the border while attempting to cross without documentation. However, using border apprehensions was a mistake, because this figure failed to account for outflows and therefore grossly overestimated the undocumented population. In other words, it assumed that most unauthorized persons who entered the United States were settling there, when in fact most of them were returning to their home countries after short stays (Bean et al., 2001).

As another example of problematic estimation, in 1974, the INS hired the outside research firm Lesko Associates to determine the number of undocumented immigrants (Corwin, 1982). For the task, Lesko used a survey of experts known as a Delphi panel. Six knowledgeable respondents (who remained unnamed in the final report) were chosen to give an independent estimate and offer their reasoning for the judgment. Lesko then compiled a report from these estimates, sent it back to the six respondents, and asked them if they would like to revise their initial assessments. This procedure was repeated twice before a final average was computed from the six guesses. In the first round, estimates ranged from 2.5 to 25.1 million; by the third round, the range was narrower at 4.2 to 11 million with a mean of 8.2 million (Kelly, 1977, 478). In retrospect, the obvious problem with the final estimate was that there were no suitable data sources, nor an appropriate rationale, available to the respondents at that time. According to numerous observers, including researchers from the Congressional Research Service who released a critical review of Lesko's report, the results of the Delphi panel told us

Grand Contradictions

very little about the size of the undocumented population (Kelly, 1977). To be fair, the panel was designed as a preliminary study and was not meant for drawing final conclusions. Moreover, the panel did provide an important lesson—namely, that educated guesswork is insufficient and naturally produces wide-ranging estimates.

Just as many of NASA's early rocket tests failed, preliminary efforts to count the unauthorized population proved difficult. But over the years, demographers established sounder methodologies and acquired the needed funding for serious data collection and analysis. Eventually, the variance in the approximations diminished and an expert consensus formed (Espenshade, 1995). Key to this progress was the residual method developed by Passel, Warren, Woodrow, Herr, and others starting in the early 1980s (e.g., Passel & Woodrow, 1984 and 1987; Warren & Passel, 1987; Heer & Passell, 1987). Estimates based on the residual method rest on the difference between two population figures: the total number of foreign-born people (legal and unauthorized) and the number of authorized immigrants (people with green cards, refugees, people granted asylum, and workers and students with temporary visas).

The first number is determined by a census or large-scale national survey. The Pew Research Center uses the Census Bureau's Current Population Survey (CPS) and the American Community Survey (ACS), which ask people about their place of birth and citizenship, but do not ask about their immigration status, legal or otherwise. Both represent massive data collection efforts compared to almost any other study of people. For instance, in 2014, the ACS carried out interviews with 2.3 million households.[1] The second number—total authorized immigrants—is based on data from the Department of Homeland Security and in the case of refugee numbers the Department of Health and Human Services. The difference between the first figure (the total number of foreign-born people) and the second figure (the total number of authorized immigrants) is the number of unauthorized immigrants living in the country. All the major research organizations that use the residual method assume that unauthorized immigrants are more reluctant to be counted than other people and therefore make upward adjustments to their final estimates of the unauthorized migrant population. Based on several studies, Passel (2007) and others (Bean et al., 1998; Capps et al., 2002) assume that unauthorized persons are two to three times more likely to be missed than legal immigrants. The residual model also calls for a number of other standard demographic adjustments to be sure that the counts of both the total foreign-born population and authorized population are accurate.

A fortuitous opportunity for a more direct count of the unauthorized population emerged with the landmark legislation known as the *Immigrant Reform and Control Act* of 1986 (IRCA), which called for the mass legalization of

6   *Chapter 1*

undocumented immigrants in the United States, as well as tougher border security measures. The IRCA allowed for the comparison of results from the residual method and the actual count of the unauthorized persons who applied for legal status (Baker, 1990). As Passel (2007, 21) put it, "Analysis of applications and approvals for legalization found that the overall levels and their distribution across states agreed very closely with the residual estimates."

Counts of the unauthorized population based on the residual method have been verified by several other studies that have used alternative techniques, calculations, and adjustments (Van Hook et al., 2006; Bean et al., 2001). Heer and Passel (1987), for instance, compared the residual method to one based on interviews with Mexican adults from Los Angeles. The respondents were asked directly about their immigration status; if they claimed to be a permanent legal resident, they were asked to show a green card. Based on this comparison, Heer and Passel concluded that two very different techniques for estimating the number of undocumented immigrants produced similar results. Passel (2007) and others (Bean et al., 1983; Massey & Singer, 1995) have also verified numbers from the residual method by examining data from the Mexico census.

To some observers, the most convincing piece of evidence in favor of the residual method is the simple fact that almost all the major research organizations involved in the immigration debate approve the use of this technique. In 2015, virtually everyone with an expensive calculator—Department of Homeland Security, Pew Research Center, Migration Policy Institute, Center for Migration Studies—used the residual method and estimated the size of the unauthorized immigrant population at roughly 11 to 12 million. These sources also agreed that this number had peaked in 2007 at just over 12 million, and then diminished or remained relatively stable until the time of this book's publication. The consensus view on these trends included restrictionist groups such as the Federation for American Immigration Reform and the Center for Immigration Studies, as well as expansionist organizations such as the National Immigration Law Center, the National Immigration Forum, and the National Council of La Raza. Of course, scientific estimates of the unauthorized immigrant population have limits. They are, after all, estimates. Even the most reliable figures are not based on a direct count of all individuals living in the country without proper documentation. The promise of social science is not to cancel uncertainty, but rather to understand it and thereby have greater confidence in the assumptions we use to make decisions. More than three decades of research has transformed new and innovative ideas into well-respected research techniques, and has led a wide range of professional demographers, scholars, journalists, and politicians to accept, with increasing confidence, the same conclusion.

Grand Contradictions 7

IMMIGRANTS AND CRIME

The idea that immigration results in higher levels of crime is an old one. In fact, the notion has been around so long that even describing it as "old" is outdated. In the early twentieth century, Edith Abbot, the economist and social reformer who led one of the earliest major studies on the relationship between crime and immigration, put it this way:

> The theory that immigration is responsible for crime, that the most recent "wave of immigration," whatever the nationality, is less desirable than the old ones, that all newcomers should be regarded with an attitude of suspicion, is a theory that is almost as old as the colonies planted by Englishmen on the New England coast. (Abbot & Bowler, 1931, p. 23)

Despite the theory's maturity, it finds little support from empirical research. Throughout the twentieth century, numerous scholars tested this claim by comparing the rates of crime, imprisonment and recidivism across the native-born and foreign-born populations. In view of the vast accumulation of peer-reviewed studies, it seems moderately clear that immigrants did not commit crimes at a higher rate than people born in the United States (Sellin, 1938; Abbott, 1915; Lind, 1930; Taft, 1936; Von Hentig, 1945; Kelsey, 1926; Hourwich, 1912; Cohen, 1931; Martinez & Lee, 2000; Butcher & Piehl, 1998; U.S. Commission on Immigration Reform, 1994; Rumbaut 2005, 2009; Akins, Rumbaut & Stansfield, 2009; Lee, Martinez & Rosenfeld, 2001; Hagan & Palloni, 1999; Schuck, 1996; Tonry, 1997; Waters, 1999; Yeager, 1997). In addition to these individual studies, there are several literature reviews and meta-analyses on the topic, which further validate a rejection of the immigration-crime link (Martínez & Lee, 2000; Zats & Smith, 2012; McCord 1995; Hagan & Palloni, 1998; MacDonald & Sampson, 2012; Mac-Donald & Saunders, 2012; Olivas, 2013; Lee & Martinez, 2009).

By the end of the twentieth century, several scholars were taking this argument one step further. Studies increasingly showed that immigration was not only a dead end in the search for crime causes, but that immigrants may have a protective effect on the communities where they reside. In a *New York Times* op-ed that summarized the recent work of leading researchers on the topic, MacDonald and Sampson (2012) wrote:

> America is neither less safe because of immigration nor is it worse off economically. In fact, in the regions where immigrants have settled in the past two decades, crime has gone down, cities have grown, poor urban neighborhoods have been rebuilt, and small towns that were once on life support are springing back.

8   *Chapter 1*

As the studies accumulated, some authors pointed to an "emerging scholarly consensus" on this topic (Lee & Martinez 2009, p. 7), while others argued that "it is now well-established in the scholarly literature that, in fact, immigrants commit less crime" (Kubrin, Zatz & Martinez, 2012, p. 1).

Given the thorough attention to this topic in previous studies, our review will be brief, selective, and focused primarily on the historical context under study: the post-9/11 period. Here we emphasize empirical research that goes beyond the null-effects hypothesis and provides evidence that immigrants are less likely than the native-born to commit crimes, or that high-density immigrant cities or neighborhoods are safer places to live than areas where immigrants are scarce.

Throughout the 1990s and early 2000s, two key social indicators—the level of immigration and the crime rate—moved in opposite directions. As the number of immigrants increased, the rates of both property crime and violent crime declined (U.S. Bureau of Justice Statistics, 2015). This straightforward correlation inspired scholars to qualify and refine the collection and analysis of data on crime and immigration and construct a persuasive body of work that demonstrates the "revitalizing" or "protective" effects of foreign-born migration in the United States. Although a unified explanation for why this relationship exists is still developing, the evidence for the relationship itself is noteworthy in several respects.

The hypothesis has been supported by many well-respected scholars using a variety of research designs. While much of the literature relies on cross-sectional data, which is collected at one point in time, scholars have also utilized longitudinal studies, which produce observations of the same phenomenon over an extended period (Martinez, Stowell & Lee, 2010; Ousey & Kubrin, 2009; Desmond & Kubrin, 2009). The latter design can offer a clearer understanding of the dynamic relationship between immigration, crime, and other structural factors that may explain the rise and fall of both immigration and crime.

The supposition that immigration reduces crime has also been tested using different units of analysis and geographical regions. One of the most common approaches is to examine multiple neighborhoods in gateway cities such as Los Angeles, New York, and Miami as the unit of analysis. Using this approach, studies have shown that immigration generally reduces homicide and other violent crimes at the neighborhood level, even when controlling for a range of other known predictors (Lee, Martinez & Rosenfeld, 2001; Nielsen, Lee & Martinez, 2005; Lee 2003; Martinez & Valenzuela, 2006; Sampson 2008; Sampson, Morenoff & Raudenbush, 2005; Sampson, 2006; Wadsworth, 2010; Feldmeyer, 2009).

Adding a caveat to this conclusion, Kubrin and Ishizawa (2012) found that the reduction in crime due to immigration is most common in neighborhoods with high levels of immigrant concentration that exist within larger immigrant communities, as is in the case of Chicago. Immigration's protective effects may also be enhanced in certain cities where immigrants have favorable political opportunities, such as access to municipal decision making (Lyons, Vélez & Santoro, 2013). Examining New York City neighborhoods, Davies and Fagan (2012) discovered a negative association between immigration and crime, but suggested that the protective effects may vary across immigrant groups. At the same time, a study by Stansfiled et al. (2013) discovered a negative relationship between immigration and crime in cities that are not traditional destinations for immigrants, and other studies have found that immigrants of all groups tend to commit fewer crimes than non-immigrants (Nielsen & Martínez, 2011). Studies have also found similar results using large cities as the units of analysis (Reid et al., 2005), as well as by following the more common approach of studying individuals on a regional or national scale (Zatz & Smith, 2012; Martinez & Stowell, 2012).

In sum, the immigration-crime link, so popular in media coverage and political speech, has been refuted by many talented researchers, from multiple disciplines, at several points in time, using a wide array of empirical research procedures and techniques. Although, as Mark Twain quipped, "All generalizations are false, including this one," the strong, often hyperbolic claims in media and political commentary about the dangers of immigrant criminals, gang members, murders, and rapists are, in general terms, inaccurate.

IMMIGRANTS AND TERRORISM

The 9/11 attacks by nineteen foreign terrorists quickly led the U.S. government to tighten controls on immigration as a counterterrorism strategy. In October 2001, President George W. Bush issued a directive entitled, "Combating Terrorism through Immigration Policies," which outlined an aggressive plan to stop immigrants from aiding or carrying out terrorist activity (Bush, 2001). Almost immediately following the attacks the Bush administration began developing the Department of Homeland Security, which would take over the functions of the Immigration and Naturalization Service and formally make immigration a national security issue. Over the years, several immigration-related policies, from the militarization of the Mexican border to the acceptance of refugees from Syria, became part of the public discourse on international terrorism and the U.S. government's efforts to fight threats from abroad. Yet, many of the claims about the immigration-terrorism nexus do not stand up to empirical scrutiny.

To begin, it should be noted that the 9/11 terrorists were not immigrants. All of them entered the United States legally with temporary visas, which made them, in technical terms, "non-immigrants." The number of non-immigrants (temporary visitors) who travel to the United States each year to attend universities, go on vacations, and conduct business far exceeds the number of new immigrants. For instance, according to the Visa Office of the State Department, 10,891,745 temporary visitors received visas in 2015; in the same year, only 531,463 immigrants received visas.[2] Given the vast number of visitors to the United States and the tragic case of 9/11, a government effort to place restrictions on the issuance of temporary visas seems logical, but much of the discussion and new policies surrounding the immigration-terrorism nexus have little to do with this non-immigrant category of foreigners.

One of the most politicized issues has involved the U.S.-Mexico border. Border security has long been a controversial topic in the ongoing debate over unauthorized immigration (Cisneros, 2014). After 9/11, the restrictionists gained ground as funding for the Border Patrol increased significantly, along with the militarization of surveillance and other security measures (Andreas, 2003; Hammond, 2011). According to a report by the Bipartisan Policy Center (Graham, 2013, p. 3), the "Border Patrol's 2012 budget of $3.5 billion more than tripled its 2000 budget of $1.1 billion, and exceeded 1990's funding level by more than 13 times."

As will be discussed in chapter 3, political commentary on the topic swelled, politicians increasingly pointed to the threat of terrorism coming from the southern border, and the public became more supportive of spending money on border security. Most notably, Donald Trump, during his bid for the presidency in 2016, linked terrorism to border security when he declared his plans for building a wall along the U.S.-Mexico border to stop unauthorized immigration and terrorism. Republican Congressman Duncan Hunter also directed public attention to border security when he claimed that ISIS members had infiltrated the United States via clandestine border crossings. He stated unequivocally: "I know that at least ten ISIS fighters have been caught coming across the Mexican border in Texas," and suggested that "dozens more . . . did not get caught by border patrol" (Parkinson, 2014). In response, the Department of Homeland Security called Hunter's claim "categorically false" and "not supported by any credible intelligence. . . . DHS continues to have no credible intelligence to suggest terrorist organizations are actively plotting to cross the southwest border" (Parkinson, 2014).

Concerns about terrorism have also shaped the public discussion on refugees. Like his plans for the southern border, Donald Trump's restrictionist position on the Syrian refugee crisis attracted a great deal of media attention in summer 2016. In a national security address on June 13, 2016 he said: "We have to stop the tremendous flow of Syrian refugees into the United States—we don't know who they are. They have no documentation and we don't know what they're planning."[3] Across the country, most governors

Grand Contradictions

made it clear that Syrian refugees were not welcome in their states, given the perceived threat of terrorism they pose. Some state legislatures also put forth new laws to bar refugees, although neither governors nor state legislators have the authority to change federal immigration plans.

Critics argued that the security concerns presented by refugees—that is, the chance that ISIS fighters may sneak in among the newcomers—have been exaggerated. Certainly, the contention that the incoming Syrian refugees constituted a "tremendous flow" was embellished. By January 2016, only 2,647 Syrian refugees had been resettled in the United States; President Obama had proposed to bring in roughly 10,000 in total. This group represented only a tiny proportion of the more than 4.5 million people driven from Syria between the start of the war in 2011 and early 2016; some countries with much smaller populations, including Canada, Germany, and France, accepted tens of thousands more refugees than the United States (Griswold, 2016). Trump's suggestion that refugees enter the United States without background checks is also flawed. Before resettlement, three government agencies—the FBI, Department of Homeland Security, and the State Department—carryout independent checks of each refugee, including analyses of the refugee's biometric data, through a painstaking process that usually takes 18–24 months (Newland, 2015).

The number of cases in which refugees were involved in terrorist activity in the United States has been debated among interest groups, think tanks, and fact-checkers (Lee, 2015; Newland, 2015), but almost all assessments of the terrorism-refugee link remain small when compared to the threat of other everyday hazards. In a relatively balanced account, the Rand Corporation, in testimony before the Committee on Homeland Security in 2015, argued that refugees do pose a security threat and that tighter screening measures were required. But the report also moderated and contextualized the risk as follows (Jones, 2015, p. 5):

> Almost none of the major terrorist plots since 9/11 have involved refugees. Even in those cases where refugees were arrested on terrorism-related charges, years and even decades often transpired between their entry into the United States and their involvement in terrorism. In most instances, a would-be terrorist's refugee status had little or nothing to do with their radicalization and shift to terrorism.

The latter point in the Rand testimony deserves further reflection. One of the most convincing critiques of the immigration-terrorism nexus lies in the fact that deadly terrorist activity is more common among those who were socialized in American society than among recent newcomers. According to the New America Foundation, between 9/11 and the Orlando Night Club Shooting in 2016, 142 people were killed in terrorist attacks. Roughly 66 percent of these deaths were attributed to violent Jihadists and 34 percent to non-Muslim right-wing terrorists, such as those with antigovernment and neo-Nazi views. Given the dominate view of terrorism in public opinion and the news media's extraordinary emphasis, foreign terrorists linked to Al Qaeda or ISIS, these numbers alone would probably surprise most Americans. A deeper look at these cases further reveals that deadly violence committed by immigrant Jihadists is indeed rare. As illustrated in Table 1.1, seven of the ten attacks between 2001 and 2016 involved perpetrators who were U.S.-born citizens; among the 94 victims, 83 were killed not by immigrants but by Americans, born and raised. Some have attributed partial blame for these homegrown attacks on the social forces of U.S. society, such as the racial and ethnic bias experienced by the perpetrators or the lax gun regulations that allow terrorists to acquire military-style firearms. In any case, many Jihadist-inspired acts of violence cannot be validly understood as terrorist attacks by immigrants or foreigners.

What is more, the figures presented by the New America Foundation were based on a rather conservative definition of terrorism. In some cases, a homegrown, non-Muslim perpetrator signals a clear racist bias prior to a violent attack, but is not been categorized as a terrorist. For instance, as reported in the *New York Times,* a man in North Carolina, who had a history of posting online critiques of religion, was charged with fatally shooting three young

Table 1.1   Lethal Jihadist Terrorist Incidents in the United States between 9/11 and the Orlando Night Club Shooting in 2016[1]

Plot name	Year	Persons killed	Citizen status of perpetrators
Orlando Night Club Shooting	2016	49	U.S.-born citizen
San Bernardino Shooting	2015	14	One U.S.-born citizen, one legal resident
Chattanooga TN Military Shooting	2015	5	Naturalized citizen
Washington and New Jersey Killing Spree	2014	4	U.S.-born citizen
Oklahoma Beheading	2014	1	U.S.-born citizen
Boston Marathon Bombing	2013	4	One naturalized citizen, one legal resident
Little Rock Shooting	2009	1	U.S.-born citizen
Fort Hood Shooting	2009	13	U.S.-born citizen
Seattle Jewish Federation Shooting	2006	1	U.S.-born citizen
Los Angeles Airport Shooting	2002	2	Legal resident

[1] Data from the New America Foundation. See the online dataset on the New American Foundation's website, "Deadly Attacks Since 9/11"; retrieved online August 18, 2016 at http://securitydata.newamerica.net/extremists/deadly-attacks.html.

Muslim neighbors (Shane, 2015). Although many observers saw this attack as ideologically motivated violence, the New America Foundation did not include it in the database. Whenever the motive of a mass murder is unclear, such as the movie theater shooting in Aurora Colorado in 2012, the case is excluded from the analysis of terrorist activities. If terrorism was defined more broadly, the number of attacks by immigrants would be virtually eclipsed by the violence of U.S.-born citizens.

ECONOMIC EFFECTS OF IMMIGRATION

When an immigrant commits a heinous act of violence, news organizations, bloggers, and partisan think-tanks can easily collect details about the act from police reports and interviews and write stories that are at once familiar and intriguing to a broad audience. When the immigrant in question is found to be "illegal," moral outrage becomes even more palatable, and restrictionist policy prescriptions suddenly seem obvious and straightforward to many Americans. The statistical relationship between immigration and the U.S. economy, though no doubt controversial, is far less obvious. A strong argument that immigration has a negative or positive effect requires a comprehensive understanding of the abundant, if complicated, economic data on this topic. Small upticks or downticks in economic indicators potentially attributable to immigration do not usually entice mass audiences. This may partly explain, as discussed in chapter 3, why the "illegality" and "crime" frames (and the "terrorism" frame after 9/11) are more abundant in media coverage of immigration than claims that immigrants have a negative influence on the economy. With a small number of interesting exceptions, the mass-mediated discourse on the economic ills of immigration consists of either over-specific anecdotes from everyday life or over-generalized claims based on popular myths and stereotypes (Edwards, 2014).

There is, however, a systematic effort being made by anti-immigration organizations to popularize the notion that immigrants take the jobs and lower the wages of the native-born, while also using more public services than they pay for in taxes (Woods, Manning & Matz, 2015). These beliefs also appear to be quite common among many Americans. Based on a large survey conducted in April 2015, the Pew Research Center (2015) found that 50 percent of Americans believed that immigrants hurt the U.S. economy, while only 28 percent said that they were making it better and 20 percent said that they are not having much effect. Another large-scale poll—this one carried out by Reuters/Ipsos in 2014 (Bell, 2014)—found that 63 percent of people believed that "immigrants place a burden on the economy." In sum, most Americans believe that immigration has an overall negative impact on the country's economic well-being.

Yet, these perceptions contradict the views of economists (Caplan, 2002; Tremewan, 2009), as well as the great majority of economic studies conducted by scholars across multiple disciplines. In fact, aside from a few hot-button issues, there is consensus among scholars and relatively little debate on some key facts. Almost no one disagrees that immigrants make an important and sizable contribution to the economy and occupy a range of important positions in the workforce, from laborers, entrepreneurs, and teachers to business leaders and innovators (Hunt & Gauthier-Loiselle, 2008).

For obvious reasons, most immigrants come to the United States to work, and they are more likely than the rest of the U.S. population to fall in the prime working-age category. As any parent knows, raising children is a time-consuming and expensive proposition, and its price tag is not offset by labor output in the form of household chores and other good deeds. As any public official knows, a big part of the cost of raising children is covered by public funds. Given that many immigrants come to the United States having already reached prime working age, their lifetime cost-versus-contribution ratio is more favorable in economic terms than that of the average American.

This claim finds support from the Current Population Survey (CPS), which is conducted by the U.S. Bureau of Labor Statistics (2014) and based on a sample of approximately 60,000 households, including those of legally admitted immigrants, refugees, temporary residents, and undocumented immigrants. The CPS indicates that, in 2014, 66 percent of the foreign born participated in the labor force, whereas 62 percent of the native-born worked. Immigrants comprise roughly 13 percent of the population and 16 percent of the labor force. Foreign-born workers were more likely to occupy low-paying jobs in the service sector, while the native-born were more likely to work in management, professional and related occupations. Full-time foreign-born workers made on average $664 per week; the native-born made $820 per week for the same amount of work (U.S. Bureau of Labor Statistics, 2014).

These figures are important, because the population is aging quickly and the labor market will increasingly require young workers as the Baby Boomers retire. In fact, demographers have projected that, by 2050, the number of people aged 65 and over will reach 83.7 million, which is nearly two times greater than this population figure (43.1 million) in 2012 (Ortman, Velkoff & Hogan, 2014). The proposals made by anti-immigration groups to dramatically reduce immigration and deport unauthorized immigrants are not only debatable on moral grounds, but also fiscally irresponsible considering immigration's net positive impact on the economy and the expected transformation of the population.

One of the more controversial issues in the immigration debate involves the jobs and wages of native-born workers. Many Americans hold the reasonable assumption that demand for workers goes down as the pool of immigrant laborers increases, and that decreased labor demand results in fewer jobs and lower wages. Yet, according to *The Economist*, the reality is that more jobs are lost as a result of automation rather than immigrants. Although this logic follows the theory offered in most undergraduate economics courses, professional economists add a number of caveats, and in so doing the great majority of them reverse this conclusion. They argue that immigrants serve as complements to the U.S. labor force, not substitutes. Put differently, native workers and new immigrants often do not compete for the same jobs. Low-skilled immigrant workers also help businesses expand, and therefore enlarge employment possibilities and incomes for all workers.

The new arrivals also represent an increased customer base. Just as businesses close in regions where the population declines, they open and grow in response to immigrant-fueled community expansion. For these and other more nuanced reasons, most economists reject the negative-economic-effects argument. Reviews of the scholarly literature on this subject show that results vary to some extent, but that almost all the studies showing that immigration lowers wages and employment find that the decreases are very small or negligible (e.g., Card, 2005; Longhi, Nijkamp & Poot, 2005 and 2010); and several studies have found that immigration has no effect or even raises wages and employment (e.g., Ottaviano & Peri, 2008 and 2011; Nadadur, 2009).

While the overall effects of immigration produce only minor skirmishes among experts, a fiercer debate exists on whether certain groups of native-born workers—namely, those with low skills and education—suffer when immigrants enter the labor force. In a paper published in 1990, David Card, an economist from the University of California-Berkeley, analyzed the economic impact of the Mariel boatlift in 1980, when Fidel Castro allowed more than 125,000 Cubans to depart Cuba and head for the shores of South Florida (Card, 1990). The episode represented a unique natural experiment that would reveal how a large influx of refugees with low skills and little education impacts the local labor market. Using conventional wisdom, one might expect that the existing low-skilled labor force in Miami would suffer dearly, given that many more people would be going after the same jobs. But Card's main conclusion contradicted this assumption. Comparing labor-market indicators in Miami to those of other cities before and after the Mariel influx, Card found that the wage and employment levels of low-skill, native-born workers were not affected by the new arrivals.

For twenty-five years, Card's interesting paper did what almost all academic papers do. It rested quietly at the library and was rarely featured in anything aside from the reference lists of other academic and government reports. But then, in 2015, George Borjas, a Harvard economist, returned to the Mariel boatlift question and came to a contradictory conclusion (Borjas, 2015). The incongruous findings between the work of Card and Borjas set off a scientific debate among multiple economists. Giovanni Peri and Vasil Yasenov (2015) of the University of California, Davis, entered the fray not long after Borjas released his report. Their analysis, one that used measurements purportedly more robust than those of Card or Borjas, supported Card's claim that the Cuban refugees did not hurt the job outlook of the native-born. The Peri and Yasenov paper was, of course, quickly met by a rejoinder from Borjas himself (2016).

Much of the controversy in the Mariel case stems from the choice of comparison groups. To demonstrate an effect of the refugees, Card attempted to show a change in labor-market opportunities for the native-born, controlling for other economic factors, by comparing the Miami employment and wage levels to other metro areas that had employment growth trends similar to Miami's. Borjas followed the same approach, but used different cities to make the comparison. Borjas also selected an extremely narrow set of Miami workers upon which to base his estimate of the changes in wage and job opportunities before and after the Mariel surge. The spirit of the research question was to determine whether the low-skill workers of Miami were harmed by the rapid increase in the low-skill labor pool, but the final answer depended on how one identified the supposedly vulnerable Miamian workers. Peri and Yasenov argued that women, young workers, and non-Cuban Hispanics should be included in the vulnerable group, while Borjas believed these subgroups should be excluded. Put differently, most of the conflict was fought on conceptual grounds, as opposed to matters of research design. However, one purely methodological difference between the two sets of studies was that Borjas's very narrow conceptualization of the vulnerable worker group left him with a decidedly small sample for the various time periods (sometimes as few as seventeen people) for which he collected data. Borjas himself recognized this issue as an important limitation of his study.

In cases where empirical studies deliver contradictory results, most thoughtful observers delay judgment and wait for further information to arise on the given question. Many observers in the news media, however, were quick to support either Borjas or the Peri-Yasenov-Card contingent. One side not only held the valid answer, but also stood on the ethical high ground. The story was almost always depicted to broad audiences as a case in which one economist was fudging data ("data mining") to score points in the immigration debate, and another economist was debunking the ideological myth. The only thing that differed between headlines was the names of the heroes and culprits.

A final judgment on the Mariel controversy may not yet be possible, but it does offer insight. In 1980, 125,000 immigrants of low socioeconomic status showed up in Miami overnight and most of them started looking for a new job. The fact that this influx was not absolutely devastating to all low-skill workers, regardless of how they are parsed, is remarkable, and it lends credence to the argument that new arrivals to a region produce both positive and negative economic outcomes for the community.

Another unique set of historical circumstances, ideal for scientific investigation, arose in the early 2000s as some state legislatures enacted restrictionist laws to control immigrant populations. The federal government had traditionally held the sole responsibility for immigration enforcement. Although, by the end of the first decade, some states began to appropriate this responsibility directly by creating their own legislation, the earliest laws allowing state involvement in immigration law enforcement came with the adoption of 287(g) programs, a federal initiative that gave local authorities, in cooperation with the U.S. Immigration and Customs Enforcement (ICE), the opportunity to perform immigration enforcement functions.[4] Florida and Arizona were among the first to begin collaborating with ICE, and by 2010 at least eight more states had followed suit. This and several other local restrictionist laws, such as the status verification system E-Verify, were intended to reduce the unauthorized population, but authorized immigrants and ethnic minority groups were affected as well. While some states took the restrictionist path, other state and local governments designed legislation to protect and welcome immigrants, while still others made only small changes or no reforms at all.

This stark variation in state-level policies served as another natural experiment of sorts that allowed scholars to examine the economic effects of curtailing regional migration. For instance, turning again to the most vulnerable segment of the native workforce, Parrado (2012) found that the creation of 287(g) programs had no effect on the unemployment rate of native-born whites and African Americans with a high school education or less. Other researchers examined the economic outcomes for states that mandated the use of E-Verify, an immigration status verification system that creates a more restrictive environment compared to places where E-Verify is optional or discouraged. Bohn, Lofstrom, and Raphael (2015) found that mandating E-Verify hurt low-skill, authorized workers, resulting in small but significant declines in employment and increased unemployment. The subgroup whose employment rate decreased the most was lower-skilled, native-born, non-Hispanic white men. Another study found that the mandates have no effect on U.S.-born non-Hispanic whites (Orrenius & Zavodny, 2015). Rafael and Ronconi (2009) revealed a similar finding for non-Hispanic groups. According to a study by Amuedo-Dorantes, Bansak, and Zebedee (2015), foreign direct investment declined significantly in states that created E-Verify requirements. It appears, in other words, that states that pass restrictionist

18   *Chapter 1*

measures reduce the potential opportunities for people to grow businesses and stimulate the local economy.

Analyzing the effects of several state-level anti-immigration laws, Pham and Van (2010) showed that such laws brought a 1–2 percent decline in employment (337–675 lost jobs) for the average county, with payroll dropping 0.8 to 1.9 percent. Although some studies offer mixed findings across the various subgroups analyzed (Amuedo-Dorantes & Bansak, 2014), the passing of restrictive state laws has not, by any estimate, led to an economic windfall for native-born workers, and most studies indicate that restricting immigration at the state level comes with negative economic consequences.

Anecdotal accounts of these effects are in line with academic studies. For instance, in 2011, one tomato farmer, Brian Cash, estimated the financial loss due to his state's new immigration law at $100,000 in a single growing season (Pilkington, 2011). The Cash family had been farming 125 acres in Alabama for generations. For four months of the year, Cash employed more than sixty, mostly Hispanic male workers to pick the harvest. When Alabama's new, anti-immigration law came into effect, all but 11 of the workers vanished and Cash's tomatoes rotted on the vine (Pilkington, 2011). The news media is replete with similar vivid stories of rotting vegetables throughout Alabama farmlands, as well as in Georgia, which passed similar legislation.

CULTURAL IMPACT

Almost all anti-immigrant claims are, in essence, cultural critiques. Each of the restrictionist ideas discussed above—that Mexicans are illegally flooding the country, that the immigrant crime rate exceeds that of the native-born, that immigration harms the economy—suggests that the culture of today's newcomers is in some way flawed, undesirable, or incompatible with the host society. Although the immigration debate is more often carried out on the shifting, rationalized terrain of census figures, crime rates and economic indicators, much of the restrictionist ideology boils down to primitive notions of us versus them, of in-groups and out-groups, of perceived intergroup conflict and ethnocentrism. News about immigration may be filled with facts, figures, and analysis, but cultural fears lie at the bedrock of the immigration debate. Many Americans are concerned, in particular, that immigrants come to the United States, isolate themselves in ethnic enclaves, refuse to assimilate, and remain loyal to their home countries.

This classic nativist concern has been present in the public mind-set throughout American history. It has been voiced by a range of mainstream elites, from the Founding Fathers to well-known intellectuals like Samuel Huntington and Republican politicians like Donald Trump. By all historical

Grand Contradictions 19

accounts, the Founding Fathers generally favored immigration, but almost all of them also worried about the threat of foreign interests, attitudes, beliefs, and culture. Hamilton, in particular, raised the red flag. He attributed the fall of Rome to immigration and argued that the conferring of citizenship to foreigners could fatally harm the new Republic (Spalding, 1994). "Foreign influence is truly the Grecian horse to a republic." he wrote. "We cannot be too careful to exclude its entrance" (Hamilton, Madison, & Jay, 1788, p. 328).

Ben Franklin, more famously perhaps, warned his compatriots about the German immigrants of his day, suggesting in no uncertain terms that they were at once morally and intellectually inept and impervious to the mores of their new land. In a letter to Peter Collinson, Franklin (1753) referred to the Germans as stupid ("Those who come hither are generally of the most ignorant Stupid Sort of their own Nation"), as untrustworthy ("with Suspicion when Honesty would set it right"), and went into remarkable detail when justifying his claim that the Germans would not assimilate ("'tis almost impossible to remove any prejudices they once entertain"). Echoing contemporary nativist rhetoric, he complained that Germans were resistant to learning English, that they imported their books from Germany, built their own printing houses, printed their own newspapers, processed legal documents through the courts in German, and even produced signs in their native tongue.

In addition to the language gap, he suggested that German men were unwilling to obey authority, whether it was their teachers, religious leaders, or own their own mothers, to whom, per Franklin, they regularly gave beatings to demonstrate their manhood. Finally, Franklin, like so many of his ideological successors, used dramatic language to describe the rate of German immigration, evoking terms like "droves" and "streams" and suggesting that the Germans could even take over the government:

In short unless the stream of their importation could be turned from this to other Colonies, as you very judiciously propose, they will soon so outnumber us, that all the advantages we have will not [in My Opinion] be able to preserve our language, and even our Government will become precarious. (Franklin, 1753)

Concerns about the latest wave of immigrants refusing to assimilate and attempting a cultural takeover have existed since the founding of the nation. The repeated rise and fall of these worries is generally aligned with increases and decreases in the level of immigration to the United States. Despite the repetition of these periods of panic, immigrants have demonstrated time and again that such worry is unnecessary. A wealth of sociological research has shown that the immigrants of today—those who came in greater numbers in the early twenty-first century—are like immigrants of the past in terms of their willingness and ability to become integrated in American society.

20 *Chapter 1*

Compared to native-born individuals, immigrants tend to have lower levels of socioeconomic status when they arrive in the United States, but they improve their economic circumstances over time and in the face of extraordinary obstacles. Numerous studies have found that as their duration in the United States increases so do their average labor-market outcomes, including their occupational prestige and earnings (Akresh, 2007; Chiswick, 1978; Chiswick, 1983; Chiswick, 1986; Duleep & Dowhan, 2002; Kossoudji, 1988; Kossoudji, 1989; Massey, 1987; Portes & Bach, 1980; Trejo, 1997), as well as their level of wealth (Akresh, 2011). Most scholars believe that this upward mobility is a sign of assimilation. Over time immigrants gain an Americanized version of human and social capital. They pursue educations, learn English and become skilled in the jobs of the American labor market. The notion that immigrants come to the United States to better their lives is cliché perhaps, but it is no doubt a powerful force behind social integration. With incremental increases in socioeconomic status and extended residence in the United States, immigrants tend to move away from urban centers, settle in suburban areas and become more incorporated in communities with higher proportions of native-born individuals (Massey, 1985).

The subject of language use deserves a bit more emphasis, given the controversial nature of the debate on this topic. Voices in the news media—most commonly in cable news and the letters sections of newspapers—often suggest that today's immigrants are especially resistant to learning English and even that the English language may be in jeopardy. In the 1980s, English-only advocates began to push for national and state legislation to reinforce the use of English in government matters. Since that time, 27 states have mandated English as the official language. Yet, concerns about the plight of English cannot be found among the great majority of scholars who study this topic. Contrary to popular belief, Mexican immigrants and Mexican Americans value English-language proficiency highly. Based on a large random sample of adults from Texas, Dowling, Ellison and Leal (2012) found that there is no significant difference in attitudes toward being proficient in English between Anglos and Mexican immigrants who are not citizens, and that respondents who used Spanish during the interviews were significantly more likely than Anglos to say that English-language ability is "very important."

Several studies have confirmed that these attitudes and values are related to actual efforts to learn English. Based on data from the U.S. Census, Bean and Stevens (2003) showed that there is a significant positive relationship between immigrants' length of residence in the United States and their ability to speak English. Per the Pew Hispanic Center, by 2013, more Hispanics (33.2 million) were fluent in English than ever before: this group made up 68 percent of Hispanics in 2013, which was up from 59 percent in 2000 (Krogstad, Stepler & Lopez, 2015). The researchers of this study also found that while the number of Latinos with English proficiency was growing, the share that spoke Spanish at home has been in decline over the last thirteen years. It takes roughly three generations for the language spoken by immigrants to be lost on their descendants (Suro & Passel, 2003). According to a study of Mexican and Cuban immigrants carried out by Alba et al. (2002), roughly 75 percent of the third generation spoke only English and did not speak Spanish. As the sociologist Mary Waters (2011) put it: "By the third generation, English fluency is universal and the majority of the grandchildren of immigrants are monolingual and cannot speak their grandparents' language."

The number of immigrants who become naturalized citizens is probably the most obvious sign that contemporary immigrants are not withdrawing into impenetrable ethnic enclaves. Among foreign-born U.S. residents, there has been an 18 percent increase in the number of naturalizations between 1990 and 2011 (Taylor et al., 2012). Mexican immigrants have a significantly lower naturalization rate than immigrants from other countries. Yet, the percentage of Mexicans opting for naturalization increased from 20 percent in 1995 to 35 percent in 2007. Since then, the percentage of Mexicans electing naturalization has remained flat (Taylor et al., 2012).

In the mass-mediated discussion of immigration, the subject of race is less salient than the issues of crime, terrorism, the nation's economic health and usage of the English language. Overt negative expressions about a minority group's skin, hair, or eye color are almost never made in mainstream media outlets. Nevertheless, individuals and groups that oppose immigration often frame their argument in racial terms. One rather common version of this argument involves the claim that immigration is driving changes in the U.S. population's racial composition and that such changes may have negative repercussions for white people. For instance, citing data from the Census Bureau, Leon Kolankiewicz (2000) from the Center for Immigration Studies, an anti-immigration think-tank, wrote that "Sometime around 2050, non-Hispanic whites will cease to be a majority." Kolankiewicz (2000) suggests that the changing demographic picture may be problematic, because minority groups, as they grow, will likely act in threatening ways toward non-Hispanic whites: "Each group in the new 'minority-majority' country has longstanding grievances against whites." Kolankiewicz speculates further that the United States could become Balkanized or completely torn apart.

A brief reiteration may be in order. The mainstream media—even when conceptualized broadly—simply does not contain direct, unambiguous, racist claims. However, a more muted, civil discussion does exist over the changing racial composition of the population. Headlines like the following are not uncommon in newspapers and other media outlets: "Minorities now surpass whites in US births" (Yen 2012). Such items accurately report immigration growth as an instrumental factor in these changes, and usually support their claims with statistics from government reports. Based on the Census Bureau's definition of minority groups, non-Hispanic whites will likely become a minority by 2044; and the foreign-born individuals will make up roughly 20 percent of the total population by 2060 (Colby & Ortman, 2014). The coming minority status of whites, even if it is rarer in the news media than other immigration-related topics, may resonate strongly with some Americans who are concerned about the growing number of people with different traditions, cultures, skin colors, or national origins.

Anyone with the least bit of sympathy for multiculturalism would celebrate the increasing ethnic diversity projected in the latest Census Bureau reports. But even those who are concerned about the minority status of whites should consider at least one important caveat to these predictions. First, the projections are, to put it simply, wrong. As pointed out by Richard Alba (2016), the Census Bureau defines "white" in the narrowest way possible and thereby underestimates the size of this group. Alba criticizes the Bureau's adoption of the "one-drop" rule, which historically classified people as black if they had any black heritage at all. Meanwhile, there is ample evidence that inter-marriages are becoming more common, particularly among the fast-growing immigrant population (Lee & Bean, 2004; Rosenfeld, 2002; Perlmann & Waters 2004). Most of these marriages included one white person, which means that the number of children with a white parent is also on the rise. The question, then, is why should these children be classified as belonging to a minority group? There is no logical explanation, aside from the institutional bias that shapes how Americans understand and perceive race. Alba (2016, 67) imagines applying an alternative, if also flawed, method of counting white people:

> If we were to go to the opposite extreme from the bureau's official projections and adopt a white one-drop rule—that is, to classify anyone with some white ancestry as white—the data show that whites would make up three-quarters of the population at mid-century, when the Census publicly claims that whites will be in the minority.

Another caveat to the Census data has been stressed by Alba and many other sociologists: They argue that the meanings people attach to race are cultural and culture changes over time. What it means to be white, or any color for that matter, is a product of human construction. The categorization system of the Census Bureau serves as one example of such invention. Drawing on this wisdom, numerous scholars have examined how once-excluded minority groups—Jews, Irish, Italians—have become white (Brodkin, 1998; Guglielmo & Salerno, 2003). In other words, these groups have been assimilated into the mainstream and no longer suffer the same degree of racial inequality.

Grand Contradictions 23

As one contemplates the end of the white majority, it is important to reflect on the socially constructed nature of race, to acknowledge that racial bias is not inevitable, and to understand our own roles in the process of racialization. However, the future of race relations in the United States represents an empirical question and a difficult one at that. Historical analysis may reveal cases where racial boundaries have blurred and greater social harmony ensued, but more recently it has also demonstrated cases where the dividing lines were reinforced and circumstances for minority groups worsened. As argued throughout the remainder of this book, there are a number of social indicators that do not portend an optimistic future for immigrants. As the threat of terrorism continues to concern many Americans, racial and ethnic boundaries may become even more rigid and the policies and institutions governing immigration—migration from Mexico, Central America, the Middle East, and Asia in particular—may become more exclusionary and authoritarian.

CONCLUSION

If public sentiment reflected empirical reality, we would find only warmth and appreciation in the mass-mediated discussion of immigration, as well as in people's views on the topic. Instead, the early twenty-first century was marked by distorted public perceptions of immigrants and growing worries about immigration. Contrary to popular belief, not to mention the proclamations of some headline-grabbing political figures, the population of unauthorized immigrants in the United States is not growing rapidly. There is no "flood," no "tidal wave," no "invasion." Immigration metaphors involving watery death and insect-related cataclysm are as vacuous as they are irresponsible when used by public officials. The number of unauthorized immigrants in the United States reached 12 million in 2007 and remained at roughly 11 to 12 million for the next decade. The task of counting this group is difficult, but decades of improvements in methodology have led to consensus among the researchers who produce these estimates, as well as among a range of advocacy groups on both sides of the issue.

The notion that immigrants are especially prone to commit crime is one of the oldest and most persistent myths about immigration. Whether researchers are comparing rates of crime, imprisonment, or recidivism, they have found that immigrants do not carry out more destructive acts on average than native-born individuals. This conclusion can be drawn from the earliest efforts to study the crime-immigration link, as well as from the latest, cutting-edge research. In the more recent era, scholars have increasingly found that immigrants may have a protective effect on the places where they live. Areas with higher immigrant concentrations have been shown to have less crime and neighborhood deterioration than areas where immigrants are sparse. The supposedly positive relationship between immigration and violent crime, including terrorism, also finds little support from scientific research.

Some restraint is required when summarizing the effects of immigration on the economic well-being of the native-born. If an economist actively searches for a small number of cases where the wages and job prospects of native-born workers were harmed by the influx of immigrants in a region, she will likely find them. However, in the aggregate, at the national level, numerous studies have found that immigration brings positive economic outcomes. One of the most interesting and still developing research topics examines how restrictionist policies at the state level are encouraging out-migration and thereby influencing local economies. Although research on this topic continues, thus far scholars have found that states that pass restrictionist measures hurt employment levels and reduce opportunities for people to grow businesses and stimulate the local economy.

Although cultural fears may have powerful effects on public opinion, overt statements about the innate weakness or inferiority of immigrant culture have been almost entirely pushed to the margins of the immigration debate. Yet the claim is often made that immigrants from Mexico and Latin America are rejecting some aspects of mainstream culture, the use of the English language in particular. Such claims are unconvincing in light of the expansive empirical literature on this question, including not one, but two major reviews of the literature (Waters & Jiménez, 2005; Massey, 1981). As Waters and Jiménez (2005, 121) put it: "After nearly 40 years of high levels of immigration, primarily from Latin America, the Caribbean, and Asia, most careful sociological research supports the notion that immigrants are being successfully incorporated into American society."

What explains the grand contradiction between careful empirical analysis of immigration's effects on the United States and the public's perceptions of these effects? Why has political rhetoric on the topic grown harsher and less welcoming of foreigners? Why, given the positive influences of immigration on American society, has the twenty-first-century policy environment favored restrictionist positions? The next chapter begins to address these questions by examining one of the driving forces of the immigration debate in the twenty-first century. Although most arguments on both sides are as old as the country itself, the terrorist attacks on 9/11 marked a new chapter in the debate and led to changes in political culture that favored restrictionist positions.

NOTES

1. See "United States Census Bureau, American Community Survey." Retrieved online, January 13, 2016, at https://www.census.gov/acs/www/methodology/sample-size-and-data-quality/sample-size/index.php.

2. See the "Report of the Visa Office 2015." U.S. Department of State. Retrieved online on 8/17/2016, at https://travel.state.gov/content/visas/en/law-and-policy/statistics/annual-reports/report-of-the-visa-office-2015.html.

3. See the Donald Trump website, "Donald J. Trump Addresses Terrorism, Immigration, and National Security." June 13, 2016. Retrieved online August, 17, 2016, at https://www.doraldjtrump.com/press-releases/donald-j.-trump-addresses-terrorism-immigration-and-national-security.

4. See the website of the Department of Homeland Security under the section "Delegation of Immigration Authority Section 287(g) Immigration and Nationality Act." Retrieved online, April 2016, at https://www.ice.gov/factsheets/287g.

Chapter 2

The Perceived Threat of Terrorism and the Authoritarian Turn in Attitudes toward Immigration

As we discussed earlier, elite discourse on immigration in the United States has always been about openness, about our willingness as a public to offer access to our country and our civic life, as well as our perpetual insistence on labeling and defining who is not worthy of such access. In an excellent essay, Beasley (2006) confirms the two approaches to the United States' interaction with and approach to immigration—namely, that we identify specific immigrant groups, based upon the historical context, as functioning as a positive, beneficial addition to American life, while also acting xenophobically and framing immigrants and the immigration processes as detrimental, dangerous, and something to fear. Targeting certain immigrants from a specific region of the world, restrictionists have promoted similar generalizations about the target group's threatening or undesirable qualities (poor education; proclivity for criminal activity; incompatible language, religion, and political ideology; inability or unwillingness to assimilate) to justify their positions. At times, restrictionist have "won" these debates and pushed through exclusionary legislation—new laws that would harm immigrants, cost American tax payers millions, stain the country's international reputation, and fail to alleviate the problems for which the legislation was created (Arthur & Woods, 2017; Beasley, 2004).

We should keep the ideological continuity of the immigration debate in mind as we consider the contemporary context. Yet, at least one factor distinguishes the current debate from the politics of old. The attacks on September 11, 2001 (9/11) marked a turning point in immigration policy discussions. Terrorist events had occurred on U.S. soil in the past, but the response to 9/11 was unprecedented. The events of 9/11 triggered an institutional redesign of the Immigration and Naturalization Service (INS) in response to the perceived link between immigration and the threat of terrorism. The perceived danger

28 *Chapter 2*

of terrorism rose higher in the public mind-set than ever before. Given the string of subsequent attacks and mass shootings at home and abroad, people's worries about terrorism remained well above the pre-9/11 levels for much of the next two decades. With the events of that fateful day, a unique and powerful tool was added to the restrictionists' repertoire of anti-immigration arguments and framing devices. In the early twenty-first century, as people and policymakers increasingly valued safety and security and viewed outsiders as potential threats, restrictionists took the dominant position in the debate.

In this chapter, we begin by examining the terrorist threat and explaining why it has produced such high and sustained concerns among Americans. We demonstrate that the attacks on 9/11 provoked intense short-term reactions, as well as a deeply felt, widely shared, long-term understanding of terrorism as a societal threat. Next, we discuss the effects of this threat on a range of values, attitudes, beliefs, and behaviors. Although empirical research has revealed that 9/11 encouraged both anti-authoritarian and authoritarian tendencies, the latter were more prominent and lasted longer than the former. Finally, we examine how immigration policy preferences are shaped by perceptions of the terrorist threat. Drawing on four diverse research traditions, we show how and why the perceived threat of terrorism has reinforced restrictionist perceptions and attitudes on immigration.

9/11 AND THE CULTURE OF PERCEIVED THREAT

The attacks on 9/11 were an extraordinary "risk event" (Kasperson et al., 1988, p. 177). Terrorism was a new kind of trouble, an ambient horror, a plausible danger that spurred visceral reactions in some, rationalized concerns in others, but disbelief in almost no one. Captured in countless images and descriptions, the attacks took the lives of around 3,000 people, left a smoldering crash site in the Pennsylvania countryside, severely damaged one section of the Pentagon, and demolished roughly 30 million square feet of office space in lower Manhattan (Bram, Orr & Rapaport, 2002). At the time, observers from around the globe were shocked, horrified, and sympathetic toward the victims of the attacks (Shlapentokh, Shiraev & Woods, 2005). For the first time in history, the great majority of Americans were worried about being personally harmed by terrorists. Subsequent attacks and mass shootings at home and abroad sustained people's concerns and made the threat more believable and frightening. This thesis bears out in numerous polls and academic studies.

The Extraordinary Increase in the Perceived Threat of Terrorism

Although worries about terrorism were not new to most Americans, public opinion polls show that the extent and permanence of these concerns after

The Perceived Threat of Terrorism

9/11 were exceptional. The first strike on the World Trade Center in 1993 and the Oklahoma City bombing in 1995 had captured the nation's attention, but the issue of terrorism did not become an enduring narrative in the media, or a permanent fixture in the minds of most Americans (Woods, 2007). According to the Gallup Organization, the percentage of respondents who were very or somewhat worried about being personally victimized by terrorism peaked at 42 percent after the Oklahoma City attacks, dropped to 35 percent one year later (April 1996), and remained at this level until declining even further to 24 percent in April 2000.[1]

After 9/11, 58 percent of Americans were very or somewhat worried about being personally victimized by terrorists, and 66 percent believed that a new attack was very or somewhat likely. Half the population believed that "Americans have permanently changed the way they live."[2] Rather than diminishing consistently as in the case of the Oklahoma City bombings, the percentage of those who were very or somewhat worried about terrorism fluctuated, falling 23 points by November 2001 and then rising 13 points by February 2003. One year later, the level of worry began to increase steadily. Between 2005 and 2007, worry levels exceeded the peak ratings after the Oklahoma City bombings.

By the end of the decade, worries about terrorism stood at 42 percent—near the average (41%) seen on this Gallup measure since September 11, 2001 (Saad, 2010). After the killing of Osama bin Laden in 2011, however, worries rose even more, as well as people's beliefs that a new attack was coming. In May 2011, 62 percent of Americans believed that a terrorist act was either very or somewhat likely to occur in the next several weeks (Saad, 2011). Beliefs about future strikes remained high in the next years and reached yet another peak in the wake of several high-profile attacks around the world—in Paris and San Bernardino in 2015 and months later in Ankara, Turkey, and Brussels, Belgium, in 2016.

These historic trends can be seen across other measures. For instance, since 1939, the Gallup Organization has regularly asked Americans, in an open-ended question, to name "the most important problem facing the United States." Before 9/11, terrorism had never made the list. After 9/11, terrorism rarely left it. In October 2001, 46 percent of respondents named terrorism the most important problem (Lewis, 2005), which far exceeded mentions of the government and economy. Until 2008, Terrorism remained relatively high on the list, spiking in 2004 following the Madrid train bombings and again in 2005 in the wake of the London train and bus bombings. By 2008, terrorism faded as a top problem, only to spike once again after the failed "underwear bombing" in 2010. Not long after the incidents in Paris and San Bernardino, terrorism returned to the top of the list in December 2015, having been mentioned more often by Americans as the most important problem than the economy, government, and guns (Riffkin, 2015).

30   Chapter 2

The Underlying Causes of Terrorism Threat Perceptions

Several researchers have attempted to explain why people's reactions to terrorism have been so strong and prolonged. Many have suggested that people's intuitive and probabilistic understandings of the threat are flawed. Like the fear of spiders or snakes, the public's cognitive and emotional reactions to terrorism are incongruent with probabilistic estimates of a harm occurring. The number of terrorist attacks in the United States and Europe has declined since the 1970s, and especially in the years after 9/11.[3] Each year, the total number of American fatalities in terrorist incidents has been extremely small when compared to other common causes of death. According to research funded by the Department of Homeland Security, 36 Americans were killed in terrorist attacks that occurred in the United States between 2004 and 2013.[4] Just about every other perilous circumstance killed more Americans during this period, including falling down, drowning, freezing to death, heat stroke, and, of course, gun-related homicides. According to authoritative reports, even lightening is deadlier than terrorism: lightning strikes (not including fires caused by lightening) kill 79 people per year on average in the United States (1968–2010).[5]

Drawing on the psychometric paradigm and the risk perception literature (Slovic, 2004), there are at least five reasons for the public's disproportionate reaction to terrorism. First, people tend to judge the likelihood of a danger by whether an example of it easily comes to mind. After 9/11, the volume of vivid examples and specific details about terrorism in the media increased dramatically and remained elevated until the writing of this book. For instance, the *Washington Post* and *New York Times* published three times more articles on terrorism in the first three months after 9/11 than in the four years before it (Woods, 2007). As discussed in the next chapter, the same trend occurred in dozens of other newspapers, television news and radio programs, presidential speeches, congressional proceedings, and political party platforms. In this way, the sheer volume, or "availability" (Tversky & Kahneman, 1974; Sunstein, 2004), of terrorism in news and popular culture reinforced the threat in many people's minds.

Second, dangers perceived as new or changing evoke greater levels of perceived threat than old or familiar hazards (Fischhoff et al., 1978; Sjöberg, 2005; Covello, 1992). For years after 9/11, a variety of intermediaries framed the threat of terrorism in dynamic terms, as something new, heightened, or increasing. From the government's color-coded terrorism threat advisories to the news media's regular reports on enhanced threats surrounding holidays, major sporting events, and the "internet chatter" of extremist groups, terrorism has been regularly framed as something novel, even though it has existed for decades.

Third, risks that can potentially harm many people, cause catastrophic or gruesome consequences, or have lasting effects on society or the environment,

The Perceived Threat of Terrorism 31

are known to inflate risk perceptions (Fischhoff et al., 1978). The death and destruction appearing in media coverage of 9/11 and subsequent attacks, as well as the ongoing discussion of terrorists acquiring nuclear technology, have likely focused people's attention on the most severe, emotional aspects of the threat and thereby distorted their beliefs about the likelihood of attacks happening in the future. During the years of the Bush administration, Vice President Dick Cheney was especially vocal about the potential for terrorists to carryout catastrophic attacks with nuclear or biological weapons. Even after he left the White House, Cheney continued to issue warnings about terrorism and critique the Obama administration's position on national security. For instance, in 2010, on ABC's "This Week," he said: "I think the biggest strategic threat the United States faces today is the possibility of another 9/11 with a nuclear weapon or a biological agent of some kind, and I think Al Qaeda is out there even as we meet trying to figure out how to do that" (Sullivan, 2010).

Fourth, the perceived controllability of a threat is another aspect that shapes people's risk perceptions. Some political communication about terrorism contains vague or inconsistent attributions of the behavior. Several studies, starting with Iyengar's *Is Anyone Responsible* (1991), have shown that the U.S. news media in general is far more likely to use episodic frames than thematic frames in its coverage of social issues, including terrorism (Papacharissi & Oliveira, 2008). In other words, the most common news story depicts terrorism with concrete, individual cases, as opposed to offering contextual, historical, or thematic details, or providing a big-picture understanding of why attacks occur. Although this is an important caveat, there is no doubt that news coverage of terrorism has frequently discussed the motives and group identity of the perpetrators (Cisneros, 2011; Flores, (2003). In the first weeks after 9/11, President George W. Bush often referred to the perpetrators as "Islamic extremists" or "radical Islamic terrorists" and the great majority of political elites and voices in news media followed suit.[6] This characterization built on and contributed to the stereotype of terrorists as uncompromising, suicidal, religious fanatics, and led many Americans to assume that the new enemy had no logical basis for their actions, that their motives were irrational and otherworldly, and therefore obstinate, uncontrollable, and frightening.

In addition to alluding to the uncontrollable nature of the threat, the Islamic extremist frame also endows its audience with a theory or diagnosis of the problem—that terrorism is a radical religious practice. Diagnostic frames of this sort are known to have greater influence on attitudes, beliefs, and behaviors than frames that merely name a problem or risk (Cress & Snow, 2000; Benford & Snow, 2000; Gamson et al., 1992; Woods, 2011a).

32   *Chapter 2*

The five psychometric factors discussed above offer important insight into people's reactions to terrorist events, especially in the short term. But the public's reaction to 9/11 should be understood as something more than a temporary psychological response to a frightening event. The 9/11 incident was not only seen as an attack on the lives and property of Americans, but also an affront to the nation itself. The attacks were experienced as both an individual and collective threat to both material and symbolic resources. The group and ethnic identity of the enemy, whether accurate or not, became an accepted fact among most Americans. These were "foreign" intruders with the goal of harming the United States, its traditions, its values, and its people. The events of 9/11, for years after the attacks, were interwoven in elite political communication, as well as in the everyday discussions of Americans. As the War on Terrorism expanded, a generalized understanding of the terrorist threat emerged. Through a dynamic interplay between individual psychological processes and the culture of perceived threat, millions of Americans came to share an understanding of the risk of terrorism, the origin of the danger, and the appropriate means for fighting terrorism and defending the nation against foreigners. As discussed in the next chapters, terrorism became a long-term threat embedded in the culture of modern American society (Woods, 2012).

Institutionalizing the Threat of Terrorism

There is another, structural reason for the prolonged public concern about terrorism, namely, the institutional redesign of the federal U.S. Immigration and Naturalization Service (INS) after 9/11. Without producing a detailed history, we should briefly note these changes. The INS, prior to 9/11, was housed within the U.S. Department of Justice, where it had been since 1940. After a brief relationship with security during World War II, the INS moved toward a mission of enforcing immigration laws in the late 1950s through the 1990s. After 9/11, concerns increased about terrorists crossing the Mexican border and attacking domestic targets. Fourteen days after 9/11, President Bush immediately connected immigration policy to terrorism policy in a speech to the FBI. He asked for an immigration policy change, allowing the administration to use the immigration court system to handle suspected terrorists. This action began an institutional shift in both the perception and the responsibilities of the federal immigration apparatus.

About a month later, President Bush issued *The Homeland Security Presidential Directive-2—Combating Terrorism Through Immigration Policies*, which continued the institutional shift through agency budgets, task forces, and the merging of security, intelligence, and immigration through technologies and databases. In this directive, the idea was to enhance the INS and Customs ability to participate in the prevention and mitigation of terrorist-related incidents by creating an organizational overlap between their responsibilities and those of the Attorney General, the Secretary of the Treasury, and the Director of Central Intelligence. Coupling the immigration agency's apparatus and the security agency's apparatus was part of the Bush administration's new goal to "immediately develop and implement multiyear plans to enhance the investigative and intelligence analysis capabilities of the INS and the Customs Service. The goal of this enhancement is to increase significantly efforts to identify, locate, detain, prosecute or deport aliens associated with, suspected of being engaged in, or supporting terrorist activity within the United States" (Bush 2003, 1323).

President Bush put forward further structural changes with the more formal Executive Order 13228, which established the Office of Homeland Security and the Homeland Security Council. This new office within the executive branch created several structural changes that fundamentally connected immigration and terrorism institutionally. For instance, EO 13228 created a bureaucratic structure with direct access to the president and charged every federal department and agency with thinking about terrorism alongside their agency goals and responsibilities. Moreover, it established a mission statement that governed its actions, namely, to "develop and coordinate the implementation of a comprehensive national strategy to secure the United States from terrorist threats or attacks."[7] Part of the strategy and mission was to create an organizational culture, within each executive branch effort, "to detect, prepare for, prevent, protect against, respond to, and recover from terrorist attacks within the United States."[8] The prevention element to the new executive office that was most important to immigration consisted of coordination with other executive agencies. EO 13228 stated that the new structure would "facilitate the exchange of information among such agencies relating to immigration and visa matters . . . ensure coordination among such agencies to prevent the entry of terrorists and terrorist materials and supplies into the United States and facilitate removal of such terrorists from the United States, when appropriate." Functionally and institutionally, the INS was now helping with border security and terrorist-related matters, a very different responsibility to that which it had over the last half century.

Eventually, the tragic events of 9/11 compelled the Congress and the president to adopt the *Homeland Security Act* in 2002, which led to the Department of Homeland Security (DHS) in 2003. This legislation was popular in the Congress and was passed with overwhelming bipartisanship. The Senate approved the *Homeland Security Act* with 90 to 9 votes in a Senate that was comprised of 50 Republicans and 50 Democrats. In the House of Representatives, however, the vote was less bipartisan but still strongly supportive of the bill and the new agency. The vote was 295 to 132 in favor of passage, with only 88 out of 210 Democrats supporting the bill.

34   *Chapter 2*

The *Homeland Security Act* forced the largest transformation of executive and bureaucratic government since the reorganization of the Department of War into the Department of Defense in 1949. The newly created agency would take twenty-two other federal departments and agencies and compile them into the Department of Homeland Security, with the expectation that there would be more communication among the existing organizations and a more cohesive mission that would prevent and mitigate terrorist-related activities in the United States. The newly created federal agency, boasting cabinet-level status, was also concerned with working directly with both state and local governments to implement the new mission (Stephens & Wikstrom, 2007).

The U.S. Immigration and Naturalization Service (INS) was disbanded, renamed, and merged, together with other organizations, into the Department of Homeland Security (DHS). In a written history of the INS, the DHS avers that the "events of September 11, 2001, injected new urgency into INS' mission and initiated another shift in the United States' immigration policy. The emphasis of American immigration law enforcement became border security and removing criminal aliens to protect the nation from terrorist attacks."[9] The INS and its responsibilities were broken down into new separate agencies under the Secretary of the DHS:

1. Customs and Border Patrol (CBP)
2. Immigration and Customs Enforcement (ICE)
3. U.S. Citizenship and Immigration Services (USCIS)

Each agency was now charged with different responsibilities, but also the prevention and mitigation of terrorism-related issues above all other issues. Clearly, 9/11 altered the path dependency of immigration policy (Ingraham & Fraser, 2006). INS was subsumed into a more complex bureaucratic structure with a new mission statement. Not only was the organizational culture different, but its purpose had been modified. According to the DHS, the newly created agency had five core missions, of which immigration enforcement was third in priority. The core mission was stated as follows:

1. Prevent terrorism and enhance security
2. Secure and manage our borders
3. Enforce and administer our immigration laws
4. Safeguard and secure cyberspace
5. Ensure resilience to disasters

Previously, the INS had been charged with checking the papers of those crossing the border, administering green cards, and investigating violations of immigration law. Since its integration into DHS, that mission has also included thwarting terrorism and restricting those at the border seeking access. This institutional shift in mission and policy structure has normalized (securitizing government activities) an abnormal event (a terrorist act). The decisions of the Congress and the Bush administration to institutionalize the threat of terror into nearly every part of the American bureaucratic structure normalized and over-emphasized the threat of terror, which led to a great deal of public concern about a statistically improbable event. A similar argument was developed in Alexseev's (2006) book *Immigration Phobia and the Security Dilemma*, which made the case that there is no empirical evidence to justify framing the immigration debate in terms of terrorism and national security.

AUTHORITARIAN AND ANTI-AUTHORITARIAN TENDENCIES AFTER 9/11

Anti-authoritarianism

Prior to 9/11, in his book *Bowling Alone*, Putnam examined the decline of civic engagement in the United States and argued that the only thing that could bring us back together was "a palpable national crisis, like war or depression or natural disaster" (Putnam, 2000, p. 402). Within two years of writing those words, the nation faced such a crisis on 9/11, and Putnam and others argued that Americans did indeed reengage with their communities as a result (Putnam, 2002; Skocpol, 2002). The idea that an emergent national threat can lead to a broader, more inclusive form of social cohesion and community identity, and encourage individuals to carry out pro-social behaviors has been a staple of social theory and research for decades (Coser, 1964; Tajfel & Turner, 1979; Greenberg, Solomon & Pyszczynski, 1997).

Empirical studies of attitudinal and behavioral reactions to 9/11 offer at least some support for this thesis. For instance, in the wake of 9/11, Americans exhibited higher levels of helping behavior and altruism ("9/11 by the numbers" 2002; Skocpol, 2002; Penner et al., 2005; Traugott et al., 2002; Yum & Schenck-Hamlin, 2005; Mikulincer, Florian & Hirschberger, 2003; Peterson & Seligman, 2003), social trust (Smith, Rasinski & Toce, 2001; Putnam, 2002; Rasinski et al., 2002; Traugott et al., 2002; Burke, 2005), civic engagement, and collectivism (Sander & Putnam, 2002; Putnam, 2001). In addition to anti-authoritarian tendencies in people's attitudes and behaviors, several voices in the news media and popular culture urged public officials to protect civil liberties, safeguard vulnerable minority groups, and exercise restraint in foreign policy. Although it would

36   *Chapter 2*

be a conceptual stretch to categorize all of these trends as "anti-authoritarian," these studies showed that social reactions to 9/11 were complex, contradictory, and potentially dialectical (Perrin, 2005).

Authoritarianism

However, the idea that the anti-authoritarian tendencies after 9/11 represented an equal and opposing force to the rise of authoritarian sentiment is simply inaccurate. Expansive literature reviews on this topic (Woods, 2011b; Woods, 2012) concluded that the post-9/11 increases in the public's anti-authoritarian traits (or pro-social attitudes and behaviors) were smaller and lasted a shorter period than authoritarian tendencies.

People's authoritarian reactions to threatening outsiders have interested scholars throughout the ages. From the works of classic philosophers like Machiavelli (1999) and Hobbes (1950) to the influential book *The Authoritarian Personality* (Adorno et al., 1950), observers have long argued that increased worries about personal safety or threats from outsiders are associated with attitudinal and behavioral harshness and intolerance. Some of the most important works of sociology, psychology, political science, and history have examined the relationship between heightened fears and a range of important psychological and social processes. Rokeach's theory of dogmatism (1960) suggests that perceived threat is the underlying cause of people's close-mindedness, rigid categorization, defensiveness, and intolerance toward others, particularly those with differing attitudes and beliefs. Tajfel and Turner's (1979) intergroup conflict theory hypothesizes that higher levels of perceived threat are associated with increased out-group degradation, stereotyping, and attribution errors. Terror management theorists (Pyszczynski, Greenberg, & Solomon, 2003) argue that perceived threat (or "mortality salience") activates greater adherence to conventional values, conformity to group norms, submissiveness to moral authorities, and rejection of outsiders.

Although countless studies based on laboratory experiments and student samples have documented the link between perceived threat and the expression of authoritarian sentiment, relatively few researchers have examined this relationship in the context of real-life events or changing environmental circumstances. As one of the few examples, Rokeach examined archival data on several Ecumenical Councils of the Catholic Church. He acquired ratings of the level of threat experienced by the church, which had led to the need for a Council, and the level of dogmatism present in the Council's decrees (Rokeach, 1960). Rokeach concluded that the greater the threat perceived by the church, the more authoritarian were its rules for proper worship.

Drawing on Rokeach's work, Stephen Sales produced a small set of studies on the link between real-life threats and authoritarianism. In one study,

Sales (1972) identified a historical period (1920–1939) that experienced extreme variation in economic hardship (the Great Depression), but no other serious threats, such as war or environmental crises. Finding a unique set of data on the number of church converts over this period, he demonstrated that during economic hard times the rate of conversion to authoritarian churches increased, while during economic good times the rate of conversions to non-authoritarian churches increased.

Sales (1973) adopted the same approach in another study, this time identifying one low-threat period (1959–1964), and one high-threat period (1967–1970). This study is more relevant to our thesis, because the differences between the two periods involved levels of extreme violence. People living during the high-threat period experienced a much greater rate of violent crime, civil disorders, and troop casualties in the Vietnam War than during the low-threat period. Tapping a dizzying range of archival sources, Sales found that under the high-threat condition, Americans were more attracted to the tough sport of boxing and purchased more conservative periodicals; they bought and registered more attack dogs; they exhibited higher levels of cynicism, superstition, and support for the death penalty; police budgets grew and the punishment of sex offenders also increased.

One critique of the study by Sales (1973) was that his low-threat period occurred before the high-threat period, which did not allow him to account for the possibility that authoritarianism had naturally increased over time owing to alternative explanations, such as the growing size and complexity of the population and other trends. To suspend this doubt, Doty, Peterson, and Winter (1991) replicated the study, but used a high-threat period (1978–1982) that occurred prior to the low-threat period (1983–1987). In addition to replicating most of the findings of the previous study (Sales, 1973), they expanded it by examining new measures of prejudice, including anti-Semitic incidents, Ku Klux Klan activity, and responses to a battery of survey questions related to prejudice. The results further supported the assumption that when social environments become more stressful and threatening, people are more likely to condemn, reject and punish outsiders, especially those who violate conventional norms.

The terrorist attacks on 9/11 presented a unique opportunity for researchers to expand our understanding of the link between authoritarianism and threat in real-life circumstances. Given the diversity of this literature, we use the term authoritarian loosely here to categorize several related changes, from shifts in people's values to specific policy preferences. In the wake of 9/11, U.S. voters, in the aggregate, altered the way they evaluated leaders and public policies. They suddenly became more receptive to male leaders with stereotypical attributes of power, toughness, and resolve, who used quasi-patriotic rhetoric and proclaimed a determination to respond aggressively to

38 *Chapter 2*

the threat of terrorism (Pyszczynski, Geenberg & Solomon, 2003; Cohen et al., 2004; Gaines, 2002; Landau et al., 2004; Gailliot, Schmeichel & Baumeister, 2006; Gordijn & Stapel, 2006; Abramson et al., 2007; Falk & Kenski, 2006; Lawless, 2004).

Americans increasingly valued safety, order, and social stability (Verkasalo, Goodwin & Bezmenova, 2006), and they grew more likely to accept rigid hierarchies and differences in power in organizational contexts (Olivas-Luján, Harzing & McCoy, 2004; Skitka, Bauman & Mullen, 2004; Pyszczynski et al., 2006; Hastings & Shaffer, 2005; Crowson, Debacker & Thoma, 2006; Jarymowicz & Bar-Tal, 2006). Support for a military response to 9/11 and increases in defense spending spiraled upward. Public approval of using "military action against terrorism" hovered around 90 percent for no less than six months after the attacks (Huddy, Khatib & Capelos, 2002; Gallup Organization, 2001). A great majority of Americans (65–71%) approved the use of military force even if it resulted in "civilian causalities" and the use of "ground troops" (Huddy, Khatib & Capelos, 2002). The events of 9/11 also brought an increase in public support for the assassination of terrorist leaders (German Marshall Fund, 2002), and the nation uniformly celebrated the killing of Osama bin Laden in May 2011 (Stanley, 2011).

People began to favor stricter, more rigorous law enforcement and security measures after 9/11, even at the cost of their rights and liberties. Several studies demonstrated that the public's elevated readiness to give up some civil liberties to curb terrorism was substantial and long-lasting (Huddy, Khatib & Capelos, 2002; Huddy et al., 2005; Greenberg, Craighill & Greenberg, 2004; Best, Krueger & Ladewig, 2006; Davis, 2007; Hetherington & Weiler, 2009). The public's favorable views on such matters as requiring people to carry a national identity card at all times, racial profiling, warrant-less search and seizures, wiretapping and making it a crime to belong to any organization that supports terrorism remained quite high and stable from November 2001 to November 2004 (Greenberg, Craighill & Greenberg, 2004).

The attacks on 9/11 resulted in harmful circumstances for many Muslims and Arabs living in the United States. The prevailing climate of fear and distrust encouraged a range of offenses, from name calling and illegal prohibitions against head scarves in the workplace to falsified police reports, violent harassment, and murder. According to the Federal Bureau of Investigation, the number of hate crimes against Muslims rose considerably in 2001 and remained above the pre-9/11 level for more than a decade (Byers & Jones, 2007). A number of indicators suggest that public opinion of Arabs and Muslims also declined considerably in the years after 9/11 (Byers & Jones, 2007; Newport, 2009; Schafer & Shaw, 2009; Gallup Center for Muslim Studies, 2010). For instance, the percentages of Americans who believed that "mainstream Islam encourages violence against non-Muslims," and that "the attacks on America represent the true teachings of Islam" increased steadily in the years after the attacks (Panagopoulos, 2006).

THE EFFECTS OF PERCEIVED THREAT ON ATTITUDES TOWARD IMMIGRATION

Almost all the authoritarian reactions to 9/11 discussed above are ideologically aligned with restrictionist positions on immigration. Greater dogmatism and conformity to group norms among white Americans should hinder the multicultural spirit that drives support for progressive immigration policy. An increased use of stereotypes should strengthen negative attitudes toward immigrant out-groups, particularly Muslims, Arabs, and those whose skin colors and ethnicities differed most from the dominant Anglo norm. An amplified tendency for errors in attribution should make it easier for pundits to use immigration as a scapegoat for unemployment and crime. A growing concern among Americans about personal and national security, as well as the increased willingness to trade civil liberties for safety, should encourage support for stricter border controls, stricter enforcement of immigrant employment policies, stricter efforts to police "illegal immigration," including racial profiling, and greater support for the creation of new federal and state institutions to oversee immigration "problems."

There is also ample direct evidence that the perceived threat of terrorism directly affects attitudes, beliefs, and policy preferences on immigration. These studies fall into four categories: public opinion polls, panel studies, cross-national research, and experiments.

Public Opinion Polls

Public opinion experts have characterized the nation's views on immigration prior to 9/11 as "quite favorable" (Esses, Dovidio & Hodson, 2002, p. 72); after the attacks, there were "rapid, steep increases in anti-immigrant sentiment" (Muste, 2013, p. 398). Among the most common polling questions were items that asked about people's satisfaction with immigration, whether they wanted an increase or decrease in it, and how they judged the consequences of immigration. These questions were asked frequently by multiple firms, allowing for an extended time series. According to the Gallup Organization, the number of Americans who were dissatisfied with "the level of immigration into the country" stood at 55 percent in January 2001. This indicator jumped by 10 percent after the attacks and remained well above the pre-9/11 through 2012. When asked in a follow-up question about whether immigration should be "increased, decreased or remain about the same," 36

40 *Chapter 2*

percent favored a decrease prior to 9/11 and 52 percent said the same after 9/11. This indicator also stayed well above the pre-9/11 levels through 2012.

Gallup also regularly asked respondents about their preferred level of immigration without using the follow-up procedure described above. The results were roughly the same: the number of Americans who thought that "immigration should be decreased" stood at only 38 percent in September 2000. Roughly one year later, as the nation faced 9/11, this indicator rose to 58 percent (Gallup Organization, 2007). This twenty-point jump was noteworthy, given the steadiness of this measure over the prior two years, during which the indicator moved by no more than five points between polls. Also, per Gallup polls, the number of Americans who thought that "immigration is a bad thing for this country" increased from 31 percent in June 2001 to 42 percent in October of the same year.[10] This indicator fluctuated over the years, but on average remained above the pre-9/11 level for more than a decade. In a review of public opinion data from multiple polling organizations, Muste (2013) showed that academic survey firms, including the American National Election Studies (ANES) and General Social Survey (GSS), found a post-9/11 spike in anti-immigration views using similar questions.

Though asked less frequently, several other immigration-related survey questions revealed the same trend. According to a review of 9/11 effects by Traugott (2002), respondents who agreed that "immigrants make America more open to new ideas and cultures" dropped from 87 percent before the attacks to 81 percent after them. There was a five-point increase in the percentage of Americans who believed that immigrants increase the U.S. crime rate. After 9/11, Americans became particularly worried about "illegal immigrants." In April 2001, only 28 percent of respondents said that they were "greatly concerned" about illegal immigration; as late as April 2007, 45 percent of respondents reported the same thing (Segovia & Defever, 2010). Support for federal spending on border security and preventing illegal immigration also increased after the attacks (Kam & Kinder, 2007). In late 2000, 53 percent of Americans favored an increase in such spending; this indicator spiked to 70 percent in late 2002 and remained above pre-9/11 through 2004.

Data from multiple other polling firms and individual researchers illustrate a mild, yet long-term backlash against immigrants in the years following 9/11 (Pew Research Center, 2006; Newport, 2007; Jones, 2007; Moore, 2002; Panagopoulos, 2006; Esses, Dovidio & Hodson, 2002; Nagel, 2002). Some scholars have even shown that a similar 9/11 effect occurred in other countries. Based on pre-post 9/11 data, negative attitudes toward immigrants and immigration increased significantly in Germany (Schuller, 2012). Other studies revealed anti-immigrant backlashes in public opinion in the aftermath of other terrorist incidents, such as the Madrid bombings in Spain in 2004 (Legewie, 2013; Echebarria-Echabe & Fernández-Guede, 2006).

Panel Studies

The comparison of cross-sectional polling data from before and after 9/11 is interesting and informative, but it can only speak to changes in the aggregate, not at the individual level, and such studies cannot exclude alternative explanations of the pre- to post-9/11 differences. More robust research on 9/11's effect on immigration attitudes is rare. As one of the few examples, Hopkins (2010) used panel data to investigate how 9/11 shaped Americans' attitudes toward immigration. He argued that public concerns about immigration are influenced by media coverage on the topic and the framing of immigration as a political issue. After 9/11, when the national news regularly linked immigrants to terrorism and framed immigration as a security issue, public attitudes, especially in neighborhoods that had experienced a recent influx of immigrants, became significantly less favorable toward immigration. Using an expansive content analysis of news media and nationally representative survey data from the same individuals before and after 9/11, Hopkins showed that the salience of the immigration-security nexus in the news media did indeed spike after 9/11, along with the percentage of Americans who perceived immigrants as threatening (Hopkins, 2010).

To our best knowledge, the only other pre-post comparison based on panel data was a study by Bar-Tal and Labin (2001) that examined a small sample of adolescents from Israel. Data were collected from the panel before and after a major terrorist event in the country. Although not directly focused on immigration policy preferences, the study found that stereotypical perceptions of and negative attitudes toward three out-groups (Palestinians, Jordanians, and Arabs in general) increased significantly among Israeli youth after the terrorist incident.

Cross-National Research

The third approach to studying the link between immigration attitudes and perceived threats are cross-national studies that use aggregated data from multiple countries as units of analysis. Inglehart and Baker (2000), for instance, showed that people in societies where survival is threatened are more likely to see foreigners as dangerous and feel more threatened by diversity and cultural change than people in societies where physical safety and well-being are not major concerns. Based on data from 17 countries, Cohrs and Stelzl (2010) showed that perceptions of resource-based threats, such as unemployment, were correlated with unfavorable views of immigrant groups. More to the point of this book, Doosje et al. (2009), using data from nine European countries, found that people with higher terrorism threat perceptions were significantly more likely to support a policy to reduce the inflow of immigrants than people with lower terrorism threat perceptions.

Experiments

The fourth approach involves laboratory experiments, which allow researchers to control for a variety of variables and more clearly demonstrate the causal link between the perceived threat of terrorism and attitudes toward immigration. This literature, however, suffers from at least two shortcomings. One, there is little of it. Experimental manipulations of the terrorist threat are far less common than manipulations of other types of threat, such as economic competition (e.g., Jackson & Esses, 2000), mortality salience (e.g., Weise et al., 2012), or cultural threat and ethnic group cues (e.g., Brader Valentino & Suhay, 2008). And two, even the few studies that do manipulate terrorism threat must contend with matters of ecological validity. Terrorist attacks are extraordinary events and attempting to replicate public reactions to them in a laboratory is fraught with methodological limitations. Even with these weaknesses in mind, evidence from experimental research adds much to our argument.

One line of inquiry has shown that Americans are more concerned about foreign terrorists than homegrown ones. To make this point, Woods (2011a) developed an experiment where he manipulated three frames in a test article about a federal commission's evaluation of security risks in American cities. The article utilized news content from the Associated Press and was designed to resemble the layout and formatting of an actual newspaper article. Evoking the image of violent foreign zealots, some subjects read about the threat of "radical Islamic terrorists," while others read about the threat from "American citizens who view their government as the enemy." After reading the article, both groups answered questions about their reactions to the threat. Compared to the homegrown terrorism treatment, those subjects exposed to the radical Islamic frame reported significantly higher ratings of the likelihood of an attack (as described in the news article) occurring. They also gave significantly higher estimates of the number of people who would likely be killed if such an attack took place, and reported significantly higher levels of worry about the threat described in the news article. In an expansion of this study, Woods (2012) also demonstrated that those subjects who experienced heightened worry about terrorism were more likely to support aspects of the Bush Administration's war on terrorism, which, among others things, gave rise to several restrictionist immigration policies (Arthur & Woods, 2017).

The study by Woods (2011b) contributed to a well-established theory in the risk perception and decision science literatures: People react to a given danger based on characteristics of the threat that are unrelated, and sometimes negatively related, to the probability of the threat causing harm (Slovic, 2004). The foreignness of immigrants, as discussed at length in chapter 1, does not make them more likely to commit a crime, take the jobs of American workers, or carry out terrorist attacks. But the characteristic of foreignness itself may explain, in part, why people's fears of crime, job loss, and terrorism increase when they are associated with immigrants, and especially immigrant groups such as Muslims, Arabs, and Mexicans that have long been stigmatized in news media and popular culture. In some cases, the news media covers the issues of crime, job loss, terrorism, and immigration separately. Yet, as demonstrated in the next chapter, these threats are often linked in newspaper articles, broadcast news, and radio programs, which may compound public concerns about each of them and move public opinion toward restrictionist positions on immigration.

As mentioned, numerous researchers have used experimental designs to study the link between various types of threat and attitudes toward immigration, but the effects of the *terrorist* threat have been explored by only one additional experiment. Starting with the assumption that immigration threat is multidimensional, Lahav and Coutemanche (2012) manipulated three types of danger commonly associated with immigration—economic, cultural, and terrorist threat—and found that respondents who read about the terrorism frame were more likely to support restrictionist positions than those who received the economic or cultural threat news frames. They also discovered that the terrorism frame had a greater effect on liberals than conservatives. In this way, the ongoing discussion of security issues related to immigration in the years after 9/11 likely produced attitudinal convergence in the population, at least along ideological lines (Lahav & Coutemanche, 2012).

CONCLUSION

Why did public opinion on immigration sour in the early twenty-first century? Why did exclusionist immigration policies blossom during this period? Part of the answer lies in the events of 9/11. After the disaster, more Americans believed in and worried about the threat of terrorism than ever before. Although the number of fatalities due to terrorism has been extremely low compared to almost any other public health concern, the perceived threat of terrorism remained elevated in the public mind-set for at least two decades. As demonstrated by the massive flow of research in the years after 9/11, the public's new concerns about terrorism influenced a range of other attitudes, beliefs, and behaviors. In some respects, 9/11 encouraged Americans to be more pro-social. They reached out to their neighbors, contributed more to charities, supported their communities, learned more about current events, and became more civically engaged. But it also encouraged authoritarian sentiments, such as support for war, assassination and tougher law enforcement practices. Among the latter tendencies, which were generally more prominent

44 *Chapter 2*

and lasted longer, many Americans came to view immigrants and immigration policies in a less favorable light.

The individual-level psychological processes that explain the relationship between the perceived threat of terrorism and negative attitudes toward immigration are vital for understanding how restrictionists took the upper hand in the immigration debate in the early twenty-first century. As discussed in this chapter, certain characteristics of the terrorist threat are known to increase people's worries about both terrorism and immigration, and encourage the perceived link between them.

But how do people become aware of these characteristics in the first place? Although thousands of people tragically experienced the attacks firsthand, the clear majority of Americans learned about 9/11 through intermediaries. Broadcast news networks were among the most influential intermediaries in the first days after 9/11. But over the years, a variety of other individuals, groups, and organizations—presidents, the Congress, the newly created Department of Homeland Security, social media among others—disseminated information about 9/11, as well as subsequent attacks, and shaped the public's understanding of terrorism.

Most Americans also lack direct experience with immigrants, and the same intermediaries have shaped and filtered information about how this group affects society. The immigration debate itself is a contest between intermediaries who wish to either amplify or attenuate people's concerns about immigrants for the sake of shaping public policy. As discussed throughout the remainder of this book, restrictionist intermediaries took the upper hand in this contest after 9/11. The most powerful intermediaries in American society—the news media, interest groups, presidents, the Congress, and state legislatures—increasingly linked the dangers of terrorism to immigration, which amplified people's worries and risk perceptions of both issues and bolstered public support for restrictionist laws and government measures.

In the next chapter, we turn our attention to the news media. Moving from the social psychology of immigration attitudes to the political culture of the immigration debate, we examine the structural and cultural factors that shaped the discussion in major newspapers, television broadcasts, and radio programs of the 2000s and 2010s.

NOTES

1. See the Gallup data in a Continually Updated Report ("Terrorism in the United States"), online at www.gallup.com.

2. See the Gallup data in a Continually Updated Report ("Terrorism in the United States"), online at www.gallup.com.

The Perceived Threat of Terrorism

3. See a report by the Rand Corporation, "Do Significant Terrorist Attacks Increase the Risk of Further Attacks?" Retrieved online in July 2016, at http://www.rand.org/pubs/perspectives/PE173.html.

4. See a report by National Consortium for the Study of Terrorism and Responses to Terrorism (START), which is supported by the U.S. Department of Homeland Security Science and Technology Directorate's Office of University Programs and based on the Global Terrorism Database. Retrieved online in July 2016, at: https://www.start.umd.edu/pubs/START_AmericanTerrorismDeaths_FactSheet_Oct2015.pdf.

5. See a report by the Center for Disease Control and Prevention, "Number of Deaths from Lightning Among Males and Females—National Vital Statistics System, United States, 1968–2010," online at http://www.cdc.gov/mmwr/preview/mmwrhtml/mm6228a6.htm.

6. George W. Bush, "Address to a Joint Session of Congress and the American People," September 20, 2001. Retrieved online at www.whitehouse.gov; George W. Bush, "Remarks by the President upon Arrival," September 16, 2001. Retrieved online at www.whitehouse.gov.

7. See Executive Order 13228, October 8, 2001, "Establishing the Office of Homeland Security and the Homeland Security Council." Retrieved online on December 9, 2016, at http://fas.org/irp/offdocs/eo/eo-13228.htm.

8. See Executive Order 13228, October 8, 2001, "Establishing the Office of Homeland Security and the Homeland Security Council." Retrieved online on December 9, 2016, at http://fas.org/irp/offdocs/eo/eo-13228.htm.

9. See the U.S. Citizenship and Immigration Services, "Overview of INS History," USCIS History Office and Library, Washington DC, 2012. Retrieved online at https://www.uscis.gov/.

10. See a Continually Updated Survey by the Gallup Organization, "Gallup's Pulse of Democracy: Immigration," online at www.galluppoll.com.

Chapter 3

The News Media, Terrorism, and the Immigration Threat Nexus

Research on media portrayals of immigrants has examined a range of topics, but most studies follow one of three objectives.[1] They describe media coverage of specific groups, investigate how historical events shape the immigration debate, or look at differences in messages across media organizations (Branton & Dunaway, 2009a; Chavez, 2008; Montalvo & Torres, 2005; Cisneros, 2008; Fujiwara, 2005; Keogan, 2002). In this chapter, we attend to all three of these goals. First, using news stories from eight, large-circulation newspapers, we identify the five most common framing devices used by restrictionists in the immigration debate. These frames—illegality, crime, terrorism, economic threat, and cultural threat—represent enduring cultural scripts that can be found in news media, political rhetoric, and popular culture. As discussed in this chapter, the use of these negative frames in news media increased after the September 11, 2001, terrorist attacks. We also found that some immigrant groups were more likely than other groups to be associated with these frames.

This chapter places a special emphasis on two opinion-leading newspapers—one known for its liberal slant (*New York Times*) and one known for its conservative slant (*Wall Street Journal*)—to show how the political ideology of the news source shapes the story of immigration in the United States, even when controlling for a variety of other variables. Although the proportion of negative immigration framing increased in both newspapers after 9/11, this shift was much stronger in the conservative *Wall Street Journal*. We conclude this chapter by examining data from a computerized content analysis of a much larger sample of news outlets over a longer period. This analysis further contributes to our main argument that 9/11 brought a long-lasting authoritarian turn in the dominant symbolic repertoire on immigration.

48 *Chapter 3*

FRAMING IMMIGRATION

News Frames as Cultural Elements

As discussed in chapter 2, the assumption that threat perceptions activate authoritarian sentiments, such as negative views on immigration, is usually substantiated at the individual level and rooted in psychological processes (Dovidio & Esses, 2001; Feldman, 2003; Feldman & Stenner, 1997; Greenberg et al., 1990; Jackson & Esses, 2000; Lavine, Lodge, & Freitas, 2005; Pyszczynski et al., 2006; Tajfel & Turner, 1979; Pyszczynski, Greenberg, & Solomon, 2003). In contrast, this chapter evaluates the presence of authoritarianism in the form of cultural elements in leading news outlets—a proxy for elite political discourse (Bennett, 1990). Authoritarian elements (or frames) in media content may involve 1) a professed willingness to reject outsiders, 2) arguments in favor of punishing people who violate conventional values or traditions, or 3) the use of stereotypes or punitive categories in the discussion of outsiders (Perrin, 2005). Although our goal is to reveal changes in the use of these frames in media coverage after 9/11, we recognize that the post-9/11 framing of immigration is rooted in long-standing cultural elements, and that the events of 9/11 were only one of multiple factors that influenced and interacted with the dominant political culture on immigration.

Any differences in immigration news coverage after 9/11 should be traced to the "cultural tools" utilized by news organizations, as well as to the unwritten norms and roles of the broader culture. This perspective, most notably developed by Swidler (2001), is echoed in what Maney, Woehrle, and Coy (2005) and Williams (2002) refer to as the "dominant symbolic repertoire." Maney, Woehrle, and Coy (2005) noted that their concept draws on the ideas of Swidler (1986), Gamson (1992), Tarrow (1992), and Nagel (1994). To this list of helpful perspectives, we add the concept of "national cultural repertoires," developed in studies by both Lamont and Thévenot (2000) and Benson and Saguy (2005). The dominant symbolic repertoire can be generally defined as the "enduring norms, beliefs, language, visual images, narrations, and collective identities circulating widely among the general public" (Maney, Woehrle, & Coy, 2005, p. 358). The leading voices in the immigration debate are both the creators and the products of the dominant symbolic repertoire. Existing within the boundaries of the given historical context, the dominant repertoire is like a smorgasbord of symbols and ideas that both enables and constrains the meanings of immigration that journalists, politicians, and average people can produce and consume.

The immigration debate is only possible because people share an understanding of the foreign-born population. Over years of being socialized in the political culture of the United States, people come to accept and take for granted the meanings of the dominant repertoire. These predispositions allow them to easily translate and understand new events using an old, stable set of ideas. Although the repertoire changed in response to 9/11, the change itself was made possible by the stable meanings that people attached to its various aspects.

Immigrant Threat Narratives

After 9/11, some observers regarded the Bush administration's "War on terrorism" as something new and extraordinary. In many ways, it was, but it tapped into a preexisting cultural script—a way of seeing the world that formed over decades, not months or years. The United States has been involved in military conflicts for much of its history. Regardless of what originally caused these wars, they reinforced ideas, outlooks, and behaviors that increased the ease and likelihood of people understanding future wars in a similar light. For this reason, there was no need for the Bush administration to invent a new ideology on 9/11. The norms and values that cultivated public support for war and other aggressive policies, including tighter restrictions on foreigners and harsher immigration law enforcement practices, were already in place. Government officials have pushed for restrictions on the foreign-born or those believed to be loyal to a foreign country because of their immigrant ancestry at many times in response to public hysteria or concern, resulting in regrettable policies such as the *Chinese Exclusion Act* of 1882 and the forced internment of Japanese, Germans, and Italians during World War II.

Prior to 9/11, news stories linking immigrants to various deviant or criminal behaviors were already common in mainstream media. Newsmakers often created spectacles around the so-called foreign invasion and associated the influx of immigrants with social problems such as crime, economic decline, cultural degradation, overpopulation, and disease (Chavez, 2008). After 9/11, the immigration threat narrative was refined, institutionalized, and increasingly invoked by public officials, government agencies, and the mainstream news media. Only days after the attacks, officials identified the prime suspects as foreigners, and the security breach itself was later traced to failures within the Immigration and Naturalization Service (Mitchell, 2001). Thousands of immigrants instantly became suspects and many were detained in the ensuing investigation (Bernstein, 2004). Although Arabs and Muslims were especially prominent in the media's rising negative coverage of immigration, the threat of terrorism became part of a more generalized immigrant threat narrative involving Latinos and other groups (Chavez, 2008).

President George W. Bush and other White House officials made it clear that the U.S.-Mexico border was now a primary homeland security concern, although none of the 9/11 terrorists had entered the United States illegally through Mexico.[2] The Bush administration carried out one of the largest bureaucratic reorganizations in U.S. history when it placed the Department of Immigration and Naturalization Services under a new agency, the Department of Homeland Security. The change reshaped the mission statement of the agency to one involving terrorism management and prevention. The idea of a "borderless world" went out of fashion in Washington policy circles, while pundits and anti-immigration groups made sweeping claims about the link between immigration and terrorism (Andreas, 2002; DeParle, 2011; Elliot, 2011) and used the new threat to legitimize their calls for enhanced border security (Shenon, 2003), a crackdown on illegal immigration (Sterngold, 2001), and the legalization of racial profiling.[3]

As discussed in chapter 2, the supposed link between terrorism and immigration also appeared in American public opinion. After 9/11, the number of Americans that favored a reduction in immigration increased considerably. The proportion of people with unfavorable attitudes toward immigration fluctuated over the years, but generally remained above pre-9/11 levels for more than a decade.

Hypotheses

Given the four factors discussed above—the preexistence of an anti-immigrant discourse, the persistent link between terrorism and immigration in public opinion, the rise in authoritarian scripts in political culture (Perrin, 2005), and the permanence of harsher, more restrictive immigration policies and law enforcement procedures—it is plausible that the mass-mediated discussion of immigration contained greater concern and intolerance toward foreigners and more discussion of immigration as a national security issue after 9/11. Specifically, we propose that the eight, large-circulation newspapers in our sample will contain a greater number of negative news frames in the post-9/11 period than in the pre-9/11 period.

As mentioned, one element of authoritarian political culture is the use of stereotypes, rigid social categories, and the rejection of outsiders (Perrin, 2005). For this reason, differences in the extent to which certain immigrant groups are portrayed in media as foreign or *outside* the dominant Anglo norm should be considered. Numerous studies have reported racial and ethnic biases in news coverage and oversimplified media representations of minorities, including immigrant groups (Branton & Dunaway, 2008; Branton & Dunaway, 2009b; Fryberg et al., 2011; Hood & Morris, 1998). Drawing on these studies, we expect that non-European immigrants, whose national origin has been racialized in the U.S. cultural context and ranked lower in the social hierarchy, are more likely to be portrayed with negative frames than Europeans, whose race and ethnicity are widely perceived as closer to the traditional Anglo norm. In addition to the research on racial bias in media, a number of studies have demonstrated that public attitudes toward immigrants are influenced by symbolic orientations and ideologies, including racial prejudice (Ayers et al., 2009; Dustmann & Preston, 2007; Fetzer, 2000; Hood & Morris, 1997; Loveman & Hofstetter, 1984; Short & Magana, 2002). As an investigation of political culture, however, this study must remain agnostic on whether racial prejudice (at the level of individuals) influences the portrait of immigrants in the news. We argue instead, as we did previously, that differences in the portrayals of European and non-European immigrant groups should be traced to the cultural tools or symbolic repertoires used by newsmakers within a particular historical context. Specifically, we hypothesize that newspaper articles on immigration will associate negative news frames with non-European immigrants more often than with European (or Canadian) immigrants.

Following both the psychological and cultural literatures on authoritarianism, it is reasonable to assume that a newspaper with a decidedly conservative or right-leaning political ideology will tend to express more authoritarian cultural scripts than a liberal or left-leaning newspaper. For the same reason, it may be further hypothesized that a newspaper with marked authoritarian tendencies is more likely to circulate negative framing of outsiders such as immigrants than a newspaper without these tendencies.

To explore these assumptions, the first task is to consider whether the political ideologies of the newspapers in this study can be accurately measured and compared. After some consideration, we determined that categorizing the ideologies of all eight newspapers in this study was not possible. Many newspapers do not make clear statements about their political affiliation or even endorse presidential candidates. Although all the newspapers in our sample have large circulations, they have not all drawn the attention of scholars. For these reasons, we will focus our analysis of ideological effects on the *New York Times* and *Wall Street Journal,* which are somewhat easier to place in political ideological categories.

At the same time, we should stress that any attempt to classify a daily newspaper as having a "liberal" or "conservative" bias is a challenging and controversial endeavor, and one whose results should be interpreted with caution. Nevertheless, there is some agreement among social scientists that the *New York Times* conveys a more liberal slant and a pro-Democrat bias, and that the *Wall Street Journal* is a more conservative, Republican-leaning newspaper.

The scientific measurement of "slant" often involves a comparison between a newspaper's language use and the words and phrases uttered by Republicans versus Democrats in their official congressional statements. Following this line of research, Gentzkow and Shapiro (2006) used a computerized "text

52   *Chapter 3*

categorization" procedure to identify certain phrases in the *Congressional Record* that are likely to be informative about partisanship.[4] For instance, Republicans are more likely to use the phrase "death tax" to describe the federal tax on assets of the deceased than by Democrats who tend to use the alternative phrase "estate tax." Incidentally, Gentzkow and Shapiro (2006) also found that the phrase "illegal immigrants" is uttered more frequently by Republicans than by Democrats. Using their findings on a large number of common partisan phrases, the researchers then computed the slant of newspapers based on how often each used the specified sets of phrases. According to Gentzkow and Shapiro's slant index (2006, 2010), the *Wall Street Journal* is more likely to utilize Republican phraseology and less likely to use the Democrats' favored terms than the *New York Times*. Their study also noted that a large (though non-random) sample of website users (www.mondotimes.com) rated the ideological leaning of the *Wall Street Journal* as far more conservative than the *New York Times*.

The slant of news outlets has also been measured using the self-reported political views of the readerships. According to a study by the Pew Research Center (2010), among the regular readers of the *New York Times,* only nine percent report being Republicans and 11 percent characterize their political ideology as conservative (a plurality of these readers report being Democrats and Liberals). Among the *Wall Street Journal's* regular readers, 36 percent are Republicans and 45 percent report being conservative (only 22% are Democrats and 12% are liberal). The two readerships also diverge consistently on specific political attitudes. *New York Times* readers are significantly more likely than *Wall Street Journal* readers to consider themselves "environmentalists," "progressives," and "gay rights supporters," whereas *Wall Street Journal* readers outnumber their counterparts as self-described "Christian Conservatives," "NRA supporters," and "Tea Party supporters" (Pew Research Center For The People & The Press, 2010).

Although these findings indicate that the two newspapers do indeed represent different ideological frameworks, the issue of immigration may, as a special case, cut across these contexts. Historically, the editorial staff at the *Wall Street Journal* has taken a neoliberal conservative stance on immigration and favored open borders as a strategy for economic growth. Although the *Wall Street Journal* may be more conservative than the *New York Times* on most issues, immigration may be an exception. In our sample of articles, especially those published in the years prior to 9/11, we found several *Wall Street Journal* editorials that support this notion. In an April 2000 editorial, for instance, the staff criticized "the arbitrariness that characterizes the Immigration and Naturalization Service's (INS) approach to people whose only crime is to have arrived here in search of a better life for themselves" (*WSJ* editorial, 2000). The editors further argued that the executives of large corporations who need foreign workers and favor open borders are better equipped to decide who can enter the country. An editorial published in July 2001 promoted a quicker, easier pathway to citizenship for immigrants, and described three dramatic cases of immigrants who risked everything to reach the United States, worked hard, and achieved much (*WSJ* editorial, 2001).

According to a study by Page (1996), if the editorials in the *Wall Street Journal* generally offer a positive take on immigration, it is likely that other parts of the newspaper follow suit. Furthermore, in a study of the press in France and the United States, Benson (2009) found that financial newspapers in both countries emphasized the economic benefits of immigration and produced more favorable coverage on this issue. Given the contradictory nature of previous studies, we investigate the effects of the news source on the framing of immigration as a research question. We wish to determine, more specifically, whether the articles on immigration published in the *Wall Street Journal* contain a greater number of negative news frames than those appearing in the *New York Times*.

In addition to the three variables above, we also consider whether the use of negative frames in press coverage of immigration depends in part on the article's type (news vs. opinion), location in the newspaper (sections A, B, C, or D), and the extent to which the topic of immigration itself plays a central or peripheral role in the story (salience). To our best knowledge, there are no previous studies that provide guidance for developing hypotheses about these variables. Conventional wisdom may suggest that negative frames are more common in the opinion pages where strong polemics and emotional debates are welcomed by editors. However, news articles about the immigration debate also contain opinionated statements, slogans, and emotive sound bites from both sides. The location where articles are placed should also be taken into account, because articles located in the front of newspapers are more likely to be read and therefore more likely to influence public perceptions of immigration (Bogart, 1989; Graber, 1988). The extent to which the topic itself is covered in a given newspaper article must be considered as well. Immigration is the main subject in some articles, but receives only a minor mention in others. Although we expect, based on common sense, to find a greater number of negative frames in articles that spend more time on the topic, the extent to which this assumption holds true is unknown, and therefore examining this variable may provide new information. Moreover, controlling for each of these variables (article type, section location, and salience) will help guard the validity of other possible predictors of negative framing in our multivariate analysis. Given the general lack of previous research on these variables, we investigate these variables as research questions, as opposed to hypotheses.

54   *Chapter 3*

The Framing Nexus

Each of the hypotheses and research questions discussed above involves an assumed coalescence of various images and ideas about immigrants or immigration. We refer to such a communicative package as a "framing nexus." A nexus, as its dictionary definition specifies, is a connection or link between objects. Cellular biologists define a nexus as the fusion of the plasma membranes of two or more adjacent cells (Dewey & Barr, 1964). Nexuses permit chemical or electrical communication to pass between cells, enabling the organization and operation of complex biological functions. In cardiac muscles, for instance, nexuses allow the muscles of the heart to contract in tandem. In a similar fashion, a framing nexus involves the fusion of two or more news frames in a newspaper article, television show, or political discourse that enables the transmission of a more complex message.

A framing nexus refers merely to a co-occurrence of carefully identified words, phrases, or images (e.g., "immigrant," "Mexican," "illegal," "terrorism"). Three related issues—to what extent framing nexuses exist in the mass media, why they exist as they do, and whether they influence human consciousness—represent a challenging set of empirical questions to which there may not always be straightforward answers. In the immigration debate, framing nexuses are used by some elites to denounce and limit immigration and curb dissenting voices, but they are also used by frame-challengers to defy the dominant symbolic repertoire and push for more open or humane immigration policies (Entman, 2003). In short, a framing nexus is a conceptual tool, not a predictive or theoretical model.[5]

METHOD

Data

One of our aims is to analyze news stories about immigration in the "opinion-leading" (or elite) press in the United States. Based on previous studies (Hertog, 2000; Horvit, 2003; Swain, 2003; Ten Eyck & Williment, 2003), we focus on the *New York Times* and the *Wall Street Journal* as proxies of the elite press. Both of these high-circulation newspapers play key roles in national decision making and influence the news coverage of other media outlets (Baumgartner & Jones, 2009; Gans, 1979; Gitlin, 1980). As previously discussed, the former newspaper is known for its liberal slant, and the latter is thought to be more conservative, which makes it possible to simultaneously investigate the effects of 9/11 on leading newspapers in general and also examine the potentially divergent reactions in liberal versus conservative news outlets. Put differently, the choice of these two newspapers represents a purposive sample that will offer preliminary findings upon which to establish a broader investigation of the relationship between terrorist events, political ideology, and the public discussion of immigration in the United States.

In addition to the *New York Times* and *Wall Street Journal*, we also extracted samples from six other large-circulation newspapers, including *USA Today*, *Washington Post*, *San Jose Mercury News*, *Houston Chronicle*, *Philadelphia Inquirer*, and *Denver Post*. These were the largest available newspapers, as reported by the Audit Bureau of Circulation.[6] These publications represent a much broader news environment, both in terms of their geography and impact on national politics. Analyses of these newspapers will allow us to determine whether the hypothesized post-9/11 changes in the mass-mediated immigration debate occurred across diverse news outlets.

We utilized two online databases (Lexis-Nexis Academic & Proquest) to construct a large sampling frame of articles that were published over a six-year period centered on the events of 9/11 (September 11, 1998, to September 10, 2004). All the articles contained at least one of the four designated search terms: immigrant, immigrate, immigration, and alien. We used a systematic random sampling technique, stratified by year, to select 180 articles from each newspaper (90 from the pre-9/11 period and 90 from the post-9/11 period) for a total sample of 1,440 articles.

Several articles in the sample mentioned immigrants from more than one country of origin. In some cases, immigrants of two different nationalities were associated with different negative frames. For instance, an article might mention *illegal Mexican* immigrants, as well as discuss a *terrorism* suspect from *Egypt*. If such an article appeared in the sample, it was broken into two separate recording units, one for each country of origin mentioned. A limit of five recording units per article was instated to moderate the influence of any one article on the overall results. In total, 2,268 recording units were extracted from the 1,440 articles in the sample.

Coding the Anti-Immigration Framing Nexus

Each recording unit was coded on ten variables, including the period of publication (1 = After 9/11; 0 = Before 9/11), the type of article (1 = opinion; 0 = news), newspaper section (1 = Section A; 0 = Sections B, C, D, and deeper), the salience of immigration as a topic in the article (1 = majority of paragraphs are on-topic; 0 = majority of paragraphs are off-topic), the region of origin of the immigrant in the story (1 = Non-European/Non-Canadian; 0 = European/Canadian), as well as five variables designed to identify whether an immigrant was associated with undesirable actions, outcomes, or labels (1 = Mentioned; 0 = Not mentioned). Before the quantitative coding procedure began, we identified four dimensions (illegal, criminal, terrorism,

56 *Chapter 3*

and economic threat) as the most common negative framing devices by examining more than 100 newspaper articles using an open coding procedure. In addition, we included an "other/specify" category in our quantitative coding scheme, which allowed us to determine that the four selected frames did indeed rank among the most common negative descriptors in our large sample of articles. In the process of collecting data in the other category, we identified a fifth dimension, which can be broadly understood as the "cultural threat" frame.

The first negative framing nexus involves the mentioning of an immigrant's illegal or undocumented status. Although there are various examples of this nexus, the most common case is the label "illegal immigrants" (or "illegal immigration"). For instance, as reported in the *New York Times*, Texas Congressman Lamar Smith criticized a new federal rule, suggesting that it "encourages more illegal immigration" (Brinkley, 1999). The second nexus can be found in stories that associate immigrants with various other crimes (not including immigration violations or terrorism), such as the sale of illicit drugs, prostitution, gang violence, and human trafficking. As one example, the *New York Times* reported on a law enforcement operation in San Diego that involved the arrest of immigrants on "weapons and drug charges" ("Cab Drivers & Guards Detained," 2003).

The third nexus was operationalized as any reference, direct or indirect, that links immigrants or immigration to terrorism. In a *Wall Street Journal* op-ed piece, for instance, Griffen Bell, a former U.S. attorney general, defended the Justice Department's post-9/11 roundup and detention of terrorism suspects, many of them immigrants, stating that "The new provisions of the Immigration and Nationality Act, which permit the indefinite detention of suspected terrorists pending criminal or removal proceedings, are consistent with the discretion afforded the administration in fighting this unique threat" (Bell, 2001). The fourth category of analysis involved the supposed link between immigration and a range of economic threats. An article might suggest that immigrants take away jobs from American workers, drive down wages, hurt tax payers, weaken real estate values, inflate hospital costs, or harm the public education system. For instance, a *New York Times* article attributed the problem of overcrowding in New York City schools to "an influx of immigrants, mainly from the Dominican Republic" (Archibold, 1999). Finally, the cultural threat frame encompassed a range of controversial claims, such as concerns about immigrants' English-language acquisition and other aspects of assimilation, and critical comments about immigrants' attitudes, beliefs, rituals, or moral qualities. As one example, an op-ed in the *Denver Post* came out strongly in favor of Initiative 31, a 2002 ballot measure that would have required that all public school students in Colorado be taught in English. The author argued against bilingual education and suggested that immigrant students who lack English-language ability cannot be successful in the United States. It should be noted that blatantly racist statements about immigrant culture were extremely rare.

Reliability

A great deal of time and energy went into testing the reliability of the data. Standard inter-coder agreement tests were conducted on all the variables using roughly 30 percent (105 articles) of the total articles in the sample. The percentage of agreement on the eleven variables ranged from 86 percent to 100 percent. Scott's Pi, which corrects for chance agreement, ranged from .78 to .95 on these variables. Compared to other acceptable reliability coefficients, such as Cohen's Kappa, Scott's Pi is a more conservative measure (Riffe, Lacy, & Fico, 2005). Krippendorff (1978) has suggested that Alpha levels of .80 or higher indicate adequate reliability. This standard is also commonly found in published research (Riffe, Lacy & Fico, 2005). Only one of the eleven variables (the variable measuring the salience of immigration as a topic in the article) had an Alpha that was slightly below the .80 standard at .78. Overall, the inter-coder reliability tests returned results that far exceeded conventional standards.

This method of testing reliability involved two, well-trained coders who spent several hours perfecting their ability to interpret newspaper articles independently in roughly the same manner. One critique of this method suggests that the careful training of coders may ensure reliability, but it also produces an artificial, specialized set of interpretations. Put differently, the statistical validation of inter-coder reliability does not ensure that members of the general population will draw similar conclusions as the well-trained coders. To explore this concern, we carried out an additional reliability assessment using twelve coders who received only cursory training on how to categorize content according to the codebook and protocol. These tests showed that a very high level of intersubjectivity exists on each of the issues in the codebook.

The twelve coders were asked to read fifteen abbreviated portions of articles from the sample and identify the country of origin of any immigrant mentioned (or indicate that no country was mentioned), and whether the given immigrant or source country was associated with any of the negative frames (illegal, criminal, terrorism, and economic threats). On thirteen out of fifteen units of analysis, all twelve coders, working independently, identified the same country of origin. The average percentage of agreement among the twelve coders was roughly 92 percent on mentions of illegality, 98 percent on mentions of other criminal acts, 98 percent on references to terrorism, and 94 percent on mentions of immigrants as economic threats. As mentioned,

58   *Chapter 3*

the cultural threat frame was developed from the entries listed in the "other/specify" category. For this reason, it was not scrutinized with this additional, twelve-coder reliability test; however, there was 100 percent inter-coder reliability on this variable using the dual-coder method. In short, the coding scheme proved to be highly reliable based on both standard and extraordinary tests.

MEASUREMENT

Dependent Variable

The dependent variable is the frequency of negative frames in newspaper articles on immigration. We measure this variable in three ways. Each of these measurements reveals a different aspect of the news coverage. First, we calculate the *mean* number of distinct negative frames per recording unit. Given the fact that there are five different negative frames (illegal, criminal, terrorism, economic threat, and cultural threat), this measure ranges from 0 to 5. We refer to it as the *threat index.* The purpose of this variable is to highlight the intensity and diversity of negative framing of immigrants in a given unit. Second, we dichotomize the variable and determine whether *at least one* negative frame was used in the given recording unit. This operationalization has the advantage of parsimony. The variable allows us to make simple percentage comparisons across the categories of the independent variables. This operationalization rests on the most meaningful difference between newspaper articles, as it differentiates those which contain no negative frames from those which contain at least one. Third, we also report on the varying prevalence of each of the five negative frames separately (illegal, criminal, terrorism, economic threat, and cultural threat).

Independent Variables

All the independent variables are dichotomous. Essentially, we ask the same question over and over: Are negative frames involving immigrants more common under Condition A or Condition B? We answer these questions by 1) comparing the percentage of units containing *at least one* negative frame across the two conditions and by 2) comparing the *mean* number of frames per unit across the two conditions. In the first case, we test the variables with a chi-square test for independence. The test demonstrates whether at least one negative frame appeared in significantly more post-9/11 articles than pre-9/11 articles, in more articles about non-European immigrants than European/Canadian immigrants, and in more *Wall Street Journal* articles than

New York Times articles. In the second case, we retest the hypotheses with a one-way analysis of variance, which will determine whether the mean number of distinct negative frames varied significantly in the expected directions.

After concluding the bivariate investigation, we create a binary logistic regression model to explore the predictive ability of the independent variables on the categorical dependent variable, while controlling for the effects of the other predictors in the model. We also run a multiple regression model for the same purpose but switch in the terrorism index (a ratio-level, continuous variable).

RESULTS

Bivariate Analysis

Confirming our general hypothesis, 9/11 had a strong and consistent effect on the framing of immigration. As shown in Table 3.1, the percentage of units containing at least one negative frame increased from 34 percent before 9/11 to 50 percent after 9/11. The change was significant for all five frames (illegal, criminal, terrorism, economic threat, and cultural threat). Not surprisingly, the immigration-terrorism nexus showed the greatest increase in prevalence. Using the threat index as the dependent variable, the mean number of negative frames was significantly higher after ($M = .76$) than before ($M = .43$) the 9/11 attacks ($F(1, 2,267) = 97.20$, eta squared $= .041$, $p < .001$). As shown in Table 3.3, the increase in negative news coverage of immigration increased significantly in six of the eight newspapers in the sample, including the *New*

Table 3.1 Effects of 9/11 on the Use of Negative Immigrant Frames

	Before Sep. 11% (units)	After Sep. 11% (units)	Δ%	χ^2	P^1
At least one negative frame mentioned	34 (369)	50 (591)	+16	58.97	<.001
Illegal mentioned	23 (251)	28 (330)	+5	6.73	.011
Criminal mentioned	10 (112)	15 (173)	+5	9.53	.002
Terrorism mentioned	1.5 (16)	21 (245)	+19.5	205.62	<.001
Economic threat mentioned	4 (44)	6 (69)	+2	3.77	.054
Cultural threat mentioned	4 (39)	7 (79)	+3	10.91	.001
Total units	1,085	1,183			

[1] P values are based on two-sided significance tests.

60   *Chapter 3*

York Times, Wall Street Journal, USA Today, Washington Post, San Jose Mercury News, and *Houston Chronicle.* There were only small, insignificant changes in negative framing in the *Denver Post* (plus 2%) and *Philadelphia Inquirer* (minus 2%).

European immigrants were linked to at least one negative frame in 19 percent of the units, while non-Europeans were cast in an unfavorable light in 47 percent of the units (see Table 3.2). The percentage difference was significant for four of the five negative frames. Non-Europeans were more likely to be linked to illegality, crime, terrorism, and economic threats than their European counterparts. There was little difference in the use of the cultural threat frame across the two immigrant groups. Based on the threat index, non-Europeans (M = .67) were also associated with significantly more negative frames per unit than Europeans (M = .27) (F(1, 2267) = 80.25, eta squared = .034, p < .001). Following 9/11, the amount of negative coverage of non-European immigrants increased considerably from 38 percent prior to the attacks to 55 percent after 9/11 (χ^2 = 55.76, p = <.001). However, there was no significant change in the rate of negative framing of European immigrants (χ^2 = 2.54, p = .111):

Moving to our analysis of the *New York Times* and *Wall Street Journal,* it seemed, at first glance, that the two ideologically diverse newspapers produced similar coverage of immigration. About the same percentage of units from the *New York Times* (35%) and *Wall Street Journal* (37%) contained at least one negative frame. The differences between the news sources were trivial on all but one of the four frames. The *Wall Street Journal* (20%), however, did use a significantly greater percentage of terrorism frames than the *New York Times* (10%)(χ^2 = 9.48, p = .002). On the threat index, there was only a

Table 3.2   Effects of Immigrant Group on the Use of Negative Immigrant Frames

	Europeans % (units)	Non-Europeans % (units)	Diff.%	χ^2	P
At least one negative frame mentioned	19 (77)	47 (883)	28	104.43	<.001
Illegal mentioned	9 (35)	29 (546)	20	71.69	<.001
Criminal mentioned	7 (29)	14 (256)	7	12.24	<.001
Terrorism mentioned	6 (23)	13 (238)	7	15.55	<.001
Economic threat mentioned	0.3 (1)	6 (112)	5.7	22.82	<.001
Cultural threat mentioned	5 (20)	5 (98)	0	.031	1.0
Total units	398	1,870			

minute, insignificant difference of .03 between the two newspapers (F(1, 535) = .146, eta squared = .000, p = .702). (These figures are not shown in tables.)

After further analysis, however, we discovered that the post-9/11 increase in negative coverage was substantially greater in the *Wall Street Journal* than in the *New York Times*. Surprisingly, the former newspaper contained 10 percent fewer negative frames in the pre-9/11 period than the latter newspaper, but then the relationship flip-flopped after 9/11. In the *New York Times*, the percentage units with negative frames rose from 27 percent to 43 percent, while in the *Wall Street Journal* the same indicator jumped from 17 percent to 57 percent. In short, the *Wall Street Journal* was significantly less likely to offer negative news coverage of immigration before 9/11, and significantly more likely to contain such framing after the tragic events.

Mixed results were found in regard to the other research questions. First, negative news coverage of immigration did not vary much by article type. The percentage of news articles (42.2%) with at least one negative frame was not significantly greater than the percentage of opinion articles (42.6%) with one negative frame. The difference between article types was also trivial on the threat index. However, articles appearing in Section A (51%) were far more likely to contain at least one negative frame than articles in Section B and beyond (33%) (χ^2 = 70.55, p < .001). Based on the threat index, the mean for articles in Section A was .73, while the mean was .45 in articles appearing in Section B or later (F(1, 2265) = 69.04, eta squared = .03, p = <.001). Finally, the salience of immigration as a topic was a strong predictor of the use of negative frames. Among articles coded as "mostly on-topic," 52 percent contained at least one negative frame, whereas only 28 percent of articles coded as "mostly off-topic" included such a frame (χ^2 = 134.87, p < .001).

Table 3.3   A Comparison of the Effects of 9/11 on the Use of Negative Immigrant Frames by News Sources

	Before 9/11 % (units)	After 9/11 % (units)	Δ%	χ^2	P[1]
News Source (units with at least one negative frame)					
New York Times	27 (41/150)	43 (59/136)	+16	8.08	.004
Wall Street Journal	17 (22/126)	57 (71/125)	+40	41.64	<.001
Washington Post	26 (29/111)	39 (54/140)	+13	4.33	.043
Denver Post	49 (63/129)	52 (85/165)	+2	.208	.724
Houston Chronicle	48 (81/170)	58 (112/194)	+10	3.699	.059
Philadelphia Inquirer	33 (51/156)	31 (44/140)	−2	.054	.901
USA Today	24 (25/105)	71 (87/122)	+47	50.943	<.001
San Jose Mercury News	37 (51/138)	48 (78/161)	+11	4.000	.048

[1] P values are based on two-sided significance tests.

62   *Chapter 3*

The mean difference between these conditions was also highly significant on the threat index (mostly on-topic mean = .78; mostly off-topic mean = .33) (F(1, 2267) = 87.55, eta squared = .072, p < .001).

Multivariate Analysis

To further investigate the individual predictive power of the relationships discussed above, we conducted a multiple regression analysis. The threat index served as the dependent variable. The independent variables were the four significant predictors of negative framing, as established by the bivariate analyses (majority of paragraphs on-topic, published after 9/11, non-European immigrants, and published in Section A). In constructing the model, the basic assumptions and potential shortcomings of regression were considered and found to be unproblematic.[7] As shown in Table 3.4, all four independent variables contributed significantly to the explained variance of the threat index, while controlling for the other factors. Articles published after 9/11 contained significantly more negative frames than those published before. Country of origin was another powerful predictor of negative framing, with non-European immigrants being significantly more likely to be associated with negative frames than European immigrants. The salience of immigration in the given article and the location of the article in the newspaper were also significant predictors. Articles that were mostly on-topic were far more likely to contain negative frames than mostly off-topic articles. Articles located in the first section of the newspaper were also significantly more likely to contain such frames.

To test the power of these predictors on the dichotomized dependent variable (*at least one* negative frame used), we conducted a logistic regression. As shown in Table 3.5, with all the variables in the model simultaneously, each of the predictors was significantly associated with the probability of a news article containing at least one negative frame. Holding all the other variables constant, articles published after 9/11 were more than two times more likely to contain a negative frame than articles published before 9/11. Compared to

Table 3.4   Regression Model Showing Standardized Regression Coefficients for Four Predictors of the Number of Negative Immigrant Frames in News Articles

	Standardized Regression Coefficients	*p*
Majority of paragraphs "on-topic"	.256	<.001
Published After 9/11	.214	<.001
Non-European Immigrants	.147	<.001
Published in Section A	.132	<.001
R Square	.160	<.001

The News Media, Terrorism, and the Immigration Threat Nexus

Table 3.5 Odds Ratios from Logistic Regression Models of the Use of At Least One Negative Frame in News Articles

	B	Standard Error	Wald	Odds Ratio	P
Majority of paragraphs "on-topic"	1.113	.098	129.87	3.04	<.001
Published After 9/11	0.812	.094	74.60	2.25	<.001
Non-European Immigrants	1.261	.142	78.84	3.53	<.001
Published in Section A	.646	.093	48.04	0.52	<.001

European immigrants, non-European immigrants were three and a half times more likely to be linked to at least one of the threatening frames. Articles that were mostly on-topic were about three times more likely than articles mostly off-topic to contain a negative frame. And, articles located in Section A were fifty percent more likely as articles in Section B and beyond to contain such a frame.

DISCUSSION

Interpretive Summary

This chapter makes a number of important theoretical and methodological contributions to research on framing, authoritarianism, and the immigration debate in the United States. Building on Perrin's (2005) study of authoritarian sentiment in letters to the editor, we demonstrated that negative news coverage on immigration increased substantially after the attacks on 9/11. Although authoritarian discourse was not actually coded in this study, our results were consistent with an authoritarian shift in language. Our study contributes in particular by showing that the general cultural shift discussed by Perrin (2005) materialized in the framing of a specific political issue. While our study can only speak to immigration, media discourses on other topics, such as crime, war, Middle East politics, and gay rights, may have changed in similar ways.

As discussed in chapter 2, the rise of the immigrant threat narrative after 9/11 represents one case of a more general coarsening of political culture—a trend we referred to as the *authoritarian turn* (Abramson et al., 2007; Cohen et al., 2004; Gailliot, Schmeichel, & Baumeister, 2006; Gaines, 2002; Gordijn & Stapel, 2006; Landau et al., 2004; Pyszczynski, Greenberg, & Solomon, 2003; Skitka, Bauman, & Mullen, 2004; Smith, Rasinski, & Toce, 2001; Verkasalo, Goodwin, & Bezmenova, 2006). Three of our major findings offer further evidence that is consistent with the authoritarian turn.

64 *Chapter 3*

First, while there was a significant increase in negative framing of non-European immigrant groups, there was only a small, non-significant climb in negative framing of European immigrants. As Americans responded to the most vivid foreign attack in U.S. history, the news coverage of immigrants was least kind to those whose skin color and culture differed most from the dominant Anglo norm. This finding is consistent with conventional theories of authoritarian responses to threats. Second, the negative shift in coverage was more pronounced in the conservative *Wall Street Journal* than in the liberal *New York Times*. In fact, the post-9/11 increase in negative framing was two times greater in the *Wall Street Journal*. We were most surprised to find that, prior to 9/11, the *Wall Street Journal* was less likely than the *New York Times* to link immigrants to illegality, crime, terrorism, or economic, and cultural threats. After 9/11, it seemed that the *New York Times* adopted a watchdog stance on immigration and became a protector of the image of immigrants, while the *Wall Street Journal* took a more pronounced authoritarian turn, and focused more on the security issues posed by open borders. Finally, the substantial increases in negative coverage of immigration was found in six out of the eight newspapers in our sample, indicating that the authoritarian turn was indeed a general culture shift, which included news outlets of different sizes, geographical locations, and ideologies.

Also indicated by the data, the immigrant threat narrative was more prevalent in articles that appeared in the front of the newspaper than in back sections. The placement of articles in traditional newspapers is a powerful cue that allows editors to influence how readers process and consume the news. As shown by Graber (1988) and others (Bogart, 1989), the great majority of reading—up to 72 percent of it—is done in the first section, where negative frames, according to our study, are far more likely to appear. This means that the typical reader is more likely to be exposed to the immigrant threat narrative. This finding likely holds for the online versions of newspapers, given that some article links are more prominent than others.

In a related finding, we also showed that articles in which the subject of immigration was central to the story were more likely to contain negative coverage of immigration, suggesting that serious or in-depth analyses rarely avoid references to crime, terrorism, or other forms of deviance. In other words, the more clearly the subject of immigration is brought to a reader's attention, the more likely he or she is to read about various dangers or perilous circumstances related to immigration.

The descriptive results should also be recognized as a contribution (Noy, 2009). Using an innovative conceptual tool (the *framing nexus*) and a highly reliable coding procedure, we identified the five most common news frames in the immigrant threat narrative (illegal, criminal, terrorism, cultural threat, and economic threat), determined the relative prominence of each in the opinion-leading press, and highlighted the differences in negative framing across immigrant groups, news sources, and historical contexts. These straightforward descriptions may be informative and useful to agencies and individuals who wish to counter the dominant threat narrative, ensure the safety and civil rights of immigrants, and call into question the "immigration industrial complex" (Brotherton & Kretsedemas, 2008; Díaz, Jr., 2011; Fernandes, 2007; Golash-Boza, 2009; Lee, Martinez, & Rosenfeld, 2001).

An Additional Empirical Note

As discussed, our analysis covered a relatively small number of newspapers over a short period and does not attempt to parse out the changes in news coverage between yearly intervals. If we are to substantiate the supposed transformation in political culture, we would need to demonstrate the continuity and longevity of the authoritarian turn across multiple media outlets. Given our detailed (descriptive) knowledge of the anti-immigration framing nexus, we can investigate its main components over a longer period using electronic search engines instead of human coding. As a preliminary step in this direction, we searched back to the 1980s for articles in the *New York Times* and *The Wall Street Journal* that contained the words "immigrant" or "immigration" as well as at least one of the main components of the anti-immigration framing nexus: "illegal," "crime," "terror." We did not attempt to include the economic and cultural threat frames, because no single search term can encompass the discussions of immigration's impact on the economy and culture. Although we cannot tell how the illegality, crime, and terror frames were arranged or contextualized in the articles, the results provide an intriguing indication of the strength and longevity of the post-9/11 authoritarian turn.

As illustrated in Figure 3.1, throughout the 1980s the amount of negative coverage of immigration was quite stable, ranging from 32 percent to 43 percent in both the *New York Times* and the *Wall Street Journal*. Prior to the first bombing of the World Trade Center in 1993, the percentage of articles with one or more negative frames stood at the low end of the range in both newspapers. After this attack, the percentages spiked to 47 percent, but then dropped and remained on a steady downward trend until 2000. Following the 9/11 attacks, the increase in negative frames was even greater and lasted longer, jumping from the 30 percent baseline to more than 50 percent. In the decade following 9/11, the percentage of negative frames never returned to pre-9/11 levels, and has seemingly found a new equilibrium (Baumgartner & Jones, 2009). While the negative framing rate fluctuated between 30 percent and 40 percent throughout much of the 1980s and 1990s, the post-9/11 news era saw a range between 40 percent and nearly 60 percent. In this period, the *Wall Street Journal,* as expected, offered consistently higher rates of negative

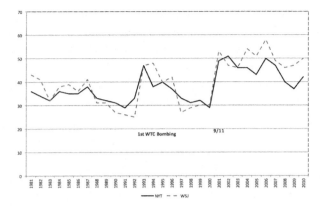

Figure 3.1 Percentage of *New York Times* and *Wall Street Journal* articles on immigration containing references to illegality, crime, or terrorism. *Source:* The data used for this figure come from a computer-aided search of *New York Times* and *Wall Street Journal* articles from 1981–2016, as shown in the X-axis. It provides a visual, detailed picture of the percentage of articles that reference the immigration frames, illegality, crime, or terrorism, as shown in the Y-axis.

framing than the *New York Times*. Although forecasting changes in U.S. immigration policy goes beyond the scope of this chapter, the social conditions underlying the immigration debate of the twenty-first century favored anti-immigration groups and proponents of increased border security and harsher law enforcement procedures.

We used the same computer-aided coding procedure on a variety of other news outlets to determine the breadth of the authoritarian turn in political culture. Lexis Nexis and Proquest collect and store the archives of twenty-seven of the 100 largest newspapers in the United States.[8] They also house transcripts of television news programs from six networks, including CBS, ABC, CNN, FOX, MSNBC, and NBC, as well as radio programs aired on National Public Radio. We searched these media outlets' coverage of immigration over a three-year period prior to 9/11 and compared it to coverage after 9/11.[9] As shown in Table 3.6, the number of items about immigration that contained at least one negative frame increased after 9/11 in almost all the outlets we searched. There was only one news organization—*Florida Times-Union*—where the anti-immigration framing nexus was notably less prevalent in the three years following the attacks. Three other organizations showed small, unsubstantial decreases in negative framing, while the thirty remaining outlets were more likely to link immigration to illegality, crime, or terrorism after 9/11 than before it. These data make it clear that the authoritarian turn in political culture included a wide range of news outlets and involved a meaningful shift in the immigration debate wherein the foreign-born were more likely to be described as threats to the lives and property of the native-born.

The News Media, Terrorism, and the Immigration Threat Nexus

Table 3.6 Effect of 9/11 on the Number of Newspaper Articles, Television News Shows, and Radio Programs with One or More Negative Immigrant Frames

	3 years before 9/11(total articles)	3 years after 9/11 total articles)	Increase/Decrease after 9/11
USA Today	392	829	+437 / 111%
Wall Street Journal	1,202	1,482	+280 / 23%
New York Times	3,316	4,820	+1504 / 45%
Washington Post	2,261	4,018	+1,757 / 78%
Philadelphia Inquirer	843	1,390	+547 / 65%
Denver Post	756	1,161	+405 / 54%
San Jose Mercury News	1,082	2,180	+1098 / 101%
New York Post	625	753	+128 / 20%
Atlanta Journal Constitution	1,334	1,643	+309 / 23%
Tampa/Petersburg Times	778	1148	+370 / 48%
Orange County-Register	848	1,064	+216 / 25%
St. Louis Post-Dispatch	1,028	1,459	+431 / 42%
The Tampa Tribune	387	516	+129 / 33%
Pittsburgh Post-Gazette	919	1,450	+531 / 58%
Daily Oklahoman	202	384	+182 / 90%
Buffalo News	426	480	+54 / 13%
Richmond Times Dispatch	202	702	+500 / 247%
Austin American- Statesman	740	732	–8 / 10%
Palm Beach Post	542	794	+252 / 46%
Florida Times-Union	577	272	–305 / 53%
Chicago Daily Herald	407	904	+497 / 122%
Dayton Dailey News	188	175	–13 / 7%
Sarasota Herald-Tribune	192	227	+35 / 18%
Salt Lake Tribune	188	504	+316 / 168%
Philadelphia Daily News	224	257	+33 / 15%
Daily News of Los Angeles	578	888	+310 / 54%
CBS	359	420	+61 / 17%
ABC	511	449	–62 / 12%
CNN	1,989	3,041	+1,052 / 53%
FOX	414	1,287	+873 / 211%
MSNBC	139	625	+486 / 350%
NBC	290	388	+98 / 34%
National Public Radio	652	1 185	+533 / 82%

Limitations

There are, of course, several limitations to the study in this chapter. One weakness lies in our discussion of the political bias and ideological forces in newspapers. We have only demonstrated that one conservative newspaper had a more adverse reaction to 9/11 than one liberal newspaper. We were

68 *Chapter 3*

not comfortable placing all eight newspapers in our sample in ideological categories. There simply were not strong enough empirical grounds for doing so. While the data shed a new and interesting light on this subject, especially given the social significance of the *New York Times* and the *Wall Street Journal*, we cannot make sweeping claims about the power of political ideology in shaping the post-9/11 immigration debate. Further research is needed on the ideological nature of local newspapers to test our hypotheses across a broader sample of liberal and conservative news outlets.

We should also qualify our claims about the authoritarian turn and acknowledge the limits of our political cultural explanation. As noted in Perrin's study (2005), an investigation of authoritarianism in the form of "cultural elements" in newspaper articles can neither confirm nor reject the classic social psychological arguments that treat authoritarianism as a psychological reaction to perceived threat or as a set of personality traits. Moreover, even though we showed that the immigrant threat narrative became more dominant in news media after 9/11, our data cannot fully explain the social processes behind this change. The news media is one part of a broader system of interdependent parts. Much of the news is shaped by political and economic elites. To better understand the cultural shift after 9/11 in general, and the social processes involved with the changes in news coverage of immigration, we now move to an analysis of presidential rhetoric to account for the role of political elites in the mass-mediated discussion of immigration in the United States.

NOTES

1. This chapter draws in part on an article published in *Sociological Spectrum* (Woods & Arthur 2014). However, the chapter contains new data and analyses that have not appeared elsewhere. Woods, Joshua, and Damien Arthur (2014). "The Threat of Terrorism and the Changing Public Discourse on Immigration after September 11." *Sociological Spectrum,* 34(5): 421–441.

2. In 2002, President Bush suggested that the flow of immigrants from Mexico served as "a conduit for terrorists, weapons of mass destruction, illegal migrants, contraband, and other unlawful commodities" (see Office of the Press Secretary 2002, retrieved online January 29, 2014, at: http://georgewbush-whitehouse.archives.gov/news/releases/2002/01/20020125.html).

3. Lawmakers in Arizona passed a measure in April 2010 that allowed the police to check the documentation of anyone they suspected of being an illegal immigrant (see Gaynor & Schwartz, 2010). In the new measure's defense, Arizona Governor Jan Brewer said that it was necessary because her state "has been under terrorist attacks . . . with all of this illegal immigration" (see a video of Governor Brewer's statements online at http://thinkprogress.org/2010/04/30/brewer-terrorist-attacks).

4. Taking a similar approach, Groseclose and Milyo (2005) count the number of references made by congressional partisans to various think tanks and policy groups, and then compare these figures to the number of times that a given media outlet cites the same groups.

5. To further clarify our definition of the framing nexus as a concept, it may be helpful to distinguish it from the closely related theory of structural intersectionality (Crenshaw, 1991; Lutz, Vivar, & Supik, 2011). The theory suggests that discourses of identity are shaped by intersecting patterns of racial, ethnic, class, and gender bias that become embedded and institutionalized in society (Cisneros, 2011; Flores, 2003). From this perspective, the American immigrant identity is influenced not only by long-standing prejudices against foreigners, but also by a set of cultural understandings that place immigrants within hierarchies based on their nationality, religion, ethnic group, skin color, age, gender, and economic standing (Flores, (2003). The theory may lead to hypotheses about how certain intersectional identities—for instance, young, male Muslim immigrants from Middle Eastern countries—are portrayed in media. Although the framing nexus may be an especially helpful tool in such an investigation, it does not explain why a given news portrayal is likely or unlikely, how it is related to social structure, or what effect it may have on audiences.

6. To determine the size of newspapers, we used circulation figures from the Audit Bureau of Circulation (see http://www.auditbureau org). In 2012, this organization changed its name to the Alliance for Audited Media, which continued to report circulation figures (see http://auditedmedia.com/). We accessed most of the newspaper articles using Lexis Nexis. Some newspapers with large circulations, such as the *Los Angeles Times*, were not available in Lexis Nexis. In such cases, we selected the next largest newspaper for our sample. It should be noted that we do not assume that these newspapers approximate public opinion on immigration in the United States. Audiences for these papers tend to have higher levels of income and education than the average citizen and may hold distinct views on immigration (Schudson, 2011; Shoemaker & Reese, 2014).

7. The dependent variable was normally distributed. We checked for multi-collinearity and found that the four significant predictors in the model had very weak correlations with each other and strong correlations with the dependent variable. By adding these variables into the model one at a time, we also found that each increased R Square substantially.

8. This search procedure was carried out in July 2016. The availability of newspapers via Lexis Nexis can change over time and the title of newspapers can also change. As one example, the *Houston Chronicle* was available at the initial point of data collection, but was no longer offered when we began collecting data for this computer-aided content analysis.

9. Anyone with access to Lexis Nexis should be able to confirm our findings, using Boolean logic, and the following search terms: "immigrant" or "immigration," and "crime" or "criminal," or "illegal" or "unauthorized" or "undocumented," or "terror" or "terrorism" or "terrorist."

Chapter 4

The President Goes Negative

Few observers of political life in the United States would be surprised to find that a politician's speech on a given topic sometimes varies depending on where and to whom the speech is given.[1] On occasion, the news media picks up on key differences between speeches and makes a story of it. One of the most famous recent cases of this occurred during the run-up to the 2016 presidential election when GOP nominee Donald Trump gave two provocative speeches on immigration—one in Mexico City, Mexico, and one in Phoenix, Arizona—on the same day, August 31, 2016 (Partlow, Sullivan & DelReal, 2016). As discussed in the final chapter of this book, the tone and policy prescriptions in the two speeches were jarringly dissimilar. A polite, diplomatic Trump stood before a crowd in Mexico City and discussed the common interests of the United States and Mexico. Only hours later, in Phoenix, out came the ill-tempered Trump and his fiery statements about building a great wall on the southern border and carrying out the mass deportation of unauthorized immigrants.

Put simply, Trump's two speeches were clearly influenced by the social context in which they were given. In this chapter, we begin by explaining how context shapes presidential speeches. We identify a number of contextual variables that may predict the way presidents talk about immigration. These variables include the terrorist attacks on September 11, 2001, the geographical locations of speeches, the health of the economy, the president's approval rating, the type of speech (major speech vs. other types of presidential communication), and others. To develop this perspective, we offer a comparative, qualitative analysis of the presidential rhetoric of W. J. Clinton, G. W. Bush, and B. H. Obama. Comparisons are made between presidents, as well as between each platform of the political parties. We use the party platforms as a baseline for each president's stance on immigration, which reveals how presidents sometimes deviate from their expected positions as the social context changes. This analysis offers a descriptive understanding of how contextual factors, particularly terrorism, are associated with the use of negative frames in presidential immigration rhetoric.

Next, we examine data from a quantitative content analysis of all presidential speeches on immigration given between January 20, 1993, and November 7, 2011. There are clear differences between the three presidents. The results also show that there are significant associations between our contextual variables and the presence of negative immigration frames. We conclude this chapter with a discussion of the significance of our findings and make suggestions for future studies on the context of presidential rhetoric.

THE CONTEXTUAL PRESIDENCY:
A THEORETICAL FRAMEWORK

The available theories for explaining the tone and content of presidential rhetoric tend to be materialist in nature and focus on the power of presidents to produce and disseminate strategic information for the sake of influencing public opinion, setting the news agenda, and winning points in policy debates (Smith, 1983). As Neustadt (1991) put it, presidential power is the *power to persuade*. Likewise, Kernell (2007) argued that presidents "go public" with their requests with the hope that it will translate into policies. The most celebrated studies of presidential rhetoric study the presidents' intent as a change agent, one who can or cannot shape the agenda with major speeches such as the *State of the Union Addresses* (Cohen, 1995; Edwards & Wood, 1999), influence the Congress (Canes-Wrone, 2004; Barrett, 2005), control news media coverage (Eshbaugh-Soha & Peake, 2008; Cohen, 2008) and structure the bureaucracy (Whitford & Yates, 2009), elevate their own public approval ratings (Druckman & Holmes, 2004; Edwards, 2003), and influence specific attitudes and public policy preferences (Eshbaugh-Soha & Peake, 2006; Edwards, 2003; Brace & Hinckley, 1992; Welch, 2000).

Previous research tends to treat the president's words as more *strategic* than *discursive* (Perrin, 2005). Such an approach deemphasizes the role of external forces that limit and guide presidential communication. Presidential behavior is no doubt entrepreneurial and tactical, but it is also situated within a social and cultural structure and incentivized by historical context. Drawing on cultural theory in sociology, we think of culture as providing the dominant repertoire of symbols, codes, conventions, representations, and frames that can be used by presidents and other powerful intermediaries. These cultural elements allow for a range of choices, and the choices presidents make often serve their material interests, but they also guide and constrain presidential

The President Goes Negative 73

speeches (Swidler, 2001; Swidler, 1986, Bourdieu, 1990, Sewell, 1992; Maney, Woehrle & Coy, 2005; Williams, 2002).

Not unlike Donald Trump's dual immigration speeches in Mexico City and Phoenix, the elite discourse on immigration is replete with contradictions, with warm acceptance of immigrants as well as nativism and xenophobia, with images of immigrants as innovators and strivers, as well as criminals and terrorists. These contradictions, whether observed on a single day or over the course of history, can often be understood and resolved by examining the context of the communicative act (Beasley, 2005).

We argue that negative rhetoric on immigration, a highly salient and controversial policy, is often the result of the context in which presidents find themselves speaking. Aside from Arthur's (2014) study on the constrained effects of the president's rhetorical economic leadership, Rottinghaus' (2006) study on public opinion, Peterson and Djupe's (2005) study on negative primary campaigns, Wood's (2007) study of presidential rhetoric and the tone of the economy, and Hart's (1989) analysis of rhetorical leadership, a literature on rhetoric as a dependent variable has not been fully developed. Zarefsky's (2004) assessment of presidential rhetoric says that it is theoretically possible that presidents pay attention to the context of their speeches, but does not provide substantial empirical analysis that addresses the issue. Identifying the contextual variables that predict the president's use of negative frames on immigration will contribute to a literature that generally treats rhetoric as a mechanism of power or as a tool through which presidents accomplish their goals (Canes-Wrone, 2004; Woods, 2007).

Terrorist Attacks

Space limitations prevent a full consideration of all the potentially influential contextual variables. Here we include a discussion of our main variables—the events of 9/11, economic indicators, and the geographical place and audience to whom the speech is given—as well as a brief account of additional control variables. As discussed in detail in chapter 2, the increasing fear of terrorism after 9/11 hardened public attitudes toward immigration and encouraged negative stories about immigrants in the news media (Woods & Arthur, 2014; Golash-Boza, 2009; Segovia & Defever, 2010; DeParle, 2011). This authoritarian turn was also reflected in the Bush Administration's responses to 9/11, including military actions in foreign countries, increased security efforts at home, the militarization of the southern border, and the securitization of immigration policies. Rising economic insecurities in the wake of the attacks only added to the culture of perceived threat that shaped the immigration policy landscape of the early twenty-first century. In line with chapter 3's hypotheses about the news media, we predict that presidential rhetoric,

74 *Chapter 4*

despite the meaningful ideological differences between presidents Clinton, Bush, and Obama, will contain more negative immigration frames after 9/11 than before it, controlling for the other contextual variables.

Economic Indicators as Predictors of Negative Framing

Cohen (1995) claims that a weak economy can draw negative attention to the president. Moreover, economic indicators are directly correlated to reelection and presidential approval (Vavreck, 2009; Wood, 2007). When the economy does not do well, the public typically holds the president accountable. As Edwards and Wayne (1985) maintain, the presidents' responsibilities toward the economy have increased, but their abilities to meet those expectations have decreased. According to the Gallup's "Most Important Problem" list, the economy, or an economic issue such as unemployment, has topped the list nearly every year since 1936 (Dolan, Frendreis, & Tatalovich, 2008). When the economy is doing well, Americans tend to say that the president is doing his job well. The inverse is true when the economy is doing poorly.

Nonetheless, when economic indicators are not where the presidents think they need to be, they often attempt to refocus the public's attention from the economy and direct it to something that can rally constituency support (Wood, 2009; Baum, 2002). Doing what is politically viable is the best economic strategy (Edwards & Wayne, 1985). Given the public's sentiment toward immigration, the president knows that immigration "saber-rattling" can create the "rally" effect they need to boost approval ratings, their reelection, or policy proposal successes (Wood, 2009). Therefore, we hypothesize that when economic indicators (unemployment, inflation rate, gross domestic product [GDP], and the misery index) are at levels that are not conducive to the presidents' plans, they discuss immigration negatively in order to refocus the public's attention. In other words, presidents are going to be more negative about immigration when unemployment is high, which enables them to blame immigration policies and immigrants for the rise in unemployment. The same is true when the inflation rate increases. Moreover, as the GDP decreases, presidents will resort to the aforementioned. We have chosen these economic indicators, as well as the Consumer Confidence Index, because they are those that best represent the health of the overall economy (Dolan, Frendreis, and Tatalovich 2008).

Geographical Location of Speech as a Predictor of Negative Framing

Presidents are constantly advocating for polices that reflect their agenda. In the past, much of their effort was directed at the Congress and the task of bargaining and negotiating to accomplish their goals. More recently, there has been an increase in divided government and party polarization, and less willingness among legislators to work together and compromise. Therefore, presidents have increasingly taken their agendas to the public. However, following the changes in the media establishment the public's preferences for content have also changed. As Cohen (2010) argues, in the 1980s, the president began losing his influence with the mass media. They were less likely to provide him with the airtime necessary to promote his programs and policies to the public. Such actions seriously limited his ability to "go public" in the same capacity.

The new strategy was to "go narrow" in local venues. In other words, presidents think they can have greater influence over the coverage of themselves in local newspapers, which can help their ability to lead the public and compel the Congress to adopt their policy preferences. Essentially, Cohen (2010) maintains that presidents have simply adjusted their behavior to meet the demands of their office by appealing to their "party base, interest groups, and opinion in localities." In this environment, presidents are more likely to adapt their communication strategies and the content of their messages to the ideological climate where they give their speeches. Given that news media coverage of immigration, as well as public opinion, are more likely to reflect negative aspects of immigration in southern border states than in other regions of the country, presidential communication in these areas is more likely to contain negative immigration frames. Presidents may also make a point of visiting southern border states and voicing local concerns about immigration in order to generate public support, particularly during an election campaign, or foster a restrictionist policy agenda. In either case, we should see more negativity in speeches given in southern border states than in other areas of the country.

Control Variables

The variables discussed above were the primary justifications for the analysis; however, we also consider how negativity differs among the control variables: whether or not there was an election transpiring, whether or not the audience to which the president is speaking has a vested interest in immigrants or immigration, the major political parties, the type of speech given, how the discussion of the different types of social identifiers of the immigrant groups contribute to the negativity, how the make-up of government contributes, how the presidents' approval ratings play a role, whether there is a recession, and how the president's calls for congressional action affect negativity and the president's political party affiliation.

76 *Chapter 4*

QUALITATIVE ANALYSIS OF PARTY PLATFORMS AND PRESIDENTIAL RHETORIC

The 1992 Democratic Party Platform was completely positive about immigration and immigrants, all 47 words of it. In addition to its brevity, the discussion was about two-thirds of the way through the document, which indicates that immigration policy was not one of President Clinton's major policy initiatives. His platform statement simply said that he "support[s] immigration policies that promote fairness, non-discrimination and family reunification, and that reflect our constitutional freedoms of speech, association and travel" (Peters & Woolley, The *American Presidency Project*, 2011). Though succinct, the platform generally suggested that Clinton would take a humane, progressive stance on most immigration issues.

However, not long after President Clinton took office, in February 1993, the World Trade Center suffered its first terrorist attack. As the FBI called it, "Middle Eastern terrorism" had penetrated America's borders (FBI, 2008). According to their interpretation, a group of radicalized Islamists exploded a truck in the World Trade Center, with the hopes of knocking it into the other tower and killing thousands of people. The FBI was able to track the group and make arrests. These terrorists were tried and convicted in a Federal Court in the United States and given life sentences. As we will see later in the book, this is a radically different response to terrorism than what transpires after the terrorist attacks on 9/11, on the same building, wherein the response to a terrorist act creates major institutional and policy shifts and becomes the responsibility of the military rather than our legal system.

A few months after the first terrorist attack on the World Trade Center, President Clinton offered a statement regarding the connection between immigration and terrorism. On July 27, 1993, President Clinton made the following remarks to reporters:

> Several weeks ago, I asked the Vice President to work with our Departments and Agencies to examine what more might be done about the problems along our borders. I was especially concerned about the growing problems of alien smuggling and international terrorists hiding behind immigrant status, as well as the continuing flow of illegal immigrants across American borders.
>
> The simple fact is that we must not, and we will not, surrender our borders to those who wish to exploit our history of compassion and justice. We cannot tolerate those who traffic in human cargo, nor can we allow our people to be endangered by those who would enter our country to terrorize Americans. But the solution to the problem of illegal immigration is not simply to close our borders. The solution is to welcome legal immigrants and legal legitimate refugees and to turn away those who do not obey the laws. We must say no to illegal immigration so we can continue to say yes to legal immigration.

The President Goes Negative 77

> But to treat terrorists and smugglers as immigrants dishonors the tradition
> of the immigrants who have made our nation great. And it unfairly taints the
> millions of immigrants who live here honorably and are a vital part of every
> segment of our society. Today's initiatives are about stopping crime, toughening
> the penalties for the criminals, and giving our law enforcement people the tools
> they need to do their job. (Clinton, July 27, 1993)

As can be seen by President Clinton's comments, he clearly identifies the connection between the policies of immigration and terrorism. At the very least, he says that one important counterterrorism strategy is to seal the borders and stop terrorists from mixing into the flow of immigrants entering the United States. This argument would become one of the most common ways restrictionists used the immigration-terrorism nexus to advocate for tougher border controls and immigration law enforcement in the post-9/11 era. Although President Clinton rarely used this frame compared to the frequent references made by President Bush, it would seem that the security dimension of immigration policy is difficult for presidents to ignore in the context of what is perceived by many Americans as an obvious terrorist threat. In spite of the generally favorable positions toward immigration held by President Clinton in the past and noted in the 1992 Democratic Party Platform, he clearly acknowledged the potential link between immigration and terrorism, especially when answering questions with reporters (though less so in major speeches).

For instance, President Clinton seemed to struggle with the temptation or pressure to connect these policies when questioned during a satellite interview with the California media about five months after the first World Trade Center attack:

> We're trying to deal with, in effect, three different problems. We're trying to
> deal with the problem presented by the fact that our airports are too porous and
> terrorists or potential terrorists can get in, and we're trying to tighten up all those
> procedures in foreign airports and here. We're trying to deal with the problem of
> alien smuggling, which is something California is familiar with, by tightening
> the control procedures and also increasing penalties for that. And finally, we're
> trying to deal with illegal aliens coming into the country generally. (Clinton,
> July 30, 1993)

This example demonstrates, again, President Clinton's willingness to connect the policies of immigration and terrorism, but the two examples above also illustrate his willingness to push back and obscure this link. In the first excerpt, President Clinton said that linking the policies "dishonors" the status of immigrants. He seemed aware that the practice of framing immigrants as terrorists or criminals is a problem itself. It appears that Clinton's rhetorical tactic is to acknowledge the loose connection between the policies and then redirect the attention of the audiences to separating terrorism from immigration, particularly by highlighting the differences between the agencies that deal with each and the institutional functions they play in the processes and policies. In the second example, in particular, he refers to three *different* problems, categorizing terrorism in the domain of airport security, linking smuggling with border controls, and characterizing unauthorized immigration as a general problem that is distinct from terrorism and crime.

In the next years, while continuing to address terrorism and immigration separately, he does not substantively address or acknowledge a connection between these policies after October 1993. Even when signing *S. 735*, the *"Antiterrorism and Effective Death Penalty Act of 1996,"* Clinton continues to resist the temptation to link the two policies. Even in the midst of the 1996 presidential election, he said of *S. 735*, "This bill also makes a number of major, ill-advised changes in our immigration laws having nothing to do with fighting terrorism."

During that presidential election campaign, the 1996 Democratic Party Platform was more specific on policy recommendations and details about the Clinton administration's approach to immigration. Again, the platform was substantively positive about the integration of immigrants into American life. The platform, however, does clarify its seemingly open immigration stance with a discussion of what the administration has done to combat illegal immigration (Peters & Woolley, *The American Presidency Project*, 2011). Moreover, throughout his last term in office, Clinton discussed terrorism, weapons of mass destruction, and the administration's efforts to combat and mitigate it. He also discussed illegal immigration and the problems associated with it. However, he did not substantively connect the two policies in a discussion of "comprehensive reform" in the way that Edwards and Herder (2012) have defined it. The 2000 Democratic Party Platform did not make the connection either.

The 2000 Republican Party Platform is different in some ways from the previous platforms. With just over 500 words, it contains no mentions that link terrorism and immigration policies. The language is more positive than the 1996 Republican Party Platform was toward immigration, particularly immigration that has occurred in the past. The platform makes a point of discussing how important immigrants have been for the United States, those that have come into the country "legally," according to their clarification.

In other ways, however, this platform is more negative. It spends considerable time discussing English as the language they need to assimilate into American life. Moreover, the platform calls for reforms to the immigration process as well as the institutions regulating immigration into the United States. The platform only addresses illegal immigration reforms and solutions

The President Goes Negative 79

for Central America and Mexico (Peters & Woolley, *The American Presidency Project*, 2011).

According to our research, President Bush mentioned immigration only nineteen times from when he entered the White House on January 20, 2001, to September 10, 2001, prior to the attacks on 9/11. Granted, this is a short time of his presidency, essentially eight months, but we can still assess the tone in which he addresses immigration before 9/11. During this period, he used one of the negative immigration frames we examined—illegality, crime, economic threat, and terrorism—in only four of his 19 references to immigration, including three uses of illegality frame and one use of the criminality frame. He does not use the terrorism or economic threat frame before 9/11.

In his first immigration speech following the attacks he immediately connects immigration policy to terrorism policy. Prior to this address, he had only mentioned immigration once after 9/11 on September 18 in a written document regarding refugees. It is telling that the first time he mentions immigration after the attacks he makes the case for the link between terrorism and immigration; he makes the policy connection to a federal agency not charged with immigration, but rather domestic terrorism. It appears to be the perfect opportunity for political symbolism, both in terms of timing and audience. To begin making the institutional connections between terrorism and immigration policy, President Bush argues,

> We're asking Congress for the authority to hold suspected terrorists who are in the process of being deported, until they're deported. That seems to make sense—[laughter]—that if a suspected terrorist is detained, and our Nation has decided to deport the person, then they ought to be held in custody until the action actually takes place. We believe it's a necessary tool to make America a safe place. Now, this would of course be closely supervised by an immigration judge. Now, the only alternative is to let suspected terrorists loose in our country. I don't think anybody wants to do that. [Laughter] I certainly hope not. (Bush, September 25, 2001)

Formally created by President Bush about a month later, on October 30, *The Homeland Security Presidential Directive-2—Combating Terrorism Through Immigration Policies*—did much to institutionalize the link between immigration and terrorism policy. The *Directive* begins: "The United States has a long and valued tradition of welcoming immigrants and visitors. But the attacks of September 11, 2001, showed that some come to the United States to commit terrorist acts"—highlighting the two main types of immigration discourse (American Presidency Project, 2016; Beasley, 2006). This statement is indicative of the profound changes that transpired after 9/11; the terrorist attacks engendered another negative frame for the restrictionists to

80   *Chapter 4*

incorporate into the negativity in immigration rhetoric. Moreover, this *Directive* signals the dramatic and lasting institutional change in these two policies. Under the fear that terrorists will utilize the immigration system, the *Directive* creates six institutional changes:

1. Create a "Foreign Terrorist Tracking Task Force" to coordinate various federal agencies to deny "aliens" entry, deport others, and streamline the communication between each agency.
2. Establish an enhanced INS and customs enforcement capability, wherein the institutional immigration apparatus is securitized with intelligence gathering and enforcement powers.
3. Limit and restrict certain "sensitive" areas of study for international students, adding more difficulties to the student visa process.
4. Seek a uniform customs and immigration system and database with Mexico and Canada so as to have a say in the immigration policies of those countries that border the United States.
5. Recommend streamlining the advanced technologies and databases of all federal agencies so that the government can better assess immigration, enforce existing laws, and apprehend any threat.
6. Develop budgetary standards for maintaining the new terrorism and immigration institutional structures across each federal agency (Bush, October 29, 2001).

In addition to issuing *Executive Order 13228—Establishing the Office of Homeland Security and the Homeland Security Council,* wherein immigration and terrorism are formally institutionalized, President Bush acknowledges the institutional and policy shift as early as February 2002. In off-the-cuff remarks he says,

> when I first came into office—or, not first came into office—well, first came into office, and actually right around the September the 11th period—the FBI's function was really to run down spies or white-collar criminals. And there's nothing wrong with that; that's an important function of the FBI. But I can tell you with certainty they've got a new major focus, and that's preventing an attack. (Bush, October 8, 2001)

Moreover, President Bush's rhetoric, in his first term, continued to make the connection between terrorism and immigration. Repeatedly making statements such as "A new terrorism task force is tightening immigration controls to make sure no one enters or stays in our country who would harm us." While at the same time, President Bush said,

> And so a good immigration policy recognizes there are people in the United States who want to employ Mexicans who want to work, and we've got to

The President Goes Negative 81

facilitate them coming together. That has nothing to do with the war on terror; that has everything to do to make sure that our economy grows. (Bush, March 20, 2002)

Yet, each action he took during his administration after 9/11, and much of his overall rhetoric engendered an institutional policy shift. Despite each institutionalizing action, President Bush thought that he could "have an immigration policy that's wise and an antiterrorist homeland security for both countries that is effective." Therefore, President Bush continued, throughout both of his terms in office, to strengthen the connection between terrorism and immigration in his rhetoric, his requests to the Congress, and his administration's institutional decisions, eventually signing into law the largest reorganization of American bureaucracy since World War II—namely, the creation of the Department of Homeland Security (DHS), which was devoted to the prevention and mitigation of terrorist-related acts.

Each of these actions, coupled with the rhetoric, created not only policy and institutional changes, but they created political changes as well. As Winkler (2006) argues, Bush used a "labeling strategy" from the Clinton administration, wherein he claimed that the terrorist attacks were a "unique challenge in the nation's history." Such a strategy enabled the administration to construct new norms for addressing the new threat, the new enemy, and the new problem. These changes were highlighted in the first major party platforms after the attacks on September 11, which would drive the political polarization that followed in the years afterward The 2004 Republican Party Platform began right away with a discussion of how immigration policy is now about connecting border security, terrorism, and immigration. The Party Platform calls for institutional and process changes to immigration policy. In fact, the platform now has its own section about border security and the administration's response and efforts to keep out "illegals" who might harm our way of life through terrorism or by taking jobs from Americans (Peters & Woolley, *The American Presidency Project*, 2011).

The 2004 Democratic Party Platform, however, was quite different in tone and policy recommendations. This is the first platform to move away from language that addresses immigrants as "illegal" and begins referring to them as "undocumented" immigrants. This platform is mostly positive about immigration; however, there are many statements that call for the assimilation of immigrants, particularly their language and education. Most importantly, however, this platform, with one sentence, places terrorism and immigration together. The platform states "we will work with our neighbors to strengthen our security so we are safer from those who would come here to harm us" (Peters & Woolley, *The American Presidency Project*, 2011). The policy is subtler and less direct in its connection, yet acknowledges it

82 *Chapter 4*

nonetheless. This is indicative of where the policy conversation had gone since 9/11. The difference, however, mainly consists of the calls for fundamental and comprehensive reform to the entire immigration processes and policies (Edwards & Herder, 2012). Nevertheless, again, we find the Democratic Party acknowledging the connection between terrorism and immigration. Having said that, they are not calling for the institutional and systemic connection of immigration and terrorism to the same extent found in the Republican Party Platform.

The 2012 and the 2008 Republican Party Platforms are not much different than the 2004 platform, with the exception of the number of words used. There is essentially no difference in the two; they are still connecting the issues of terrorism and immigration. For instance, the 2008 Republican Platform reads,

> Immigration policy is a national security issue, for which we have one test: Does it serve the national interest? By that standard, Republicans know America can have a strong immigration system without sacrificing the rule of law. Border security is essential to national security. In an age of terrorism, drug cartels, and criminal gangs, allowing millions of unidentified persons to enter and remain in this country poses grave risks to the sovereignty of the United States and the security of its people. (Republican Party Platform, 2008)

The 2008 and 2012 Democratic Party Platforms are not much different than the 2004 Democratic Party Platform, which offered a change in the language used to discuss immigration. The negative frames used by President Obama changed significantly from that of the Bush administration. This change transpired, primarily, in the use of terrorism frames. President Obama only used the terrorism frame once from 2009 through 2011. How he used that frame is also important. He did not use the word "terror" when connecting the policies. He simply acknowledged that the United States had to review its immigration policies in the aftermath of 9/11, that it was important to do so in the interest of the safety of the citizenry.

Since the inception of Obama's campaign for the presidency, he tried to act as a policy entrepreneur and redefine the issue of immigration, changing the dominant policy idea that the largest concern pertaining to immigration is the control of the U.S. border—an idea that was championed by his predecessor. Or, at the very least, President Obama tried to convince the Hispanic voting population that the aforementioned shift is necessary and that he has passionately advocated for it. Mostly, his issue redefinition attempts have centered on allowing the most qualified immigrants access to the legal immigration apparatus, which will, according to him, enhance the economy. Nevertheless, as another chapter in this book shows, this is not really the best political framing strategy. The public seems to only care about the legal status of the immigrant in question.

President Obama has signaled—in his rhetoric, administrative policy decisions, and dealings with the Congress and the public—that he simply wants to remove the unauthorized immigrants who pose a threat to public safety and the American way of life. He argues that he will focus on "actual threats to our security: felons, not families; criminals, not children; gang members, not a mom who's working hard to provide for her kids." Scholars have, however, taken issue with this rhetoric, given that it is not entirely true, according to the data (Golash-Boza, 2012a & 2012b & 2013; Gottschalk, 2015). For instance, Golash-Boza (2015) argues that the United States has adopted a deportation policy based upon race and gender, rather than criminal action.[2] From 1997 to 2015, the United States deported twice as many immigrants than all deportations prior to 1996. Nearly 90 percent of the deportees were male and sent to a Latin American country. She argues that the deportations are less about actual crimes being committed and more about the criminalization of black and brown men. Therefore, in her estimation and research, "deportation has become a state strategy of social control," coupled with the economic restructuring of neoliberal reforms, rather than a deliberate strategy of differentiating between families, criminals, security threats, and those seeking more economic security (Golash-Boza, 2015).[3]

The Party Platforms of both Democrats and Republicans from 1992 through 2000 are generally positive about immigration. It is only the party platforms that are adopted after 9/11, wherein blatant negativity and policy connections between terrorism and immigration are established, that we find a substantive shift in tone and policy recommendations. These platforms, particularly that of the Republican Party, change the conversation entirely to immigration policy control as a way to mitigate terrorism and related activities such as border control. The 2008 Democrat Platform is mostly positive about immigration, however, with the one exception in the sentence mentioned earlier. Both the Democratic and Republican Party Platforms of 2016 are addressed in the last chapter of the book.

A QUANTITATIVE CONTENT ANALYSIS
OF PRESIDENTIAL RHETORIC

The empirical approach described in this section builds on a study by Arthur and Woods (2013). The aim is to identify contextual patterns in the immigration rhetoric of presidents W. J. Clinton, G. W. Bush, and B. H. Obama. We have selected these administrations because they cover ample historical periods from both before and after the terrorist attacks on 9/11. We used the *American Presidency Project* to collect the presidential speeches by keyword from January 20, 1993, through November 7, 2011. The *American Presidency*

84   *Chapter 4*

Project is a digital search technology that allowed us to search the *Public Papers of the President*. This enabled us to document when and how often the presidents used negative frames in their discussions of immigration. We analyzed the speeches using human coding, as opposed to computer-aided coding, based on a detailed codebook and protocol (Arthur, 2014; Cameron, 2000; Arthur & Woods, 2017; Barrett, 2005; Barrett, 2004; Woods & Arthur, 2014; Arthur & Woods, 2013).

Many of the speeches mention "immigration" multiple times. Therefore, the word "immigration" was our coding trigger and the *day* is the unit of analysis. In many instances, there are different social identifiers or negative frames in the same thought that includes the word "immigration" in the speech. For instance, a speech might mention "immigration" and "Mexico" and "securing the borders" from "terrorists" and "drug cartels" as well as discuss the "Canadian border" and the issue of "illegality." In such an instance, the coding was consistently treated in the same fashion: we took the closest coding trigger for each mention of "immigration" in the speech. We broke each mention of "immigration" into as many separate recording units that the speech included, one for each "immigration" word mentioned. In total, 1850 recording units were found in the 769 speeches from January 20, 1993, through November 7, 2011.[4]

Coding of Independent Variables

Each presidential mention of immigration was coded with fifteen variables, including whether the speech was made before 9/11 or after (1 = after; 0 = before), the audience the president was addressing (1 = groups with a vested interest in immigration or immigrants; 0 = groups with no apparent vested interest in immigration or immigrants), the party of the president (1 = Democrat & 0 = Republican), whether or not there was an election transpiring when the speech was given (1 = election year; 0 = no election year and 1 = midterm election; 0 = no midterm election), divided government (1 = president and Congress are a *different* party; 0 = president and Congress are a *same* party), Chamber Control (House - 1 = Democrat; 2 = Republican) & (Senate[5] - 1 = Democrat; 2 = Republican), the approval rating of the president the day before the speech (expressed as a percentage = 0% to 100%), type of speech given (1 = News Conference; 2 = Town Hall Meeting; 3 = Other (Written, Proclamations, Radio Addresses); 4 = Major Speech (Televised); 5 = Interview; 6 = Remarks, whether the president proposed legislation dealing with immigration (1 = yes; 0 = no), whether there was a recession happening (1 = yes; 0 = no), the unemployment rate (continuous variable expressed in percentage), the Consumer Price Index (continuous variable), the inflation rate (continuous variable expressed in percentage), the GDP (continuous variable expressed in Billions of Chained Dollars), the Misery Index (inflation rate + unemployment rate - continuous variable expressed in percentage), the social identifiers (1 = Mexico, Central America, Caribbean, South America (also Latino or Hispanic); 2 = Europe; 3 = Asia; 4 = Africa; 5 = Arab/Middle East; 6 = Oceania; 7 = Canada; 8 = none mentioned), as well as the geographical area wherein the speech was given (1 = Northeast; 2 = South; 3 = Midwest; 4 = West; 5 = DC; 6 = Outside of the U.S.),[6] whether or not the president mentioned reforming the immigration process (1 = Immigration Reform and 0 = Reform not mentioned), and whether the speech was given in a Border State (1 = yes; 0 = no).

Coding of Dependent Variables

The main dependent variable is the presence or absence of negative immigration framing. We measured this variable in two ways. First, we determine whether any of the negative frames were present. The outcome variable in this case is dichotomous, wherein "1" indicates that at least one negative immigration frame was present and "0" represents no negative immigration frames present. Second, we coded the presence of each type of negative frame. The outcome variable is multinomial, wherein "1" represents a mention of illegal immigration, "2" represents discussion of criminality in relation to immigration, "3" represents the mention of terrorism with immigration, and "4" represents discussion of immigration as an economic threat to the United States. A more detailed description of these negative frames—illegality, criminality, terrorism, and economic threat—can be found in chapter 3.

Measurement

This analysis will determine the difference in the frequency and type of negative frames in the presidential "immigration" rhetoric before 9/11 and the negative "immigration" rhetoric after 9/11. Analyzing the data in this way will allow us to determine the shift in negativity that transpired. The variables enabled us to create various pertinent measures of percentages and bivariate relationships with the other independent variables (See Table 4.1). One logistic model (M1) and one multinomial logistic regression model (M2) were used to predict the frequency with which negative frames were utilized by the presidents. Moreover, by using these regression analyses, we model and graph the predicted probabilities that the independent variables can have on the frequency of the negative immigration framing, controlling for the other variables.

In the first model, to find the predicted probability of the specific indicators on the presence of at least one of the negative frames in the immigration

86   Chapter 4

Table 4.1   Bivariate Relationships between Immigration Narratives and Presidential Speeches Results[1]

	Clinton	Bush II	Obama	n
Terrorism	4/1%	186/23%	1/.30%	191
Criminality	55/8%	25/3%	5/2%	85
Illegality	221/31%	157/19%	90/27%	468
Economic Threat	55/8%	6/1%	13/4%	74
No negative frame	372/52%	436/54%	224/67%	1032
Total Immigration	707	810	333	1850
Mentions				

[1] Expressed as the overall percentage of each president's total immigration rhetoric, including rhetoric with no negative frames and each of the other negative frames present.

rhetoric of presidents W. J. Clinton, G. W. Bush, and B. H. Obama, a logistic regression analysis was performed. Logistic regression uses a *Maximum Likelihood Estimator*, an iterative method that measures the effect of the predictor variables on the use of at least one negative frame. Tables 4.1 and 4.2 present the coefficients, odds ratios, and p-values as well as the standard errors and the measures of fit. The model, overall, is in line with our theory. The predictor variables in this analysis significantly affect whether the president uses a negative immigration frame in his rhetoric.

The log odds of a negative frame occurring after 9/11 (versus before 9/11) increases by 2.736, showing that it is significantly more likely for presidential rhetoric to contain negative immigration frames after 9/11 than before it. In fact, when presidents discuss immigration after 9/11, the presence of a negative frame increases by a factor of 15.43. This was highly significant, both statistically and in terms of the magnitude of the odds ratio.

Table 4.2   Summary of Logistic Regression Analysis (logit) for Variables Predicting the Presences of at Least One Negative Frame in Presidential Immigration Rhetoric

Dependent Variable: Pr (Success = 1) N = 1850				
Log Likelihood	-1149.6984	$\chi^2 = 239.97$ $(p < .0000)$		
	Coefficients	Odds Ratios	p values	standard errors
Period	2.736	15.43	.000	.4079
Border State	.7200	2.054	.001	.2266
Mexico	.4325	1.541	.003	.1463
Africa	1.659	5.252	.003	.5652
Middle East	−.1183	.8885	.935	1.459
Europe	−1.063	.3455	.049	.5409
Recession	.3535	1.424	.175	.2604
Inflation Rate	.1849	1.203	.016	.0770
Unemployment	.0514	1.053	.276	.0472
GDP	−.0009	.9991	.000	.0001

In the second model, a multinomial logistic regression analysis, our results showed that 9/11 affected the use of each of the negative immigration frames. Post-9/11 presidential rhetoric is more likely to contain the criminality, illegality, terrorism, and economic threat than the rhetoric of the pre-9/11 period (see Table 4.3). The coefficients are quite large and highly statistically significant.

During the Clinton administration, the percentage of the rhetoric with at least one negative frame actually increased until his first midterm election. From 1993 through 1996, President Clinton's overall "immigration" rhetoric was negative over 50 percent of the time, topping 70 percent in 1994 and 1995.[7] He was not as negative for the rest of this administration, however, with the exception of 41 percent negativity in 1999. For instance, in 1998 only about 8 percent of his rhetoric was negative. Moreover, in 1995 and 1996 over 45 percent of his "immigration" mentions discussed the illegality frame. After the midterms, his use of negative frames dropped significantly. There were similar numbers in 1997 (25%) and 2000 (14%). There was a slight increase, however, in 1999; about 40 percent of his rhetoric was negative. President Clinton rarely mentions the other negative frames, with two exceptions. In 1995, 17 percent of his "immigration" rhetoric mentioned the criminality frame, which was 28 percent of all criminality frames for each president. Moreover, in 1994, 34 percent of his "immigration" rhetoric mentioned the economic threat frame, which was nearly 45 percent of the total economic threat frames for all presidents.

In 1995, this number was about 10 percent of his "immigration" rhetoric, which was nearly 18 percent of all economic threat frames. We speculate that the budget battle of 1996 and the opposition Congress that President Clinton faced, after the midterm elections, engendered the perfect opportunity

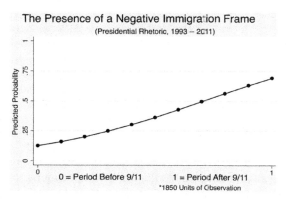

Figure 4.1 Presence of a negative frame in presidential rhetoric as a result of the period in which the speech was given. *Source:* The data used for this figure are coded by the authors from all presidential speeches pertaining to immigration from 1993–2011. It provides a visual, detailed picture of the probability of a negative immigration frame existing before and after 9/11.

Chapter 4

Table 4.3 Summary of Multinomial Logistic Regression Analysis (mlogit) for Variables Predicting the Type of Negative Frame in Presidential Immigration Rhetoric, 1993–2011

Dependent Variable: Pr (Success = 1 Illegality, 2 Criminality, 3 Terrorism, 4 Economic Threat) N = 1850

Log Likelihood - 1845.2282 χ^2 = 668.22 (p < .0000)

	Illegality	Criminality	Terrorism	Economic Threat
Before & After 9/11	1.961 ***	3.60 **	3.758 ****	5.091 **
	(.665)	(1.786)	(.807)	(2.429)
Border State Speech	.318 **			1.073 ****
	(.162)			(.291)
Approval Rating	−.040 ****	−.033 **		−.081 ****
	(.008)	(.014)		(.023)
Misery Index Rate			.063 ***	
			(.024)	
Consumer Price Index	−.041 ****	−.090 ****	−.067 ***	−.098 ***
	(.010)	(.020)	(.022)	(.034)
Hispanic Identifier	.452 ***	.731 ** (.287)		
	(.158)			
Asian Identifier				−14.078 ****
				(.581)
African Identifier	1.815 ***	−13.402 ****	−12.512 ****	−12.893 ****
	(.605)	(.557)	(1.069)	(.780)
Middle Eastern Identifier	−19.838 ****	−19.704 ****	2.263 **	−19.482 ****
	(1.121)	(1.216)	(.984)	(1.225)
Immigration Audience		−0.557* (.317)		
Major Speech	1.163 ***		1.115 ***	1.795 ***
	(.379)		(.401)	(.684)
Divided Government	−.363 **	.919 *** (.358)		−0.757 *
	(.153)			(.459)
Presidential Party	1.209 ****		−2.873 ****	4.136 ****
	(.280)		(.558)	(.796)

*p < .1; **p < .05; ***p < .01; ****p < .001

for presidential rhetoric to be responsive to context rather than create entrepreneurial meaning. Most importantly, however, we argue that the backlash President Clinton faced from the signing of the North American Free Trade Agreement (NAFTA) increases the likelihood that he mentioned NAFTA and immigration together. On multiple occasions, President Clinton, in his rhetoric, responded to the criticisms of NAFTA and argued that it will significantly decrease the amount of "illegal" immigrants who come to America. In fact, he claimed that NAFTA will or has created the type of economic growth in

Mexico that will lead to the slowing of "illegal" immigration, which, in turn, will keep "legal" immigration running smoothly. These conditions motivated him to deviate from the tone of his Party Platform. Given the decreasing percentage of negative frames and the lack of mentions of NAFTA in his rhetoric after 1996, one has to consider this rationale.

During the Bush administration, the trend of negative immigration rhetoric changed significantly. The negativity in his rhetoric was consistently over 30 percent, until 2008 where it was 21 percent. His negativity peaked in 2004 (52%), 2005 (69%), and 2006 (52%). The year 2006 accounts for about 20 percent of the total negative rhetoric for all of the presidents. For instance, about 39 percent of Bush's "immigration" rhetoric used the negative frame terrorism in his first year in office. The percentage dropped slightly in 2002 (29%), 2003 (29%), and 2004 (23%) before rising again in 2005 (34%), right before the midterm elections. There was a steady decline in the terrorism frame in 2006 (25%), 2007 (13%), and 2008 (10%). In 2006, however, President Bush used the terrorism frame 74 times, which is about 39 percent of the total terrorism frames for all of the presidents in this study. The next closest negative frame President Bush used regularly was the illegality frame, in 2004 (20%), 2005 (26%), and 2006 (26%). In 2006, he used this frame the most, 77 times, which is almost 17 percent of the total illegality mentions for all of the presidents.

Directly after 9/11, the president's approval rating and image as a leader was unparalleled. His approval topped 85% at one point. The president did not need to remind the public of 9/11 directly after the event to garner any support for his policies, particularly the largest reorganization of American bureaucracy since the creation of the Department of Defense. Again, as his approval rating was still high in 2003 (70% at some points), the Republican Party took the House and Senate, which gave them a unified government, and he initiated the invasion of Iraq; the conditions were not conducive to negative rhetoric. However, the conditions in which President Bush found himself governing began to change in 2004 and 2005 and after his second election. The context had changed; his approval ratings were dropping (36%), people were growing weary of the wars, and the midterm elections were nearing. This context is where we start to see the increase in President Bush's negativity. For instance, we do not see the negative frames of "terrorism" and "illegality" reaching their peak until 2006. We observe President Bush increase his usage of the negative frames the closer he gets to the 2006 midterm elections, wherein the Republicans are expecting to lose many House and Senate seats. As President Bush's conditions changed, the perfect context was created for presidential rhetoric to respond to externalities rather than set or create new agendas. As we discuss in greater detail in chapter 5, President Bush resorts to the authoritarian script in a playbook designed to foster fear and concern in an attempt to keep his party in power.

The negativity in President Obama's rhetoric was higher than expected. His total "immigration" rhetoric was negative, however, over 25 percent for 2009 (30%), 2010 (40%), and 2011 (26%). Moreover, he uses about 18 percent of the total economic threat frames. One might speculate that his use of the economic threat frame is a response to the economic crisis he encountered upon entering the presidency. President Obama's use of the illegality frame, in 2009 (24%), 2010 (37%), and 2011 (18%), is similar to that of other presidents in that it decreases the longer they are in office, with the exception of the midterm elections.

The economic variables are significantly related to the frequency of negative immigration frames. The indicators consist of the inflation rate, the unemployment rate, and the gross domestic product (Wood, 2007; Dolan, Frendreis, & Tatalovich, 2008). When the inflation rate increases by .11849, the presence of a negative frame increases by a factor of 1.203. This is exactly what we would expect it to do. When the purchasing power of the public is mitigated, they want action from the president (Beck, 1982). When the unemployment rate decreases by .052, the president becomes more negative. This is not, on the surface, what one would expect the president to do. One would expect the president to become more negative as the unemployment rate *increased*. High unemployment is detrimental to presidential reelections. We speculate that low unemployment might keep the president from "rattling the immigration saber" and securing his policy goals (Wood, 2009). Nonetheless, the presence of a negative frame in his rhetoric increases by factor of 1.053 when this economic indicator decreases. The result was not statistically significant, however.

In M1, when the GDP decreases, the president is more negative in his discussion of immigration; in fact, the presence of a negative frame in his immigration rhetoric increases by a factor of .999 (See Figure 4.2). Again, this is exactly what one would expect. If the GDP decreases too much, the United States slips into a recession, which is consequential for an incumbent president (Dolan, Frendreis, & Tatalovich, 2008). In M2, the effect of the Misery Index was indistinguishable from zero, except in the case of the terrorism frame, making a modest effect.

Our results show that the geographical location where speeches are given predicts the use of negative immigration frames. In M1, for every one-unit change in whether the speech occurred in a state that borders Mexico, the odds of it being negative toward immigrants increase by a factor of 1.541. However, the majority of the negative frames (507) presidents used occurred while they were in Washington, DC. Slightly over half of the negative frames (156) used outside of Washington, DC, occurred while they were in a state that bordered Mexico. The second model (M2) shows that presidents are significantly more likely to use the "Economic Threat" and "Illegality" frames when speaking in the states that border Mexico.

The President Goes Negative

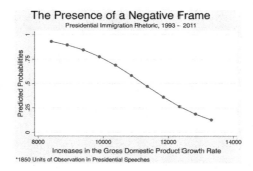

Figure 4.2 The presence of a negative frame in presidential rhetoric as a result of the gross domestic product growth rate when the speech was given. *Source:* The data used for this figure are coded by the authors from all presidential speeches pertaining to immigration from 1993–2011 and GDP data from the U.S. Bureau of Economic Analysis. It provides a visual, detailed picture of the probability of a negative immigration frame existing as the gross domestic product increases.

Many of our control variables were statistically significant predictors of negative presidential rhetoric (See Table 4.4). We were concerned that the audience that the president addressed might have some effect on the rhetoric they choose to use. We identified those groups/audiences that are closely tied to immigrants and immigration, those groups that have a direct and substantial interest in making sure that immigrants are treated positively and that the immigration process works well for those that are trying to migrate to the United States. We identified these groups by their mission statements to ascertain the audiences, particularly specialized groups, to which the presidents are speaking such as the National Council of La Raza. Those groups that identified immigration or immigrants as crucial to the mission of their

Table 4.4 Summary of Logistic Regression Analysis (logit) for Variables Predicting Negativity in Presidential Immigration Rhetoric

Dependent Variable: Pr (Success = 1) N = 1850				
Log Likelihood	−1149.6984	$\chi^2 = 239.97$ ($p < .0000$)		
	Coefficients	Odds Ratios	p values	Standard Errors
Proposed Legislation	0.4393	1.552	.000	0.1255
Approval Ratings	−0.0194	0.9808	0.011	0.0077
Major Speech	1.156	3.176	0.001	0.3357
Divided Government	−0.1884	0.8283	0.334	0.1949
Audience	−0.2774	0.7577	0.03	0.1276
Election Year	−0.0214	0.9788	0.902	0.1742
Midterm Election	0.1472	1.159	0.461	0.1997
Democrat House	0.0012	1.001	0.997	0.3007
Democrat Sen.	−0.3318	0.7177	0.278	0.3059
Republican House	−0.0012	0.9989	0.997	0.3007
Republican Sen.	0.3317	1.393	0.278	0.3059

92   *Chapter 4*

organization were included in this variable. Not conducting the analysis in this way would mean that every group the president addresses has a vested interest so there would be no variation and the "audience" would not matter, particularly given that presidents have a great deal of say in the audiences they address.[8] We determined that when the president addresses these groups, he is less negative about immigration. In fact, when presidents address these groups, the negativity in their speeches decreased by a factor of .7577 in M1 and was only significant in relation to the "Criminality" frame in M2, which is, again, evidence that the context in which the president speaks has an impact on the tone of their speeches about salient policy topics.

We were also interested in whether or not negative rhetoric increased during an election year. This addition provided a unique element to the analysis, particularly the substantive differences between the amount of negative frames in the presidents' rhetoric in the midterm elections and the general presidential elections. Of the 817 total negative frames in the presidents' rhetoric, 402 of them occurred during an election. Presidents are significantly more negative during the midterm elections (301 negative frames) than they are during the general presidential elections (101 negative frames). Our analysis, however, suggests that there is no statistically significant difference between the negativity in an election year or non-election year. We speculate that presidents are simply trying to appeal to their party (ideological) bases during the midterms and are vying for the more moderate voters during the general presidential elections; again, this is another instance wherein presidents respond to their context.

We also examined whether the type of speech the president gives influences the use of negative immigration frames. By far, the president mentions immigration more in his various remarks (989 total and 404 negative frames), interviews (146 total and 76 negative frames), and news conferences (173 total and 80 negative frames), as well as their written rhetoric (452 total and 204 negative frames), which is essential for establishing and maintaining an engendered environment of policy perspectives. However, the public is more likely to pay attention to their major speeches (49 total and 35 negative frames), the ones televised for extended periods of time. Therefore, we controlled for this in our analysis and found that the presence of a negative frame in presidential rhetoric in a major speech increases by a factor of 3.176 in M1 and was highly significant in M2, as seen in Tables 4.2 and 4.4

A serious concern of ours was the social identification of the immigrant mentioned in the speech. Our analysis found that it does make a significant difference in the frequency of negative immigration frames used in presidential rhetoric. Overall, however, we find that the presidents' use of social identifiers before 9/11 rather than after the attacks is more apparent, with just three exceptions. Table 4.3 illustrates this point wherein 1) "Hispanic" is significant when presidents are referring to "Illegality" and "Criminality," 2) "African" is significant when presidents are referring to "Illegality," and 3) "Middle Eastern" is significant when referring to "Terrorism." We were concerned with what type of social identifications presidents would discuss negatively when considering immigration, particularly after 9/11. One might simply assume it would be Arabs/Middle Easterners, especially given the fact that the United States was involved in two large-scale wars after immigrants of Arab/Middle Eastern social identification used the immigration system to enter America and then commit terrorist attacks. Presidents did mention Arabs/Middle Easterners with the "Terrorism" negative frame attached to it in a significant way after 9/11, but not for the other negative frames.

The most significant social identifier within presidential immigration rhetoric, as seen in Tables 4.2 and 4.3, consists of Mexico, Central America, and the Caribbean as well as South America (also Latino or Hispanic). Presidents mention this social group 358 times of which 176 mentions had a negative frame attached to it. In other words, when presidents mention Mexico, Central America, or Caribbean as well as South America (also Latino or Hispanic), the presence of a negative frame attached to this social identification increased by a factor of 1.541 in M1 and by a factor of 2 when referring to Criminality in M2. Interestingly, when presidents are discussing European immigrants, they are significantly less likely to use a negative frame in their rhetoric. In fact, the presence of a negative frame in their rhetoric decreases by a factor of .3445. Further, when presidents are discussing African immigrants, they are significantly more likely to use a negative frame in their rhetoric. In fact, the presence of a negative frame in their rhetoric increases by a factor of 5.252.

In M1, the dynamics of congressional government and its relation to presidential rhetoric had a significant impact. The party that is in control of the Congress, as well as whether there is divided government, particularly between congressional control and presidential control, does not have a significant effect on the frequency of negative immigration frames. There were more negative frames in presidential rhetoric during Republican control of the Senate (479) than in Democratic control of the Senate (338). Moreover, there were more negative frames in presidential rhetoric during Republican control of the House (549) than in Democratic control of the Senate (268). Nonetheless, presidents are more likely to use negative immigration frames when there is no divided government.

We addressed presidential approval ratings in the model as well. Our analysis indicates that it does make a significant difference in the frequency and type of negative immigration frames used in presidential rhetoric, with the exception of the "Terrorism" frame. In fact, when the presidents' approval ratings decrease by 1 percentage point in M1, presidents use more negative frames in their rhetoric. The approval ratings only have to decrease very slightly for them to use the "Illegality" and "Criminality" frames. The reality is that the presence of a negative immigration frame increases by a factor of .988 when approval ratings decrease by slightly under 2 percent.

CONCLUSION

There are numerous studies that treat presidential rhetoric as an independent variable. Scholars often conceptualize presidential speeches as attempts to set the agenda or accomplish a task. The literature has not fully examined whether presidential rhetoric on immigration issues is responsive to context. The goal of this chapter was to explore whether certain conditions motivate presidents to use negative frames in their discussions of immigration. We were particularly interested in learning whether the negative shift in public opinion and news coverage of immigration after 9/11, as discussed in previous chapters, could also be found in presidential rhetoric (Woods & Arthur, 2014).

Our findings were based on a content analysis of 750 speeches (1,850 units of analysis) made by presidents W. J. Clinton, G. W. Bush, and B. H. Obama over a long and diverse historical period. From reading these speeches, we concluded that presidents play both an active and passive social role. On the one hand, presidents make choices about what to say and thereby shape public opinion, set the news agenda, and encourage institutional change. Presidents Clinton, Bush, and Obama, each made an important contribution to the dominant symbolic repertoire on immigration, and in so doing, influenced how subsequent presidents would talk about this topic.

On the other hand, the results of this study also showed that presidents change the level of negativity in their immigration rhetoric depending on when and where their speeches are given, and in response to externalities that they are mostly unable to control. In other words, presidents pay attention to the context in which they find themselves. They are not always setting the agenda or creating new meaning for and in the political process. As Miroff (2003) argues, presidents should be studied in the framework of leadership rather than entrepreneurship. Skowronek (1997) says that this is true because the presidents are constrained by the institutional framework created by their predecessor and that their efforts at entrepreneurship are part of a larger drama in which presidents often fail to control the arrangements that are imposed upon them. Light (1999) asserts that presidents simply do not have time for new policy perspectives or an innovative agenda. The political process is too fragmented and competitive to accommodate another entrepreneur. His "derivative presidency" shows that presidents must use "old"

The President Goes Negative

policy ideas rather than create them anew (p. 285). This forces presidents to try to accomplish their goals by responding to the context in which they find themselves.

The terrorist attacks on 9/11 and the fear of terrorism hardened public attitudes toward immigrants, encouraged negative news stories about immigration (Woods & Arthur, 2014), led to key institutional changes, and promoted a culture of fear that would shape the way Americans perceived immigrants and how presidents talked about them for decades (Winkler, 2006). The prevailing authoritarianism after 9/11 was especially prominent in the speeches of George W. Bush, who, more than any president before him, and much more so than President Obama, connected the policy issues of immigration and terrorism. Much of this rhetoric likely enhanced the notion that immigrants pose a threat to national security and encouraged the public and the government to restrict outsiders' access to public life.

In contrast, President Obama rarely used the terrorism frame when discussing immigration, and appeared to part ways with the authoritarian stance in President Bush's rhetoric. Yet, even Obama, as well as Clinton, struggled at times to remain as positive and progressive as the positions stated in their party's platforms. Obama may have made strides in taming the authoritarian turn in political culture, even during the presidential election of 2012, but he clearly did not transform it permanently. There has not been a fundamental shift in the dominant symbolic repertoire on immigration. As discussed in the final chapter of this book, the vestiges of the authoritarian turn reemerged, in full force, during the 2016 presidential campaign and helped energize Donald Trump's successful bid for the presidency. Before moving to the contemporary context, however, the next chapter will examine the post-9/11 changes in the immigration debate in the U.S. Congress.

NOTES

1. This chapter draws in part on an article published in *Presidential Studies Quarterly* (Arthur & Woods, 2013). However, the chapter contains new data and analyses that have not appeared elsewhere. Arthur, C. D. and Woods, J. (2013). "The Contextual Presidency: The Negative Shift in Presidential Immigration Rhetoric," *Presidential Studies Quarterly*, 43(3) (September 2013).

2. Please see Flores (2003) for a discussion and analysis of the deportation strategy in the early 20th century.

3. David Frum argues that those who maintain that Obama deported en masse is not statistically accurate. He argues that those numbers are "total removals" instead of a disaggregated number. Frum argued, "Deportations from the interior *plunged* under Obama: down 19 percent from 2011 to 2012, down another 23 percent between 2012 and 2013. (Note that those were years of economic recovery and expansion, when illegal immigration was rising again after the downtick in the

2008–2010 recession). Although the Obama administration claimed to focus on criminal aliens, deportation even of those tumbled in Obama's second term." Moreover he said that Obama opened the borders to teenagers who were promised. Accessed on April 1, 2017, from: https://www.theatlantic.com/politics/archive/2017/03/debating-immigration-policy-at-a-populist-moment/518916/

4. Testing the reliability of the data was a significant concern for the researchers. We employed standard inter-coder agreement tests on all the variables using roughly 30 percent of the total units. The percentage of agreement on the eleven variables ranged from 86 percent to 100 percent. We used *Scott's Pi*, which corrects for chance agreement. It ranged from .78 to .95 on the variables. According to Riffe, Lacy, and Fico (2005), this measure is a better method to determine reliability. We used alpha levels of .80 or higher as the measure of significant reliability (Krippendorff, 1970). Testing the reliability of negative frames involved two, well-trained coders who spent many hours perfecting this method. One might state that such well-trained coders would, in fact, tailor their interpretations to ensure reliability. Therefore, providing statistical validation of inter-coder reliability does not prove that others would come to the same conclusions, as did the trained coders. In order to control for this, we carried out an additional reliability assessment using twelve coders who received only minimal training on how to code the content according to the codebook and protocol. These tests showed that a very high level of intersubjectivity exists on each of the issues in the codebook.The average percentage of agreement among the twelve coders was roughly 92 percent on mentions of illegality, 98 percent on criminal acts, 98 percent on references to terrorism, and 94 percent on mentions of immigrants as economic threats.

5. If the Congressional Chamber is tied, it is assumed that the vice president will vote along with his party to break the tie. Thus, whichever party the vice president belongs to, that party is in the majority.

6. Each continuous variable in the analysis was recoded into a dummy variable so as not to bias the results.

7. President Clinton had to address the issue that was transpiring in Haiti when he assumed office, which created a significant amount of Haitian refugees in 1994. One may assume that this would account for some of this negativity. In order to correct our model to account for this suggestion, we removed all observations wherein President Clinton was addressing Haitians. We had already, as our model shows, accounted for the social identification of the immigrant community discussed by the president in each speech. This accounted for 23 observations of presidential rhetoric. According to our model, 10 of the 23 observations were negative, which is about 44 percent of presidential mentions that were negative when addressing Haitians. We ran the same regressions for each model, one that included rhetoric that addressed Haitians and another model that did not include rhetoric that addressed Haitians. There were no statistical differences in the substantive effects of the regressions.

8. We thought it interesting to note that presidents speak to these groups far more often when there is not an election year. This enables them to speak about immigration more authoritatively and negatively during the election when they are appealing to their bases and not performing the ceremonial obligations of the Office of the Presidency.

Chapter 5

Congressional Hearings

Immigration Frames in Expert Testimonies

The public's interest and attention to any political issue can change quickly as new events drive other concerns to the forefront (Downs, 1996; Baumgartner & Jones, 1993; Kingdon, 1999). All interested parties in politics are beholden to a variety of demands on their attention, and the prioritization of public concerns can easily fluctuate (Hunt, 2002; Jones, 1994). For instance, in January 2014, immigration was a concern for about 3 percent of those polled, a small share compared to the 25 percent of respondents who named government dissatisfaction as the most important problem (Gallup, 2014). By November of the same year, during the midterm election, 17 percent of Americans named immigration the most important problem (Gallup, 2014).

At the beginning of 2014, the Obama administration and many Republicans had reached agreement on some elements of immigration reform. In fact, the Republican Speaker of the House, John Boehner, and the Republican House Majority Leader, Eric Cantor, had been discussing and advancing a comprehensive immigration bill to work alongside the Senate bill that had been passed earlier (Foley, 2014). The approach to immigration reform had been advancing because reform was seen, by both parties, as a mechanism to fix the problem of having around 11 million undocumented immigrants in the United States. (Foley, 2014). The opportunity for immigration reform had all but ended by the end of July, when a perfect storm of events drew the attention of all interested parties away from "reform" to a new problem, border security, one that was defined by the restrictionists—those who defeated Eric Cantor in his primary race in May—and most importantly, by the influx of tens of thousands of migrant children crossing the border. By the time the midterm election had taken place, there were as many as 68,000 new undocumented children in the United States (Park, 2014).

The Obama administration asked for about $1.2 billion from Congress to create detention centers to house the children as they figured out what to do with them, not wanting to deport them to countries where they might be harmed. This decision triggered much criticism. Many Republicans charged that Obama was refusing to enforce the law; the children should be deported. President Obama tried to frame this incident as a humanitarian response to the migrants, with some limited success. The migrants' presence, however, began to tax the budgets and immigration centers of the states. Moreover, the Republican Governor of Pennsylvania, Tom Corbett, and other Republican members of the House of Representatives argued that the increase in migrant children was more than a humanitarian crisis; it was about national and border security.

Corbett made dubious claims about the children spreading diseases, such as the measles, swine flu, tuberculosis, and Ebola. He argued that their presence in the United States, and the mechanism by which they entered, was a threat to the security of our country, saying our borders must be secured (Lazar, 2014). Naturally, as the migrant child population continued to rise, the issue of immigration shifted from reform, where Obama and the Republican leadership wanted it, to border security. Therefore, border security and its connection to immigration policy was front and center in the midterm election, again. And it eliminated any opportunity for policy change.

Such political turbulence complicates policy efforts of decision makers to control or frame an issue such as immigration (Egan, 2013). The unpredictability of events, how those events are framed, and the attention paid to the events, present constraints that limit change. Most pertinent issues are plagued by this reality. Immigration in particular is an intricate policy domain, wherein multiple contextual factors, new information and events, as well as competing voices, play a role in shaping issue ownership and policy outcomes.

This chapter seeks to ascertain how, given the multiple influences, members of Congress and immigration experts frame immigration. Building on previous chapters, we assume that the post-9/11 authoritarian turn in immigration rhetoric will also be found in the rhetoric of congressional elites during hearings. We assess how 9/11 functions as a shock to the immigration policy monopoly, wherein the framing nexus of "terrorist" and "border control" gains a foothold. In building a substantial database on the discussion of immigration, this study coded remarks from the expert testimonies in congressional hearings from the 103rd Congress (1993–1994) through the 109th Congress (2005), mapping the framing of immigration rhetoric before and after 9/11. Rather than determining if congressional attention to immigration is capable of effecting change in the policy narrative, as an entrepreneurial mechanism of power, this study provides a discussion on the importance of "triggering events" such as 9/11 and the issue expansion in topical policies such as immigration.

9/11 AND THE AUTHORITARIAN TURN
IN IMMIGRATION POLICY

The United States Senate held a congressional hearing on April 4, 2001, entitled *Immigration Policy: An Overview*, wherein the Immigration Subcommittee sought to define immigration policy. This was the last hearing on immigration the Senate had prior to the terrorist attacks on September 11, 2001. The language used in that hearing was not completely positive, but there were only 11 negative frames out of a total of 280 mentions of immigration. Most of the negativity in the expert testimony focused on the economic relationships the United States had with other countries and the immigrants that migrated here for jobs. Seven of the 11 negative frames addressed the economic threat that immigrants can pose to U.S. workers. Nevertheless, the hearing was overwhelmingly positive in its assessment of U.S. immigration policy and immigrants migrating to the United States. The chairman of the subcommittee, Senator Sam Brownback (R-KS), began the hearing and set the tone with this opening statement:

> America is a nation of immigrants. That is what Ronald Reagan reminded us of in his first address to the nation. President Reagan saw a vision and always envisioned America as a shining city on a hill, and in his mind it was a city that teemed with people of all kinds living in peace and in harmony. Then he said, "And if this city has walls, the walls have doors, and the doors are open to those with the energy and the will and the heart to get in. That is the way I saw it, that is the way I see it." And that is the way I see it, too . . . America's greatest strength remains in its openness to new ideas and new people. That openness explains why the United States is powerful, influential, and growing. (Sam Brownback, April 4, 2001)

The context of this hearing is defined by several factors. It happened before 9/11, Republicans were in control of the Senate, the president was a Republican, overall polarization was on the decline, and the United States had just entered a recession in April 2001, per the National Bureau of Economic Research (NBER), which likely explains the hearing's emphasis on the supposed economic threat of immigration.

In the first congressional hearing on immigration after 9/11, the *Effective Immigration Controls to Deter Terrorism*, both the context of the discussion and the framing of immigration changed dramatically. The United States suffered the most catastrophic attack on its homeland since Pearl Harbor in

100 *Chapter 5*

December 1941. The Democrats were in control of the Senate (until November 25, 2002). Members of the U.S. Senate, particularly Majority Leader Tom Daschle (D-SD), were sent Anthrax, a deadly bacterium, through the U.S. Mail. The major corporate scandal involving Enron was unfolding. The Stock Market was in a serious downward spiral; the Dow Jones lost 14 percent and the S&P was down nearly 12 percent a week after 9/11 (Davis, 2011). And, the war in Afghanistan began with strong support from both parties.

In this first hearing after 9/11, the attempt to expand the immigration policy narrative from issues of "illegality" and "criminality" and "economic threats" to include "border security" and "terrorism" begins. Illustrating the changing tone and context of the immigration policy discussion, Chairman of the Subcommittee Senator Ted Kennedy (D-MA) begins the hearing with his opening statement, wherein we see the beginning of the competition for party ownership of the issue definition of immigration (Egan, 2013). He states,

> We know that there has been some news affecting exposures to anthrax to some of the staff in our buildings and that is being dealt with very effectively by the Sergeant at Arms and by the health professionals that have been assigned to deal with that job. We feel strongly, since immigration issues have important implications in terms of national security and also to terrorism, that it was important that we move ahead.[1]
>
> We are dealing as well with the challenges of immigration as well as the challenges in the intelligence community. So all of these make up very important aspects in dealing with terrorism. It was our judgment that we ought to move ahead with this hearing.
>
> It is a privilege to chair this hearing today on the critical issue of border security and its critical importance in preventing terrorism. Strengthening the security of our borders is an indispensable part of this Nation's effort to prevent future terrorist attacks. We must develop policies and enact laws that meet the serious security threats we face from abroad. (Ted Kennedy, October 17, 2001)

The first congressional hearing after 9/11 clearly showed how Congress was redefining immigration policy, expanding the issue to include border security and terrorism. The attempt to expand immigration policy continued into the next subcommittee hearing on April 12, 2002, *The Enhanced Border Security and Visa Entry Reform Act*. The testimony from Robert C. Byrd (D-WV) is indicative of the strategy to control the conflict over immigration policy and ascribe policy control and an ownership to the beneficial outcomes of the new policy to a specific party (McCool, 1998). In other words, by framing immigration policy as a border security issue that mitigates the threat of terrorism, which is popular with the public, all benefits that result will be associated with the Democratic or Republican Party, allowing the party to "own" the issue of immigration and signal to the voters that the outcome of the popular

Congressional Hearings 101

policy perspective is the result of the actions of the party in control of the policy issue. First, however, a bit of context would create a better understanding of the testimony and the interaction between the parties that transpires after Senator Byrd's prepared statement, and their attempt to define, control, and own immigration policy.

Again, this hearing occurs during the short period wherein the Democrats have control of the Senate (June 6, 2001, to November 25, 2002) and the chairmanships, which enables them to decide what individuals, groups, and interests can testify to the subcommittee; therefore, shaping the immigration narrative and defining the immigration policy image in the hearing. It is also important to note that this hearing is, in part, the result of Senator Byrd's decision not to grant unanimous consent, the previous December, to the passage of *The Enhanced Border Security and Visa Entry Reform Act*, which they were discussing in April.

Senator Byrd objected to the request for unanimous consent to pass the bill without any hearings or debate on the Senate floor. With total control of each branch of government, as well as a major national tragedy and terrorist act, the Republicans could move the legislation forward and control the immigration policy image, while excluding the perspective of the Democratic Party. Without an opportunity for the Democratic Party to debate, amend, and force Republicans to compromise on the details of the bill, the public would simply perceive the border security and terrorist mitigation efforts as the work of the Republican Party.

Senator Byrd's decision was, in part, based on his intention to frame immigration policy and its connection to border security in a manner that is also beneficial to Democrats, while highlighting the deficiencies of the Republican Party's ideological commitments to border security and terrorist mitigation, as it is being discussed in the hearing. It is an ideological fight by the parties for immigration policy control. Each party wants ownership over border security and its new connection to immigration policy. It is a popular policy, and one that involves governmental action that produces money for certain districts. It also represents a successful talking point that exemplifies the effectiveness of the party. To illustrate our argument, Byrd maintains,

> The September 11 attacks showcased the gaps in our border defenses. . . . I firmly believe that the Senate needs to pass legislation to tighten our immigration and border security laws. I devoted a large amount of my time and resources last fall to that very goal. I crafted a $15 billion homeland defense package as part of the economic stimulus bill the Senate considered last November. That homeland defense package provided $1.1 billion for border security initiatives, many of which are included in the border security bill that we are discussing today. Under a Presidential veto threat—let me underline that, under a veto

102   *Chapter 5*

threat by President Bush [a Republican], those funds were removed from the economic stimulus package by a partisan vote on a budgetary point of order, and every Republican on this committee supported that point of order to knock out that money. Not a single Republican stood with us [Democrats] in my effort to fund border security then and there, not one. . . . Because that point of order—we were not able to get the 60 votes to override it because the Republicans, to the man and woman, voted against it. We could have done things then. But every Republican on this committee voted against us [Democrats]. (Robert C. Byrd, April 12, 2002)

Senator Byrd continues this line of thought, framing the issue of border security and the failings of the United States in maintaining safe, secure borders on the political obstructionism of the Republican Party. He develops the notion that the Democrats are willing now, and have been willing in the past, to devote political capital, political will, and substantial amounts of money to the issue of border security—arguing that the Republicans want to vote in the affirmative for border security without voting for the money necessary to secure the borders. He states, emphatically, that Republicans have not been willing to do this, arguing that not one Republican voted for the money and the Republican President Bush threatened to veto the bill. In other words, they are not the party of border security, but rather the Democrats are the owners of the border security issue in immigration policy. His fear is that the Republicans would pass the bill and go home to their states and claim that they "fixed" the problem, which makes them the party of border security. Senator Byrd continues,

When I tried to get money before we went out of session, not a single Republican on this committee supported me, not one. At the time, I was told that a window of opportunity had opened to pass this legislation and that in the aftermath of the September 11 attacks, a united coalition, Democrats and Republicans, would support this authorization bill. Yes, they [Republicans] were willing to support the authorization bill, good to pass that, pass it by unanimous consent, go back home and say we have taken care of the problem, we passed an authorization bill. But not one, not one Republican—I am sorry to have to be so strong in my statement here in this regard. I very seldom criticize members of the other party, but I think I have a right to in this instance. . . . And then some of the members of this committee implored me, pleaded with me to agree to unanimous consent to pass this authorization bill. They could go home then [with complete unified party government]. They could say, oh, yes, we passed that. But when it comes to the money, I wanted to face these Republicans and say, are you going to vote for the money [the real measures necessary to fix the border security problem]? (Robert C. Byrd, April 12, 2002)

The contrast between the pre-9/11 and post-9/11 hearings is indicative of the fundamental argument in this book, namely, an act of extreme terrorism helped to redefine and expand, by adding a new framework, the authoritarian approach to immigration policy in American political affairs. The 9/11 attack refocused the attention of government on immigration, expanding the policy image to include the issue of border security, along with illegality, criminality, and economic threats. The United States went from spending $1.055 billion in 2000 to $3.531 billion in 2012, which is about a 235 percent increase in funding in just over a decade (Graham, 2013).

However, this immigration policy issue expansion does not replace the dominant "illegal" framing nexus, but rather offers terrorism and border security a place in the rhetorical palette of elite authoritarian discourse in congressional hearings. The effects of 9/11 and the immigration issue expansion set off a competition between the Republican and Democratic Parties to own the issue of immigration and its connections to border security and terrorist mitigation. Moreover, the ownership of the post-9/11 immigration policy also gave the party the reputation of being the protector of national security in the face of terrorism and immigration dangers, a strategic electoral advantage. Republicans eventually ended up "owning" the issue, but the Democrats were fighting for ownership directly after 9/11, as illustrated above. In fact, as Egan (2013) notes, the issue of immigration was the second most important policy priority the public had for both the president and the Congress in 2008 and the most important one by 2011.

It is important to note here that the congressional committees established by members of congress create policy monopolies through their stronghold on the policy turfs; the committees are a subsystem of limited participation (Worsham, 2006). Only those persons invited by the majority party can participate in the hearings. The control of the policy turf can create policy monopolies, wherein the image of the policy is completely controlled by a limited group of participants and access to that policy-making system of power is restricted by those in control, elected officials in this case (Worsham, 2006).

The interesting aspect of this shift in the immigration issue definition, however, is that there is very little resistance to including "terrorism" and "border security" in the immigration conversation, but rather the competition is more closely identified with party ownership of the idea. This is precisely why Democrats, in the limited amount of time they are in control of the Senate after 9/11, hold hearings when they know their control is limited in duration. In other words, there were no arguments about the overall policy image of immigration wherein one would say it is solely about "illegality" or "refugees," as it had been in the past, but rather it appears that including "border security" and "terrorism" as policy images for immigration are a foregone

104   *Chapter 5*

conclusion by many of the voices in the elite discourse on immigration. The expansion of the authoritarian turn in the immigration policy image in Congress can be seen in nuanced rhetoric from the elite experts in the hearings. These differentiations are more apparent from those that are from border states or those states with high immigrant populations and migrant worker economies, however. Nevertheless, the reality is that after 9/11 the dominant immigration policy monopoly is one of negativity and authoritarianism.

DATA AND SOURCES

The number of hearings on immigration policy have ranged from nearly 70 in the 80th Congress (1947–1949) to just above 20 hearings in the 82nd Congress (1951–1953). This dramatic rise and fall remains until the 95th Congress (1977–1979), wherein it hovers around 75 hearings until it drops off to under 10 hearings in the 98th Congress (1981–1983). There has been a steadier increase in the number of hearings through the 103rd Congress (1993–1995). Compared to the Senate, the House of Representatives has been a bit more consistent in the number held, dropping below 65 hearings only in the 86th Congress (1959–1961) and the 89th through the 91st Congresses (1963–1969). The fluctuation in the number of Senate hearings is indicative of the competition in immigration policy; as the majority and minority power changes, each group schedules hearings so as to frame the policy discussion in ways that benefit their party (Hunt, 2002).

Our study is interested in what was said during these hearings and who said it (Hunt, 2002). For this reason, we differentiated congressional testimonies by elected officials, government bureaucrats, and interest groups. We choose to analyze the hearings from the 104th Congress to the 109th Congress (1995–2005), giving us, a few years before 9/11 and a few years after this consequential event. As Theriault (2013) argued, this is a period when both the Senate and House are polarized. During this period, typically referred to as the *Republican Revolution*, the Republican Party's *Contract with America* was formalized, uniting the party and polarizing the Senate (Theriault & Rohde, 2011). The Republicans took control of both the House and the Senate during this time, after years of Democratic Party control and polarization began to increase.

We choose to ignore the House Hearings for theoretical reasons and took a statistically appropriate approach to narrowing down the number of Senate hearings (Garand, 2010; Lee, 2008; McTague & Pearson-Merkowitz, 2013). We would expect intense polarization and competition for control of immigration policy in the House, more so than in the Senate, as other research suggests (Theriault & Rohde, 2011; Poole & Rosenthal, 1984; Schickler, 2000; Finocchiaro, & Rohde, 2008; Eilperin, 2007). Focusing exclusively on hearings in the Senate allows us to make a unique contribution to immigration policy analysis. As Theriault and Rohde (2011) maintain, most studies have examined the House because the rules of that body encourage polarization and those of the Senate foster a more "equalitarian" approach to policy making. Yet, because the Senate has become more polarized since the *Republican Revolution*, more studies need to focus on the Senate exclusively to expand our institutional understanding of the Senate's impact on policy, especially on a contentious, polarizing issue like immigration. As discussed earlier, we expect that House members will be strongly in favor of or against various immigration ideologies, as they represent specific, localized economies and constituencies; the senators represent a larger, more diverse constituency that better reflects the views and attitudes of their entire state. Therefore, a shift in the rhetoric of the Senate hearings would be more representative of an authoritarian turn on immigration policy in society.

In addition, following a sharp decline, the number of Senate immigration hearings increased back to the level of 1985. As Figure 5.1 illustrates, there is a drop in hearings in 1999 and 2000, which indicates that the immigration policy image is established and not at risk for a challenge from the other party (MacLeod, 2002). The fact that there is a dramatic increase in hearings after 9/11 in 2001 is indicative of the challenge to the established immigration policy image and the competition for party ownership of that issue.

The increase in hearings remains steady until 2006 when the Democrats take control of the Senate, leading us to speculate that party and issue ownership has a significant effect here. Not only is each chamber vying for control of immigration policy, we can also see an attempt made by the Republican Party to elevate this issue at the beginning of their *Revolution* and maintain

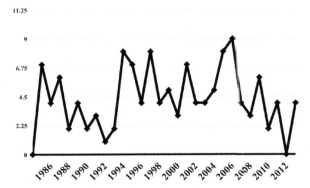

Figure 5.1 **Number of Senate hearings on immigration 1985–2013.** *Source:* The data used for this figure are from the Policy Agendas Project data set. It provides a visual, detailed picture of the total number of Congressional Hearings in the U.S. Senate differentiated by year, which is represented by the X-axis in this figure. The Y-axis shows the breakdown of the congressional hearings by the start year of the congressional session.

it throughout their time in the majority as they get more seats in the 2002 midterms, an effect of 9/11 (Hunt, 2002).

To obtain transcripts of the hearings pertaining to immigration, one cannot simply use a key word search to identify hearings by topic. The word "immigration" is often mentioned in hearings that have nothing to do with immigration per se. Therefore, to ascertain the number of hearings that specifically address immigration we went to the *Policy Agendas Project* and utilized their data, as it is accepted in the scholarly community. As Figure 5.1 shows, there were 59 hearings in the Senate from 1995 through 2005. Our next challenge was to narrow down the number of hearings and select a manageable sample (Cook, Barabas & Page, 2002). Our search led us to the Library of Congress (LOC), which houses a large collection of congressional hearings digitized in a searchable format. Partnering with Google, the LOC has collected every congressional hearing in existence. As part of a test experience, the LOC and Google selectively compiled a sample of hearings in three areas: Census U.S., Freedom of Information/Privacy, and Immigration. Thus, we had each Senate hearing from 1995 through 2005 in a searchable document.

Mentions of "immigration" number in the tens of thousands for all hearings in the Senate, especially when you consider all stem forms of the word "immigra." Trying to ascertain each relevant stem word and code it appropriately is unnecessary and burdensome (Woods & Arthur, 2014; Arthur & Woods, 2013; Hopkins & King, 2010). To reduce the impracticality of analyzing the entire population of congressional mentions of "immigra," we coded every mention of the term "immigration" in our sample of congressional hearings to create a database of elite discourse that extends around five years before and after 9/11 (Woods & Arthur, 2014; Arthur & Woods, 2013; Lohr, 2010; Barrett & Eshbaugh-Soha, 2007; Jacobs & Shapiro, 2000; Spriggs, 1996; Barrett, 2004; Peterson, 1990). There were 1,989 mentions of immigration, our unit of analysis, in the 18 hearings we read and coded (See Table 5.1).

As discussed in previous chapters, the codebook used for this project is aimed at detecting the use of four negative immigration frames, including illegality, criminality, terrorism, and economic threats (Cameron, 2000; Barrett, 2005; Barrett, 2004; Woods & Arthur, 2014; Arthur & Woods, 2013). In addition to coding the negative frames, we coded several social identifiers that are often used in the context of the immigration debate, such as the country of origin (Mexican/Hispanic, Arab, and so forth). Following previous studies, we took the closest coding trigger to the thought regarding "immigration" (Arthur & Woods, 2013; Arthur, 2014). We are highly confident in the reliability of our human coding procedure (for a detailed discussion of the inter-coder reliability, see chapter 3).

Table 5.1 Coded Senate Hearings on Immigration 1995–2005

	Extracted from the Library of Congress
May 10, 1995	Verification of Applicant Identity for Purposes of Employment and Public Assistance
Oct. 2, 1996	Immigration and Naturalization Oversight
May 1, 1997	INS Oversight: The Criminal Record Verification Process for Citizenship Applicants
July 17, 1997	The Visa Waiver Pilot Program
Dec. 17, 1997	Haitian Refugee Immigration Fairness Act
April 14, 1999	The Kosovo Refugee Crisis
Oct 21, 1999	America's Workforce Needs in the 21st Century
April 4, 2001	Immigration Policy: An Overview
Oct 17, 2001	Effective Immigration Controls to Deter Terrorism
Feb. 12, 2002	Empty Seats in a Lifeboat: Are There Problems With the U.S. Refugee Program?
Feb. 28, 2002	The Unaccompanied Alien Child Protection Act
April 12, 2002	The Enhanced Border Security and Visa Entry Reform Act
March 12, 2003	Border Technology: Keeping Terrorists out of the United States
July 29, 2003	L1 Visa and American Interests in the 21st Century Global Economy
March 23, 2004	United States and Mexico: Immigration Policy and the Bilateral Relationship
April 1, 2004	Securing Our Borders Under A Temporary Guest Worker Proposal
Sep 21, 2004	Refugees: Seeking a Solution to a Global Concern
April 28, 2005	Strengthening Border Security Between the Ports of Entry: The Use of Technology to Protect the Borders

EMPIRICAL MODEL

We used a regression analysis to facilitate our understanding of the authoritarian shift in elite immigration discourse after 9/11 and help us make sense of those changes in relation to this dramatic shock to the political system. The model also reveals how and when important social identifiers are used by elites in the immigration debate. The analyses provided predicted probabilities and odds ratios for the use of negative frames in our 1,989 units of analysis. Table 5.6 presents the coefficients, standard errors, and the measures of significance.

Variables

Our exploratory look at the data revealed that the primary participants in the process were 1) Senators, the other members of Congress, and other various elected officials invited to testify at the hearings; 2) interest groups,

108 Chapter 5

whose mission is connected and vested in U.S. immigration policies; and 3) unelected bureaucrats charged with the government operations of the immigration apparatus. Each of these experts played an important role in the messages presented in the hearings. For this reason, when breaking down the mentions of immigration, we differentiated each statement by source (elected officials, non-elected bureaucrats, or interest groups) (See Table 5.2).

The invitation of interest groups and politicians serves more than the need for expert information (Baumgartner & Leech, 1998; Kersh, 2006). The mere presence of certain political actors is a powerful symbol that can mobilize a specific set of ideas (Chock, 1991; Talbert, Jones, & Baumgartner, 1995; Birkland, 1998). Their presence and testimony represents the will of the people and offers legitimacy to whatever idea about immigration is presented. Moreover, they represent the concerns about and the solutions to the problems associated with the states the elected officials represent. Theoretically, each member of congress is concerned with making good policy and their own reelection, which leads them to use the committee system and congressional hearings to garner attention to an issue and define or redefine that issue during the hearings (Jacobs & Shapiro, 2000; Fenno, 1978; Mayhew, 1989). See Table 5.3 for a list of those "expert" politicians who testified in the time of our analysis and Table 5.4 for a list of those interest groups that testified.

The non-elected bureaucrats are invited to offer their institutional knowledge of immigration. Their presence is required to illustrate the problems with the functional mechanics of the governmental immigration apparatus. Depending on the policy image desired by the majority party, the non-elected bureaucrats are there to offer reassurance that the bureaucracy can handle whatever solution or problem the Congress presents to them. Interest groups have been an indispensable component of American politics. Their presence in congressional hearings grants legitimacy to their cause and the causes of those members who invite them to testify. Their testimonies, and any particular points of information, are important, but also their presence represents

Table 5.2 Bivariate Relationships between Immigration Frames and Elite Discourse of Expert Testimonies in Congressional Hearings

	Bureaucrats n / %	Elected Officials n / %	Interest Groups n / %
Terrorism	9/2	41/7	34/4
Criminality	12/3	5/1	13/1
Illegality	56/14	92/16	64/7
Economic Threat	13/3	15/2	24/3
No Frames	324/78	432/74	818/85
Total Number of Statements from Experts	414/100	585/100	953/100

Congressional Hearings

Table 5.3 Testimony of Elected Officials and their Immigration Philosophy[1]

Elected Official	Immigration Philosophy	Border State	Hispanic Population
Benjamin Cayetano (Gov. HI)	Economic Expansion	No	7.3%–8.9%
Barbara Boxer D-CA	Reformist	Yes	25.8%–37.6%
Bob Miller (Gov. NV)	Economic Expansion	No	10.4%–26.5%
Neil Abercrombie (Rep.HI)	Security	No	7.3%–8.9%
Charles Grassley (R-IA)	Restrictionist/Security	No	1.2%–5.0%
Christopher Dodd (D-CT)	Security: Border/Economic	No	6.5%–13.4%
Chuck Hagel (R-NE)	Reformist	No	2.3%–9.2%
Larry Craig (R-ID)	Restrictionist	No	5.3%–11.2%
Daniel Inouye (D-HI)	Economic Expansion	No	7.3%–8.9%
Dianne Feinstein (D-CA)	Illegality Problem	Yes	25.8%–37.6%
Frank Murkowski (R-AK)	Economic Expansion	No (Borders Canada)	3.2%–5.5%
Jay Kim (Rep. CA)	Economic Expansion	Yes	25.8%–37.6%
John Cornyn (R-TX)	Restrictionist	Yes	25.5%–37.6%
John McCain (R-AZ)	Restrictionist	Yes	18.8%–29.6%
Jon Corzine (D-NJ)	Security	No	9.6%–17.7%
Jon Kyl (R-AZ)	Security: Border/Economic	Yes	18.8%–29.6%
Maria Cantwell (D-WA)	Reformist/Refugees	No (Borders Canada)	4.4%–11.2%
Mazie Hirono (Lt. Gov. HI)	Economic Expansion	No	7.3%–8.9%
Orrin Hatch (R-UT)	Border Security	No	4.9%–13.0%
Patrick Leahy (D-VT)	Reformist	No (Borders Canada)	0.7%–1.5%
Bill Clinton (D- POTUS)	Refugee Protections	(n/a) US	9%–16.3%
Lincoln Diaz-Balart (R-Rep. FL)	Refugee Protections	No	12.2%–22.5%
Ileana Ros-Lehtinen (R-Rep. FL)	Illegality/Criminality	No	12.2%–22.5%
John Conyers, Jr. (D-Rep. MI)	Refugee Protections	No (Borders Canada)	2.2%–4.4%
Richard Durbin (D-IL)	Reformist: Border/Economic Sec.	No	7.9%–15.8%
Richard Lugar (R-IN)	Security: Border/Economic	No	1.8%–6.0%

(Continued)

110   Chapter 5

Table 5.3   Testimony of Elected Officials and their Immigration Philosophy[1] (Continued)

Elected Official	Immigration Philosophy	Border State	Hispanic Population
Spencer Abraham (R-MI)	Reformist: Illegality	No (Borders Canada)	2.2%–4.4%
Alan K. Simpson (R -WY)	Reformist: Processes	No	5.7%–8.9%
Bob Graham (D-FL)	Refugee Protections	No	12.2%–22.5%
Charles Robb (D-VA)	Reformist/Restrictionist	No	2.6%–7.9%
Charles Schumer (D-NY)	Refugee Protections	No (Borders Canada)	12.3%–17.6%
Ted Kennedy (D-MA)	Reformist/Security	No	4.8%–9.6%
Mike DeWine (R-OH)	Restrictionist: Security Reformist	No (Borders Canada)	1.3%–3.1%
Robert C. Byrd (D-WV)	Border Security	No	0.5%–1.2%
Sam Brownback (R-KS)	Border Security	No	3.8%–10.5%
Ileana Ros-Lehtinen (R-Rep. FL)	Refugee Protections	No	12.2%–22.5%
Saxby Chambliss (R-GA)	Border Security	No	1.7%–8.8%
Stephen Horn (R-Rep. CA)	Illegality: Government Doc.	Yes	25.8%–37.6%
Jeff Sessions (R-AL)	Restrictionist	No	0.6%–3.9%
Tom Coburn (R-OK)	Restrictionist	No	2.7%–8.9%
Tony Knowles (Gov-AK)	Economic Expansion	No (Borders Canada)	3.2%–5.5%

* These Immigration philosophy indicators do not perfectly reflect the coding we used for the statistical analysis, but rather are qualitative descriptions of the overall theme of their testimonies to the Congress in the data set we analyzed. We are aware that these figures can and do change their perspectives of immigration over time. Our assessments are for the time frame 1995–2005. For the statistical analysis we used an epidemiological approach and only coded negative frames.

a specific idea of a group or highlights their presence for symbolic reasons (Diermeier, & Feddersen, 2000). Moreover, the groups picked are typically highly organized and possess access to monies, which facilitates in the senators' attempt to advance the immigration policy image desired (Leyden, 1995). See Table 5.5 for a list of those non-elected bureaucrats who testified in the time of our analysis.

In the model, we regressed our dependent variable, whether or not there was negative immigration frame, on our key independent variable (before or after 9/11), giving us a predicted probability of the effect of the 9/11 on the framing of immigration rhetoric. We also controlled for other variables, including the type of immigration expert, the geographical locations of the expert (e.g.,

Congressional Hearings

Table 5.4 Interest Groups Testifying in Congressional Hearings, differentiated by Year and Lobbying Mission

Interest Group (Yr. Testified)	Lobbying Mission
AFL-CIO (1995)	Lobbying for Union/Labor
American Occupational Therapy Assoc. (1995)	Lobbying for Occupational Therapy
American Business Legal Immigration (1995)	Lobbying Group for Immigration
The Technology Network (1995)	Lobbying Group for Technology
Western Governors Association (1997)	Bipartisan Lobbying Group of Govern.
National Council of Agriculture Empl. (1995)	Trade Association for Agriculture
American Electronics Association (1995)	Trade Assoc. for Technology Industry
Private Attorney/Former Senate Council (1995)	Technology Frauds in Govern. Docs.
CA Department of Motor Vehicles (1995)	Frauds in Govern. Docs.
Institute of Electrical & Electronics, INC (1995)	Trade Association for Electronics
Olympus Group (1995)	Business Lobby Group
Coalition for Fair Empl, Silicon Valley (1995)	Trade Assoc. for Employees
DMV, Maryland (1995)	Frauds in Govern. Docs.
Mexican Legal Defense & Edu (1995&2004)	Legal Information Provider
KPMG Peat Marwick LLP (1997)	Legal Information Provider
Airports Council International (1997)	Trade Association for Airports
Amnesty International (1997)	International Civil Rights Organization
Governmental Accountability Office (1997)	U.S. Government Agency
Honduran Unity (1997)	Information Provider
National Governors Association (1997)	Network of U.S. Governors
Florida Immigration Advocacy Center (1997)	Legal Information Provider
Air Transport Association of America (1997)	Trade Association for Air Transport
Archbishop of Miami (1997)	Religious Information Provider
Center for Protection of Women, Kosovo (1999)	NGO Protecting Refugees
Biometric Industry Association (2001)	Trade Association for BioTechnology
National Council of La Raza (2001)	Civil Rights Organization
American Immigration Lawyers Assoc. (2001)	Legal Information Provider
Cato Institute (2001)	Think Tank
Pricewaterhouse-Coopers (2001)	Legal Information Provider
Nat. AsianPacific Ameri. Legal Consort. (2001)	Legal Information Provider
U.S. Conference of Bishops (2002)	Religious Information Provider
Fraternal Order of Police (2002)	Trade Association for Law Enforcement
Latham and Watkins (2002)	Legal Information Provider
American Federation of Gov. Emp. (2002)	Federal Employee Union
Chicago Bar Legislative Committee (2002)	Legal Information Provider
Unaccompanied Child, Foreign Country (2002)	Personal Interest Story
Lawyers Commt. for Civil Rights (2002)	Civil Rights Organization
U.S. Committee for Refugees (2002)	Resettling Refugees Organization
Families of September 11, 2001 (2002)	Nonprofit supporting the deceased of 9/11

(Continued)

112   *Chapter 5*

Table 5.4 Interest Groups Testifying in Congressional Hearings, differentiated by Year and Lobbying Mission (Continued)

Interest Group (Yr. Testified)	Lobbying Mission
U.S. Chamber of Commerce (2002)	Business Lobby Group
American Civil Liberties Union (2002)	Civil Rights Organization
Refugee Women and Children (2002)	NGO Protecting Refugees
American Council on Intern. Personnel (2003)	Employer Network
Systems Staffing Group (2003)	Business Provider
Adjunct Professor of Law, Cornell (2003)	Information Provider
Global Personnel Alliance (2003)	Forum of Companies Concerned about Immigration
The Migration Policy Institute (2004)	Think Tank
Federation for Immigration Reform (2004)	Nonprofit trying to Reduce Illegal Immigration
American Immigration Law Foundation (2004)	Public Charity
Adjunct Professor of Law, Univ. GA (2004)	Information Provider
Latin Studies at Georgetown Univ. (2004)	Information Provider
Council on Foreign Relations (2004)	Think Tank, providing information
Refugee Council USA (2005)	NGO Protecting Refugees
Haitian Refugee Homestead, FL (2005)	Resettling Refugees
Pew Hispanic Center (2005)	Provides Statistical and Survey Information

borders Mexico), and the social identifiers connected to the immigrants or immigration mentioned (e.g., Hispanic, Arab). We also included measures of congressional control to ascertain how the make-up of government and party control shaped immigration rhetoric (namely, we used variables for divided government, party control of senate, and an election year variable).

Statistical Findings

To find the predicted probability of the specific indicators on the presence of negative frames in congressional hearings between 1995 and 2005, a Logistic Regression Analysis was performed. The model, overall, is in line with our theory. The presence of negative immigration frames in congressional hearings increased after 9/11, holding all other variables constant. A one-unit change in the period, before/after 9/11, makes a significant difference in the frequency of negative immigration frames. The odds of a negative frame occurring after 9/11 increases by a factor of 5.438, which is a 443.8 percent change in odds. Our research suggests that it is significantly more likely that congressional hearings after September 11, 2001, will have a negative immigration frame, as illustrated in Figure 5.2. This finding was highly significant, both statistically and in terms of the magnitude of the odds ratio.

In our analysis of the hearings, the dynamics of congressional government and its relation to the immigration policy image had a significant impact. It

Congressional Hearings

Table 5.5 Non-Elected Bureaucrats Testifying in Congressional Hearings and the Negative Frames they use in their testimonies, differentiated by Year and Agency

Bureaucrat (Yr. Testified)	Immigration Frames	Agency
James A. Puelo (1995)	Illegality	Immigration & Naturalization (INS)
Steven L. Pomerantz (1995)	Illegality	Federal Bureau of Investigation (Criminal Justice)
Robert H. Rasor (1995)	Illegality	Secret Service
Jack Scheidegger (1995)	No Frames	Department of Justice (CA)
Richard E. Jackson (1995)	No Frames	Department of Motor Vehicles (NY)
William Florence (1995)	No Frames	Department of Motor Vehicles (NY)
Mary Ryan (1997)	No Frames	State Department
Michael Bromwich (1997)	Criminality	Department of Justice
Michael Cronin (1997)	Terrorism/Illegality	Immigration & Naturalization (INS)
Richard Stana (1997)	No Frames	Government Accountability Office (GAO)
Stephan Colgate (1997)	No Frames	Department of Justice
Julia V. Taft (1999)	No Frames	State Department
James Ziglar (2001)	Criminality	Immigration & Naturalization (INS)
Lino Gutierrez (2001)	Illegality	State Department
Michael Creppy (2002)	No Frames	Executive Office for Immigration Review
Stewart Anderson (2002)	Illegality	Immigration & Naturalization (INS)
Asa Hutchinson (2003)	Illegality	Homeland Security (Border Patrol)
Robert C. Bonner (2004)	Illegality/Criminality	Homeland Security (Border Protection)
Roger Noriega (2004)	Illegality/Criminality	State Department (Western Hemisphere)
Arthur Dewey (2004)	No Frames	State Department (Refugees)
Eduardo Aguirre (2004)	Every Frame	Homeland Security (Immigration)
Stewart Verdery (2004)	Every Frame	Homeland Security (Border Security)
David Aguilar (2005)	Illegality/Criminality	Homeland Security (Immigration)
Dr. Kirk Evans (2005)	No Frames	Homeland Security

(Continued)

114   Chapter 5

Table 5.5   Non-Elected Bureaucrats Testifying in Congressional Hearings and the Negative Frames they use in their testimonies, differentiated by Year and Agency (Continued)

Bureaucrat (Yr. Testified)	Immigration Frames	Agency
Gilbert C. Fisher (2005)	No Frames	Social Security Administration
Doris Meissner (2007)	Illegality/Economic Threat	Immigration & Naturalization (INS)

Table 5.6   Predicting the Presence of a Negative Immigration Frame in Congressional Hearings, 1995–2005

			Dependent Variable: Pr (Success = 1) $N = 1989$		
	Log Likelihood		-763.95766	Wald $\chi^2 = 311.36\ (p < .0000)$	
	Coefficients	Odds Ratios	Percent Change in Odds	p value	Robust Standard Errors
Period	1.693	5.438	443.8%	.000	.4821
Border's Mexico	1.285	3.615	261.5%	.000	.3117
Elected Official	.8394	2.315	131.5%	.059	.4445
Bureaucrat	−.9059	.4042	−59.6%	.022	.3953
Interest Group	−1.338	.2625	−73.8%	.000	.3790
Election Year	−.4687	.6258	−37.4%	.009	.1786
Republican Senate	1.913	6.776	577.6%	.000	.5216
Divided Government	1.382	3.983	298.3%	.000	.3942
Hispanic Identity	.3159	1.372	37.1%	.243	.2705
Arab Identity	2.135	8.456	745.6%	.000	.4016
Asian Identity	.8967	2.451	145.1%	.172	.6568
Reform Rhetoric	1.306	3.692	269.2%	.000	.1519
DC based Speaker Terrorism/HS	2.502	12.211	1121.1%	.000	.2661
Subcommittee	−1.267	.2817	−71.8%	.014	.5167

is one of the most important variables and contributes to the research. Our results indicate that the party that is in control of the Congress, as well as whether there is a divided government, particularly between congressional control and presidential control, has a significant effect on the presence of negative immigration frames in the testimonies of expert witnesses. There were more negative frames in congressional hearings after 9/11 during Republican control of the Senate (246) than in Democratic control of the

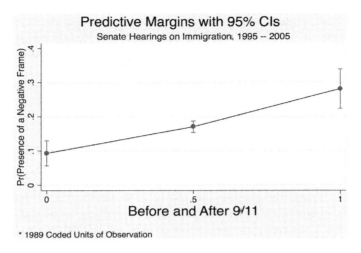

Figure 5.2 The probability of a negative immigration frame in the expert testimony during a congressional hearing, 1995–2005. *Source:* The data used for this figure are coded by the authors from all Senate congressional hearings on immigration from 1995–2005. It provides a visual, detailed picture of the probability of a negative immigration frame existing before and after 9/11.

Senate (44). Moreover, when Republicans are in control of the Senate, the presence of a negative frame in the hearing increases by a factor of 6.776, which is a 577.6 percent change in odds, as seen in Table 5.6; it is highly significant.

We maintain that the increase in frames and the inclusion of a new "terrorism" frame is specifically about party control and defining and connecting immigration policy with border security. The authoritarian approach to immigration is present in congressional hearings prior to 9/11, but it is significantly increased after 9/11. As we discussed earlier, the competition for issue ownership of immigration is not about issue redefinition in the classic sense, but rather it is about adding a new negative frame to the nexus by which we discuss immigration, namely, terrorism and border security. This new framework is advocated by the elected officials, mostly from the Republican Party leadership in the Senate and the other elected officials they invite to testify, as illustrated in Table 5.3.

After 9/11, there is a significant difference in the negativity regarding immigration in the rhetoric of elected officials. In fact, the negativity increased by a factor of 2.315. The terrorism and border security frame is not coming from the non-elected bureaucrats or the interest groups, as indicated by our regressions. Statistically, the non-elected bureaucrats and the interest groups, in their testimony, holding all other variables constant, are more negative before 9/11 and when Republicans control the Senate. Democrats use this negative frame after 9/11, and invite experts who use it, when they are in control of the Senate, but it is not statistically significant. It is, however, highly significant when Republicans use it when they are in control and determine which experts testify.

These two "expert witness" groups continue to offer a negative policy image of immigration after 9/11, wherein the non-elected bureaucrats employed 56 negative frames and the interest groups used 115 negative immigration frames after 9/11, both of which are an increase in the number frames after 9/11. Moreover, we know that the groups were utilized by the Senate and the Republican leadership to employ the illegality, economic threat, and criminality frames prior to 9/11. We maintain that the Republican leadership allowed these groups to testify as a mechanism of maintaining the current immigration policy image, one of negativity, as they did prior to 9/11. As discussed earlier, there is no attempt to replace the existing negative frames of illegality, criminality, and economic threats after 9/11, but rather an attempt to continue those discussions in order to place the new framework of terrorism and border security alongside them, creating a larger authoritarian framing nexus.[2]

Our results also suggest that it is more likely that the geographical location/state matters in the frequency of negative immigration frames. If the expert testifying is from a state that borders Mexico, they will use more negative frames than if they are from a state that does not. In other words, for every one-unit change the odds of it being negative toward immigrants increase by a factor of 3.615, which is a 261.5 percent change in the odds. As would be expected, expanding immigration policy to include border security engenders a greater concern for people in states that border Mexico, which is probably why they were invited to testify. The same is not true for the Canadian border, however.

Moreover, we were curious if the social identification of the immigrant mentioned made any difference in the likelihood that a negative frame would be used. Our analysis found that the results are mixed in the congressional hearings. Overall, however, we find that the expert witness testimony is less likely to include specific social identifiers with specific negative immigration frames; this is a different result from the chapter on presidential rhetoric. The social identification of "Arab" does make a significant difference in the frequency of negative immigration frames used in congressional hearings. There is a dramatic increase in the use of the Arab social identifier when discussing immigration after 9/11. As expected, this social identifier was not used at all prior to 9/11 and was used forty-five times afterward. Overall, when those testifying mention Arab immigrants or immigration, the presence of a negative frame attached to it increased by a factor of 8.456, which is a 745.6 percent change in odds.

It is interesting to note, however, that the Mexico, Central America, Caribbean, South America (also Latino or Hispanic) frame was not statistically significant in the model. Use of this social identifier did increase by 207 percent after 9/11 but these mentions did not predict the use of negative frames. The "Asian" social identifier was also insignificant; it was used only 26 times prior to 9/11 and was never used after 9/11.

The significant increase in both the amount and level of negativity of immigration rhetoric is indicative of congressional attempts to expand the immigration policy image to include issues of terrorism and border security. There are 154 negative mentions of immigration by the elected officials in the hearings we coded. In their official testimony and responses in the congressional hearings, elected members of the Congress only used 43 negative frames about immigration prior to 9/11 (28% of the negative frames). After 9/11, there were 111 negative frames used (72% of the negative frames). This is a 158 percent increase in negativity after 9/11.

CONCLUSION

This chapter demonstrates that the authoritarian shift in public opinion, news coverage of immigration and presidential rhetoric, as discussed in previous chapters, also occurred in congressional hearings. We used an exploratory study of senate hearings pertaining to immigration to show how the shift transpired after 9/11 and the extent to which party identification played a role in maintaining and expanding the authoritarian approach to immigration policy. The policy image of immigration was expanded and maintained by the continued use of the negative immigration framing nexus. Our research suggests that 9/11 functioned as a shock to the immigration policy monopoly, expanding the authoritarian approach to immigration rhetoric to include terrorism and border security in the anti-immigration framing nexus.

These findings were based on a content analysis of 1,989 mentions of immigration in congressional hearings that took place over a ten-year period, 1995–2015, crossing September 11, 2001. From our reading of these hearings and the expert testimony in them, we concluded that a competition for party ownership of the immigration issue transpired in the Congress; it also appears that both Democrats and Republicans were willing, in this time frame, to connect immigration to border security without nuanced qualification. Significant events can garner the attention of the Congress and shape the image of topical policies such as immigration. The Congress and the experts, through their testimonies, have shaped the immigration narrative in a substantive manner, one that continues the negativity and authoritarian approach to how immigrants supposedly participate in civic life, creating a persistent immigrant threat narrative. This

118   *Chapter 5*

dominant repertoire of immigration frames finds support from both parties and little competition from inclusive or anti-authoritarian immigration narratives.

NOTES

1. It is important to note here that party control of the Senate had already changed three times since January 3, 2001. Once when Vice President Al Gore was still the tie breaker as president of the Senate. Again, after George W. Bush and Vice President Dick Cheney are sworn in on January 20, 2001, giving the Republicans the majority and control of the committees. Again, in early June when the Republican senator of Vermont, Jim Jeffords, switched from Republican to Independent and said he would caucus with the Democrats in the Senate, giving the Democrats control. Lastly, the Democrats knew that their majority position in the Senate would be short-lived, as a special election in Missouri was underway for the seat of Mel Carnahan who died prior to winning his election. Even though the Senate would choose not to reorganize after the election results on November 25 until the new session convened in January, Democrats knew that they were going to lose their chairmanships to the Republicans and their new majority.

2. We ran separate regressions with the same variables in the model presented above, changing only the dependent variable, each time, to a dichotomous variable of the type of negative frame, illegality, criminality, terrorism, and economic threat. We did this to see if holding all other variables constant, the expert testimony of each of the groups also increased their likelihood of using each of the frames after 9/11. When the frames are differentiated from just any frame, the directions of the coefficients were correct and significant for the "criminality" frame; non-elected bureaucrats and interest groups are significantly more likely to use the "criminality" frame after 9/11.

Chapter 6

The Partisan Fear of Terrorism, the Polarization of Immigration Attitudes, and the 2016 Presidential Campaign

In September 2016, Donald Trump Jr., in his role as top adviser to his father's presidential campaign, posted a message on Twitter that compared Syrian refugees to Skittles, the popular candy. The tweet showed a bowl of Skittles with the caption: "If I had a bowl of skittles and I told you just three would kill you. Would you take a handful? That's our Syrian refugee problem. . . . Let's end the politically correct agenda that doesn't put America first." This was one of many controversial statements delivered by the Trump campaign that linked the threat of terrorism to the foreign-born living in the United States.

The public's response to Trump Jr.'s tweet illustrated the emotional intensity and extreme polarization of the immigration debate in the run-up to the 2016 presidential election. Many social media users reacted with anger and disgust. Some responded by sharing images of people who had been uprooted by the Syrian conflict—women and children who had been harmed and desperately needed aid. Many others, including Trump's running mate, Governor Mike Pence, defended the Tweet, endorsed the comparison, and pivoted to the subject of national security and the difficulty of fully vetting refugees when they enter the country.[1]

In 2014–2016, this kind of partisan divide increasingly characterized public attitudes toward immigration, popular fears of terrorism, as well as the framing of immigration in news coverage, social media, presidential rhetoric, and congressional debate. If the terrorist attacks on 9/11 popularized authoritarian political culture across differing population groups, the events leading up to the 2016 presidential elections divided the nation and polarized the political landscape. The threat of terrorism was still being felt by Democrats and Republicans alike, but authoritarian reactions to this threat were increasingly accompanied by anti-authoritarian responses.

120   Chapter 6

To encapsulate the main ideas of this book, this chapter examines the shift in political cultural in 2014–2016 by analyzing both intrapsychic and cultural phenomena. A review of public opinion data, as well as further analysis of the key intermediaries of the immigration debate—print and broadcast news, presidents (and party nominees Clinton and Trump), and Congress—shows that a new rise in authoritarian political culture, despite a growing anti-authoritarian response, helped pave the way for Trump's successful presidential campaign.

THE PERCEIVED THREAT OF TERRORISM AND ATTITUDES TOWARD IMMIGRATION

Increasing Fear

As decades of psychometric research has shown, dangers that are more "available" or easier to recall are perceived as more threatening than less available hazards, even when the former is far less likely to result in actual harm than the latter. On the eve of the fifteenth anniversary of 9/11, the Pew Research Center (2016a) asked a large random sample of Americans, "Do you happen to remember exactly where you were the moment you heard news about the September 11 attacks." More than nine out of ten said "Yes." Another question in the same survey asked respondents if they knew which year 9/11 occurred. Those who said yes were then asked to give their answers in an open-ended format. The great majority (70%) correctly named the year 2001. Fifteen years later, the tragic events of 9/11 are still with us, still inside our minds and consciousness, a frozen tragedy in the collective mind.

But the devastating events of 9/11 were not simply easy to remember and therefore frightening. They were also an anomaly, an unrepresentative case that was often brought into the discussion of subsequent terrorist attacks. In other words, this worst-case scenario was regularly discussed in the context of attacks that harmed far fewer people and resulted in material damages that were infinitesimal in comparison to the destruction that occurred on September 11, 2001. This tragic event has become part of a misleading stereotype, a cultural formation that encourages Americans to think of the most terrifying cases of terrorism when assessing the threat.

Fifteen years after 9/11, national surveys continued to show that large portions of the population were worried about being harmed by terrorists and believed that future attacks were imminent. In September 2016, nearly eight out of ten Americans believed that it was "very likely" or "somewhat likely" that "in the near future there will be a terrorist attack in the United States causing large numbers of lives to be lost."[2] When asked in June 2016 to think about "the last 5–10 years," and report whether they "feel more or less safe, living in America," the majority of respondents (54%) said "less safe"; only 10 percent said "more safe"; and 32 percent said "no change."[3] By mid-summer 2016, the potential for "lone-wolf" attacks rose in the public's consciousness. Roughly 86 percent of Americans said they were "very concerned" or "somewhat concerned" about an individual from the United States carrying out a terrorist act on their own country.[4]

According to a Pew study (2016), 40 percent of Americans believed, in 2016, that "the ability of terrorists to launch another major attack on the U.S. is greater than it was at the time of the 9/11 attacks." This indicator was higher in 2016 than at any point in the past. From 2002 to 2014, the most common response had been that the threat was "the same." But then, as the 2016 presidential election began to heat up, and a few high-profile attacks hit the headlines, the perceived threat of terrorism rose considerably in the public mind.

As people's fear of terrorism rose, the percentage of the population that favored stronger security measures against terrorism also grew. According to the Gallup Organization, 69 percent of Americans were "satisfied" with the nation's security from terrorism in 2014; this percentage dropped ten points between 2014 and 2015 and decreased an additional sixteen points by early 2016 where it stood at 43 percent (Norman, 2016). The previous low point for this indicator was 51 percent, a measure taken in January of 2002, only four months after the attacks on 9/11. Naturally, with the share of satisfied Americans declining, the level of dissatisfaction was on the rise. In fact, in 2016, for the first time in American history, most respondents (55%) reported being dissatisfied with the nation's security from terrorism; 2016 also marked the first year that dissatisfied Americans outnumbered satisfied ones (Norman, 2016).

Other related polls produced similar results. According to the Pew study, in 2015–16, Americans were more concerned about protection from terrorism than about the effect of the government's anti-terrorism measures on civil liberties. In December 2015, 56 percent of Americans said that they were more concerned about protection, while 28 percent reported more concern about civil liberties (Pew Research Center, 2015). Only small changes in these numbers were seen several months later when the survey was repeated (Pew Research Center, 2016a).

Partisan Fear

The run-up to the 2016 presidential campaign should be characterized, in general, as a period of elevated public concerns about terrorism. However, the fear of terrorism was also becoming more partisan. There have long been differences in perceptions of terrorism among Republicans and Democrats; yet these differences increased in 2015–16. According to the Pew Research Center (2016a), 58 percent of Republicans versus 31 percent of Democrats said that the terrorist threat was greater than it was around the time of 9/11. Recorded in 2016, this was the largest partisan fear gap of the post-9/11 era. The public's level of satisfaction with the government's efforts to fight terrorism also differed greatly across party lines. Between 2014 and 2016, the percentages of both Republicans and Democrats who were "satisfied with the nation's security from terrorism" declined, as mentioned above, but the drop was far greater for Republicans (-42 points) than it was for Democrats (-25 points) (Norman, 2016). Likewise, there was a 22-percentage point gap between the share of Republicans (68%) and Democrats (46%) who reported that the government had not gone far enough to protect the nation from terrorism (Pew Research Center, 2016a).

The views of Republicans and Democrats also increasingly differed on the image of Muslims and the supposed link between terrorism and the Islamic religion. Does "Islamic fundamentalism" represent a "critical threat," "an important threat but not critical," or "not an important threat at all"? Responding to this question, 66 percent of Republicans compared to 48 percent of Democrats said "critical threat" (Smeltz et al., 2015). When asked in July 2016 about Donald Trump's proposed policy to ban Muslims from entering the United States, the percentage of Republicans in favor of "temporarily banning Muslims" (56%) was almost four times greater than the percentage of Democrats (15%) who supported the ban.[5] Using the same question wording, another poll, conducted only one month earlier, found that 73 percent of Republicans and 13 percent of Democrats supported such a ban.[6] Republicans were twice as likely as Democrats to support security measures that would encroach upon the civil liberties of Muslims living in the United States, such as creating a federal database containing the names of Muslims.[7] By a two-to-one margin, Republicans were also more likely to believe that the Islamic religion encourages violence more than other religions around the world.[8]

Republicans and Democrats did not always label acts of violence the same way. For instance, there were differences in how partisans viewed the mass violence at an Orlando nightclub in June 2016. A Gallup poll conducted only days after the deadliest shooting in U.S. history found that 79 percent of Republicans saw the incident as "Islamic terrorism," while only 29 percent of Democrats viewed it the same way; by a five to one margin, Democrats were more likely than Republicans to label the Orlando shooting as "domestic gun violence" (Jones, 2016).

Partisan Attitudes on Immigration

During the period surrounding the 2016 presidential election, public attitudes toward immigration, in the aggregate, were neither especially negative nor positive. Trend data from several public opinion polls placed the nation's mind-set on immigration somewhere between the highs and lows of the past. However, like the widening gap between Republicans' and Democrats' fears of terrorism, attitudes toward immigration also became more polarized during this period. In 2015–16, pollsters found deep disagreements between Republicans and Democrats on a range of policy issues, from beliefs about the impact of immigrants on the United States to the question of what should be done about unauthorized immigrants.

In March 2016, the percentage of Democrats saying that "immigrants strengthen the country" stood at 78 percent, while only 35 percent of Republicans said the same (Pew Research Center, 2016a). The Pew Research Center had asked this question regularly for roughly twenty years, during which the gap between Republicans and Democrats (43 percentage points) had never been as great.

The partisan divide was also apparent on issues related to unauthorized immigrants. A poll carried out in May–June 2015, with a national sample of 2,034 adults, asked a question about people's views on "illegal immigrants" who were currently employed in the United States; 48 percent of Democrats and 17 percent of Republicans believed that "they should be allowed to stay in their jobs and to apply for U.S. citizenship" (Smeltz et al., 2015). The reverse was true when asked about whether unauthorized immigrants should be required to leave their jobs and leave the country: 14 percent of Democrats and 45 percent of Republicans thought they should leave (Smeltz et al., 2015). Stark disagreements also characterized views on whether the government, in its efforts to deal with unauthorized immigration, should prioritize "better border security and stronger law enforcement"; Republicans were more than four times more likely to favor such a priority (Pew Research Center, 2016b). Only a small share of Democrats supported (14%) building a wall along the U.S.-Mexico border, while a 63 percent majority of Republicans favored the wall (Pew Research Center, 2016b).

Republicans were also more supportive of negative stereotypes about unauthorized immigrants. In 2016, they were roughly twice as likely as Democrats to believe that undocumented immigrants working in the U.S. "mostly fill jobs U.S. citizens would like," and "are not as honest and hard-working as U.S. citizens." The gap was greater on the subject of crime: 42 percent of Republicans and 15 percent of Democrats believed that "undocumented immigrants are more likely than U.S. citizens to commit serious crimes" (Pew Research Center, 2016b).

The partisan contrasts were even more vivid when comparing survey results from Trump supporters to Clinton backers during the run-up to the 2016 election. Among Trump supporters, 66 percent characterized immigration as a "very big problem in the United States" in August 2016; only 17 percent of

124   *Chapter 6*

Clinton backers said the same (Doherty, 2016). The nationwide survey that found this gap also asked Trump and Clinton supporters about several other problems, including terrorism, crime, race relations, the availability of jobs, the gap between rich and poor, and the condition of the environment. The difference between Trump and Clinton backers was greater on immigration than any of the other topics. Not surprisingly, one of the other big gaps was found on the topic of terrorism, with 65 percent of Trump supporters saying terrorism is a "very big problem" compared to just 36 percent of Clinton supporters (Doherty, 2016). For those who planned to vote for Trump, the only concern that rivaled their perceived threat of terrorism was immigration.

DEBATING IMMIGRATION IN AN ECHO CHAMBER

Why do such stark differences exist in what people think and feel about immigration and the threat of terrorism? Why is the fear of terrorism experienced differently across party lines? Why are Republicans more likely than Democrats to believe that immigrants bring crime, terrorism, illness, and poverty to the United States? Why were more Republicans than Democrats swayed by the authoritarian turn in political culture during the run-up to the 2016 presidential election? From the number of undocumented immigrants living in the United States to the relationship between immigration and terrorism to the acceptance of Syrian refugees, there was little agreement in the public mind about how immigrant flows shaped the nation. At a time when quality information and education had never been more available, a consensus on even the basic facts eluded us.

This ideological rift went well beyond the issues of the immigration debate. Per an extensive study by the Pew Research Center (2014), "Republicans and Democrats are more divided along ideological lines—and partisan antipathy is deeper and more extensive—than at any point in the last two decades." Put differently, the intensity of the immigration debate rose to a boil during the run-up to the 2016 presidential election just as the conflict between partisans reached new heights.

One reason for the polarization of public views on immigration lies in the emotional nature of the debate. Most of the key issues associated with immigration engage emotions, stoke frustrations, and inevitably lead to reflections on what many Americans fear most: economic insecurity, crime, terrorism, racism, and the loss of identity. The debate itself, so ridden with emotional landmines, often takes place from a distance, in separate ideological spaces, like warring spouses who complain about each other to their respective friends and only interact by texting diatribes back and forth from different rooms in the house. The conflict is no doubt real, but meaningful communication between the two sides is often not. In a sense, the immigration debate is not a debate, but rather two, self-reinforcing discussions, occurring simultaneously, colliding occasionally, and energized continually by the partisan media systems that surround and nurture each side.

Communication scholars and other social scientists use the metaphor of an echo chamber to describe how media influence the political views of audiences. The metaphor is useful in at least two respects. First, it suggests that one source of information may sound to consumers like many voices as it receives uncritical repetition by likeminded media outlets. For instance, the findings from a single immigration study might surface in several ideologically aligned media, giving the impression that multiple independent sources came to the same conclusion. As findings from the study reverberate through the partisan media landscape, they often become abbreviated into sound bites and eventually treated as accepted facts.

The echo chamber metaphor also implies that audiences consume information about the world in semi-closed social spaces (*chambers*) where their preconceived notions are confirmed and reinforced by their chosen set of partisan media. In *Echo Chamber* (2008), Jamieson and Cappella explain how, working together, three conservative media outlets not only promoted the ideals of Reagan conservatism, but also insulated their audiences from counterarguments by systematically criticizing the Democrats, undermining liberal views, and attacking mainstream media. Through reverberation and isolation, echo chambers are thought to be making the average American more partisan.

For such a theory to hold true, however, at least two additional hypotheses require empirical support. First, news consumers must, to some degree, seek out a set of media outlets that, together, form the type of echo chamber described by Jamieson and Cappella (2008). According to several studies of media habits, this seems to be the case. In the early twenty-first century, people were increasingly placing their trust in and consuming news media that were ideologically aligned with their partisan attitudes. As Mitchell et al. (2014) put it, "When it comes to getting news about politics and government, liberals and conservatives inhabit different worlds." Mitchell and colleagues based this conclusion on a year-long study of political polarization in the United States carried out by the Pew Research Center. They found that conservatives gravitated toward Fox News, while liberals were far more likely to follow CNN, NPR, and the *New York Times*. The two groups' levels of trust in their respective news sources skewed along the same lines. In terms of social media use, both consistent conservatives and liberals surrounded themselves with people with similar views (Mitchell et al., 2014).

Second, to support the echo chamber theory, an empirical link must be drawn between self-selected partisan media exposure and public attitudes.

126   *Chapter 6*

Although evidence for this link is mixed (Prior, 2013), scholars have shown that as news audiences retreat into their protected, ideological enclaves and seek media that further confirm their divergent perspectives, the attitudes and beliefs of each audience become more extreme and polarized (Stroud, 2011; Slater, 2007). There are several case studies that show how echo chambers shape public views. As one example, echo chambers explain, in part, the divergence of public beliefs about global warming (Jasny, Waggle & Fisher, 2015). Feldman and colleagues (2014) showed that people who consume conservative media such as Fox News are more likely to reject the idea that global warming is taking place and disfavor policies designed to reverse the problem. Likewise, those who use non-conservative media such as CNN tend to believe in global warming and support climate policies. Taking this idea one step further, the researchers also discovered that people's beliefs about global warming shaped their selection of media outlets in the future. Over time, non-believers watched more Fox, believers gravitated toward CNN, and on went the reinforcing cycle of media effects on the one hand and media selection effects on the other.

Echo chambers have aided the formation of political parties (Morin & Flynn, 2014; Iyengar & Hahn, 2009), and polarized public attitudes and beliefs on a number of key issues, including the existence of weapons of mass destruction in Iraq prior to the 2003 invasion (Iyengar & McGrady, 2007; Kull, Ramsay & Lewis, 2003), beliefs about the safety of vaccinations (Dunn et al., 2015), attitudes toward education policy (Jabbar et al., 2014), and views on several other policy issues (Levendusky, 2013).

The power of echo chambers to polarize political views and groups likely increased with the rise of internet technology and social media in the late 1990s and early 2000s. Virtual echo chambers in the blogosphere and on forums like Facebook and Twitter made it even easier and more likely for consumers to find sources that matched and reinforced their ever-narrowing ideological positions (Baum & Groeling, 2008; Sunstein, 2009; Warner, 2010; Reese et al., 2007). The online experience itself changed as websites started personalizing what consumers saw as they navigated the web. In *The Filter Bubble* (2011), Pariser argued that democracy was weakened when most major websites began quietly personalizing what consumers received in their electronic search results, making it less likely for them to encounter competing views or conflicting information.

Trump's 30 Million

Echo chambers may create disagreements between partisan audiences on even the most rudimentary facts, making compromise more difficult and conflict more likely. As an example of such an echo chamber in action, let us return to the case of Donald Trump's estimation of the size of the unauthorized immigrant population in the United States. As discussed in chapter 1, in the summer of 2015, Trump launched his presidential candidacy in large part by taking a harsh stance on immigration, and "illegal immigration" in particular. To accentuate the problem, he stated that the number of unauthorized immigrants living in the United States was 30 million to 34 million. The high end of Trump's estimate was three times greater than almost any serious estimate that was being made at the time (Baker & Rytina, 2012; Passel et al., 2014), and even contrasted with the estimates of conservative think tanks such as the Center for Immigration Studies (Chip, 2015), and some right-leaning political commentators including Rush Limbaugh (Spurlock, 2013).

In some ways, the case of Trump's 30 million defies the expectations of an echo chamber. Trump was clearly able to spread his unfounded estimate beyond the conservative media machine. Between May and December 2015, he referenced the 30 million, without being disputed, on almost all the major American television news networks, including MSNBC, CNN, ABC, NBC, and FOX. The unique harshness of Trump's rhetoric and the sheer spectacle of his election campaign attracted the attention of news organizations of all types, creating a sort of rift in the echo chamber, which allowed him to circulate his views in a diverse media environment.

With this reservation aside, however, it was clear that the bloated estimate of 30 million undocumented immigrants was aired far more often on conservative media outlets, Fox News in particular, than mainstream or liberal ones, such as MSNBC, and that the estimate was asserted almost exclusively by right-wing commentators and those who support the Republican Party. More importantly, the partisan media's filtering mechanism, as anticipated by the echo chamber perspective, did generally shape the way in which television news programs covered the issue. When the 30 million emerged on liberal or mainstream news programs, the hosts or other guests on the show often asked about the source of the estimate, whereas conservative programs usually acquiesced to the claim or reinforced it.

In at least three cases on CNN, the claim was challenged directly and rather forcefully. For instance, on the MSNBC show *Politics Nation,* Al Sharpton played a clip of Trump reciting his usual talking points: 1) the estimate of 11 million is wrong, 2) the government has no idea how many there are, 3) it's probably 30 to 34 million, and 4) I've seen the estimate in various newspapers. Breaking away from the clip, Sharpton retorted: "I mean, how do you debate someone when they just make up their own facts, David?" (MSNBC, July 29, 2015, 6:00 PM EST). Sharpton and his guest that night, David Birdsell, an expert on political debate, went on to critically examine other examples of Trump's use of extreme, unsubstantiated claims. Trump's 30 million was also sharply criticized by CNN National Correspondent Sunlen Serfaty on the program *OUTFRONT*

128 *Chapter 6*

(CNN, July 24, 2015, 7:00 PM EST) and by Latin American political analyst Ana Maria Salazar on CNN's *New Day* (CNN, July 9, 2015, 6:30 AM EST).

Echo chambers may function differently across the different types of news media. As illustrated by the case of Sharpton's heavy retort, the echo chambers of mainstream cable news often function not as a filtering mechanism that cancels out dissenting voices, but rather as a mechanism of de-legitimization that inoculates viewers against competing positions. As one further example, on a Fox News show that aired in July 2014, Bill O'Reilly discussed whether the United States should accept child refugees from Central America who enter the country illegally.[9] O'Reilly and one of his guests, Mary Katherine Ham, argued in favor of deporting the children, while a third guest, Juan Williams, argued against it. The two restrictionists received far more airtime as they spouted empirically questionable claims about the financial cost of accepting the children, while the expansionist, amid rude interruptions from the restrictionists, pled the case for accepting the kids on moral grounds. The level of disgust and aggression in O'Reilly's voice and body language was palpable. Both of his guests, Ham and Williams, were Fox News analysts who regularly appeared on O'Reilly's show. And still, with violent facial expressions and while jabbing his pen toward the camera, O'Reilly, called Williams' ideas "insane," shouted over Williams several times and discredited his response as "dodging" the question at hand. In short, echo chambers often function by systematically devaluing, delegitimizing, and humiliating dissenting voices. In other cases, especially on social media sites and websites with extremist views, the messages may be one-sided and the echo chamber reverberates with the views of only likeminded commentators and thereby insulates and isolates the audience from opposing positions.

In either case, the existence of echo chambers likely explains, in part, why Republicans tend to fear immigration more so than Democrats. Anyone inhabiting a conservative echo chamber would likely perceive the "problem" of unauthorized immigration as being three times greater (i.e., the 30 million) than people in a liberal echo chamber. The ideas that the borders are porous, that unauthorized immigration is out of control, that a key national security issue resides on the Mexican border, that terrorists are sneaking into the country and plotting attacks are probably regarded as conventional wisdom in one chamber, and as dangerous, racist hyperbole in another. In a media system, replete with echo chambers, a constructive discussion of these issues, and an averaging of extreme views are not possible.

The Partisan Divide in the Elite Press

In many ways, the echo chambers of television news are an expected outcome of the proliferation of news media choices and the emergence of partisan outlets like Fox News and MSNBC. The fact that commentators on Fox News are more likely to favor increased border security and immigration law enforcement efforts than the folks at MSNBC may not be surprising. More interesting is the prospect that the opinion-leading press is following the same trend. The journalists and editors who work for award-winning newspapers such as the *New York Times* and *Wall Street Journal* have been socialized through education and job training to sidestep personal politics and provide professional coverage of the nation's most pressing matters.

In chapter 3, we showed that differences between these two newspapers were evident during much of the decade prior to the 2016 presidential election. To determine whether the gap widened during the most recent period, we returned to the electronic content analysis procedure discussed in chapter 3. Tracking changes in the rate of negative framing of immigration, we searched back to the 1980s for articles in the *New York Times* and *The Wall Street Journal* that contained the words "immigrant" or "immigration" as well as at least one of the main components of the anti-immigration framing nexus: "illegal," "crime," "terror." As illustrated in Figure 6.1, throughout

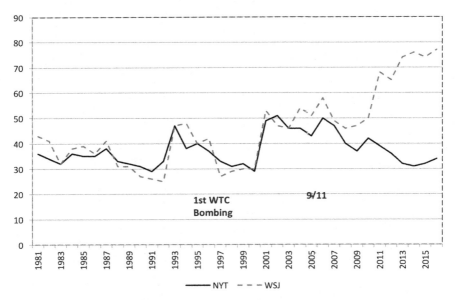

Figure 6.1 Percentage of *New York Times* and *Wall Street Journal* articles on immigration containing references to illegality, crime, or terrorism (1981–2016). *Source:* The data used for this figure come from a computer-aided search of *New York Times* and *Wall Street Journal* articles from 1981–2016, as shown in the X-axis. It provides a visual, detailed picture of the percentage of articles that reference the immigration frames, illegality, crime, or terrorism, as shown in the Y-axis.

130 Chapter 6

the 1980s the amount of negative coverage of immigration was quite stable, ranging from 32 percent to 43 percent in both the *New York Times* and the *Wall Street Journal*. The number of references to "illegal immigrants" and the coverage immigrants committing crimes or terrorist acts were relatively low and similar in the two papers.

Both the *New York Times* and the *Wall Street Journal* increased negative coverage of immigration after the first bombing of the World Trade Center in 1993, and especially after 9/11. Although there was some fluctuation until 2003, the post-9/11 news era was characterized by a growing gap in negative framing between the nation's two most prestigious newspapers. As illustrated in Figure 6.1, by 2015, the percentage of references to illegality, crime, and terror in news stories about immigration reached 74 percent in the *Wall Street Journal*, but stood at only 32 percent in the *New York Times*. Between January and September 2016, the gap increased another percentage point. It seems clear that the run-up to the 2016 presidential election marked a period of extreme polarization on immigration issues in both the partisan cable news outlets, as well as the elite press.

For a qualitative glimpse at the differences between the two papers, consider the editorial responses to Donald Trump's presidential campaign, and his harsh, anti-immigration rhetoric. The editorial board of the *New York Times* referred to Trump's presidential announcement ceremony on June 16, 2015 as a "racist speech" (Lost in the immigration frenzy, 2015), and called his campaign a "racist road show" (The anti-immigrant binge, 2015). In an August 2015 editorial, the *New York Times* called upon Trump's Republican opponents to reject his "despicable proposals" on immigration:

> Because his plan is so naked—in its scapegoating of immigrants, its barely subtextual racism, its immense cruelty in seeking to reduce millions of people to poverty and hopelessness—it gives his opponents the chance for a very clear moral decision. They can stand up for better values, and against the collective punishment of millions of innocent Americans-in-waiting. (Republicans' anti-immigrant race, 2015)

In describing how Trump had become the leader of the Republican Party on immigration issues, the *New York Times* quipped: "Like a racist pied piper, Mr. Trump has gotten his party to fall in line behind him" (The great "sanctuary city" slander, 2015). The newspaper reported this on Trump's policy on Muslims: "Donald Trump, a bigot without foreign policy experience, showed that there is nothing he won't say or support to sow hatred. On Monday he outrageously proposed barring all Muslims from entering the country" (Bizarre responses to a plea for reason, 2015). As the extent of Trump's popularity became evident, the *New York Times* on multiple occasions urged

The Partisan Fear of Terrorism, the Polarization of Immigration Attitudes 131

readers to take the candidate seriously and see his campaign as a reflection of a larger, more ominous social trend (The Trump effect, and how it spreads, 2015). Reviewing the findings from a survey cn the rising level of anger in American society, the *New York Times* wrote:

> In his pledges to banish undocumented Mexican immigrants, Muslims and most foreign competition from the American landscape, Mr. Trump plays on what the survey's authors call "the anger of perceived disenfranchisement—a sense that the majority has become a persecuted minority." These people could be Republicans or Democrats; they don't agree that immigration strengthens the nation and are "significantly" more likely to say the American dream is dead and twice as likely to say "white men are struggling to keep up in today's world." (Angling for the hopping mad, 2016)

In sum, the *New York Times* editorial board did not simply critique Trump's policies, but rather condemned the man himself, in no uncertain terms, as a racist, a bigot, and as morally unfit to be president, while also framing his supporters as dangerously, emotionally unstable. This sort of high-pitched rejection of Trump and his positions on immigration could not be found in the editorials published in the *Wall Street Journal*. Its first statement on Trump's candidacy in July 2015 suggested that he was not a serious candidate, that "he won't win a GOP caucus or primary," and that his brash statements on immigration were being used by Democratic candidate Hillary Clinton to paint a false picture of the Republican Party. The editorial went into detail about Trump's statements on immigration, but did not critique them as unacceptable or morally repugnant. The *Wall Street Journal*'s strongest critique of Trump's immigration policies was that they did not make sense in economic terms. To the contrary, "Immigration is essential to faster growth because it offsets an otherwise aging workforce, brings in new human capital and ideas, and raises the GDP of all workers."

On Trump's proposal to ban Muslims, the *Wall Street Journal*, again, argued against the position, but avoided normative condemnations. The editors' strongest reproach against a full-scale ban on Muslims was that such a policy would be "contrary to America's best traditions," and that a similar episode in U.S. history, the *Chinese Exclusion Act* of 1882, "was not America's finest hour" (The Obama-Trump Dialectic, 2015). They considered Trump's plan problematic not because it was morally repugnant, but rather because it failed as an "antiterror strategy," given the need for Muslim allies to fight the "radical Islamist infection" (The Obama-Trump Dialectic, 2015). Also in great contrast to the *New York Times*, editorials in the *Wall Street Journal* clearly linked immigration to terrorism. As one example: "The rising terror threat has also made immigration a security issue as much as an economic one. This too has given Mr. Trump potent ammunition" (The Obama

132   *Chapter 6*

Legacy Project, 2016). As far as we could tell, the immigration-terrorism nexus never appeared in a *New York Times* editorial in 2015–2016.

By the end of summer 2016, the editors of the *Wall Street Journal* could still be seen as critics of Trump's immigration policies, but they became more supportive toward Trump's supporters, and more likely to accept some of Trump's ideas on immigration, especially on issues related to national security. For instance, in a September 2016 editorial, they wrote:

> We understand that in a world of rising terror threats the U.S. needs border controls and immigrant vetting. Most Americans no doubt agree with Mr. Trump's plan to deport criminal aliens, though his claim of two million far exceeds other estimates. Mr. Trump also has a strong case against "sanctuary cities," a reference to mayors who defy federal immigration law. (Trump's fortress America, 2016)

This editorial went on to criticize Trump's plans for mass deportation of unauthorized immigrants, but once again sidestepped the moral dimension and suggested instead that such a plan was "politically impossible and economically damaging" (Trump's Fortress America, 2016). Even at the highest levels of American journalism, there were two echo chambers, one that accepted terrorism as a serious threat, prioritized national security issues and embraced the anti-immigration framing nexus, and one that questioned the terrorist threat, and denounced those who tried to use it to justify restrictionist immigration policies.

POLARIZATION IN PRESIDENTIAL RHETORIC

Policy Disputes Prior to the 2016 Presidential Election

As we demonstrated in chapter 4, public perceptions of terrorism and immigration were not only driven by media but also by presidents. Since 9/11, shifts in the tone of presidential rhetoric and administrative action have been pronounced, from President Bush's harsh, post-9/11 rhetoric and institutional changes to Obama's mild negativity in 2008–2010 and his increasingly inclusive stance after 2012 to the conversation regarding immigration and terrorism during the run-up to the 2016 presidential election between former Secretary of State Hillary Clinton and reality television celebrity and real estate developer Donald Trump. Hillary Clinton called for comprehensive immigration reform, and a continuation of Obama's progressive policies and approach, while Donald Trump called for building a wall on the southern border, a Muslim ban, a massive deportation force, the rejection of Syrian refugees, and the identification of radical Islam as a main source of terrorism.

The historical context of this increasing polarization deserves a closer look. Given our emphasis on the immigration rhetoric and stance of the Bush Administration in chapter 4, we begin here with the first years of the Obama Administration. Since taking office, Obama advocated for a bill that would comprehensively reform the immigration system. Despite having a supermajority in the Senate and a large majority in the House from 2008 to 2010, a public law never materialized. Some blamed the economic crisis and the massive stimulus that ensued. Others blamed the amount of political capital he expended on healthcare reform initiatives. Still others ascribed the failure of comprehensive immigration reform to a lack of political willingness on his part, suggesting that he wished to win political points by blaming the Republicans for the lack of reform and mobilizing the Hispanic vote against them rather than compromising and producing a lackluster reform bill.

The polarization of the elite political establishment became more pronounced as President Obama's approach to immigration shifted after the 2012 presidential election. Obama set the tone for the midterm election and presciently summarized the polarization and political strategies that would ensue in 2016 when he said,

> It's anybody's guess how Republicans are thinking about this [immigration]. If they were thinking long-term politically, it is suicide for them not to do this [reform]. Because the demographics of the country are such that you will lose a generation of immigrants which says, "That party doesn't seem to care about me." (Obama, 2014)

Facing a divided government with a history of obstructionism toward his agenda (Milkis, Rhodes, & Charnock, 2012), President Obama used his executive authority to alleviate some of the burden placed on immigrants and their attempts to navigate the political process, directing the administrative offices to essentially remove the threat of deportation for those who had resided in the United States for more than five years. This executive action expanded the 2012 *Deferred Action for Childhood Arrivals* (DACA) program. Charging the administrative agencies to use prosecutorial discretion in the deportation of undocumented immigrants, his executive action offered about 4 million more immigrants protection (Ehrenfreund, 2014).

Because of this executive action, the leadership of the Republican-controlled 114th Congress charged President Obama with overstepping his constitutional authority, and subsequently supported a law suit, brought by several attorneys general, against his administration for this executive action. Obama had stated multiple times during the year that he would use an executive order that would alleviate some of the burdens immigrants experience if the Congress did not produce an immigration reform bill. He ended up using

134   *Chapter 6*

an executive memorandum instead, but the Republicans were furious and partisan divide would only widen leading up to the 2016 primary and general elections.

Even though both Republican presidents, Reagan and H. W. Bush, in 1986 and 1990 respectively, employed similar executive measures to give relief to the immigrant population (up to 3 million immigrants for Reagan and nearly 40 percent of immigrants or 1.5 million for H. W. Bush), Republicans responded dramatically to Obama's action (Yglesias, 2014; Greenberg, 2014; Farley, Kiely, & Gore, 2014). Some called for impeachment. Others threatened to use the "power of the purse" to thwart Obama's use of the executive memorandum, particularly the use of limitation riders on the spending of bureaucratic agencies charged with immigration enforcement, despite the disagreements over whether the United States Citizenship and Immigration Services (USCIS) agency was completely self-funded through fees, and whether it was subject to congressional appropriations (Bobic, 2014). Representative Steve King, Republican from Iowa, warned that if Obama acted unilaterally, the Congress would "use the power of the purse to restrain a president who has threatened to violate the Constitution in the most obscene manner possible" (Werner, 2014). Even though many legal agencies stated that Obama was within his legal right to issue the executive memorandum, a total of 24 states sued President Obama over his executive action and a District Court in Pennsylvania ruled it unconstitutional. In 2016, the action was ruled unconstitutional by the United States Court of Appeals for the Fifth Circuit and upheld by a divided Supreme Court—after the death of Associate Justice Antonin Scalia, an open seat that the Republican Party refused to let President Obama fill. Even members of his own party asked the president to delay his executive action even further, until the Congress could pass a budget, as he did until after the Midterm elections of 2014.

President Obama issued the executive memorandum on November 21, 2014, bypassing the Congress and partially producing some of the same effects as the *DREAM ACT* he campaigned for Congress to pass. Emboldened by the fact that the U.S. Constitution provides Congress with an expressed authority over immigration, the Republican-controlled House of Representatives added fuel to the turf war (King, 1997). On December 4, 2014, they passed a budget bill that funded nearly all executive agencies except for the Department of Homeland Security, the agency charged with immigration enforcement. Many analysts and congressional insiders opined that the bill was a symbolic act intended to send the president a message about constitutional power, rather than a serious attempt to set budget policy priorities (Mataconis, 2014). Others maintained that the bill was a compromise by the Republican establishment with the Tea Party to avoid a government shutdown (Mataconis, 2014). More recently the discussion shifted to the removal of amendments to the Homeland

The Partisan Fear of Terrorism, the Polarization of Immigration Attitudes   135

Security Funding bill that would inevitably preclude passage. Nevertheless, these actions revealed the bitter tensions between the policy positions of the Republican and Democratic Parties. This polarized environment would become the battleground for the Trump-Clinton contest of 2016.

Clinton Follows Obama on Immigration and Terrorism

In her 2016 presidential campaign, Hillary Clinton embraced Obama's ideas on immigration reform. Although, it appears, she was less adamant than Obama when quelling public concerns about terrorism, and more hawkish in her approach to fighting international terrorism, her public statements demonstrated compassion for immigrants and their families. For instance, she said:

> I would not deport children. I do not want to deport family members either, Jorge. I want to, as I said, prioritize who would be deported: violent criminals, people planning terrorist attacks, anybody who threatens us. That's a relatively small universe. (Nakamura, 2016)

Although Clinton's stance on immigration should be characterized more so as a continuation of Obama's position than a break from it, in some ways she took a more expansionist approach on immigration than did President Obama. Throughout her 2016 campaign she promised to introduce a comprehensive reform bill within the first hundred days of her administration, a bill that would offer a path to full citizenship for unauthorized immigrants living in the country, a similar proposal to Obama's. She also championed herself as a sponsor of the *DREAM* Act, again following Obama. However, her approach to deportations diverged slightly from that of Obama and radically from Trump's. For instance, she has said, "The idea of tracking down and deporting 11 million people is absurd, inhumane, and un-American. No, Trump" (LoBianco, 2015).

It is well documented that the Obama administration has carried out raids and deportations in immigrant communities wherein undocumented immigrants reside, targeting individuals for petty crimes and simply crossing the border (Nakamura, 2016). Clinton, however, has been subtle in her departure from the Obama administration's deportation policy. Most of her language and tone is less specific and focuses on the notion of keeping families together. For instance, she has repeatedly said,

> As a Senator I was proud to cosponsor the national DREAM Act and to vote for it. I'm a strong supporter of comprehensive immigration reform and I believe that we have to fix our broken immigration system. We have to keep families together. We have to treat everyone with dignity and compassion, uphold the rule of law, and respect our heritage as a nation of immigrants striving to build a

better life. And so, bringing millions of hardworking people out of the shadows and into the formal economy. (Rucker, 2014)

Promising to only deport violent criminals and terrorists represented a notable change from the policy and approach of the Obama administration (Nakamura, 2016). This departure from such a key aspect of his administration's immigration policy indicated her attempt to function within an expansionist perspective on immigration. Of course, her position strays even farther from the harsh, restrictionist immigration policies of Trump. For instance, in response to Trump's proposed religious ideology test for Muslims and his idea that they should be banned from entering the country, Clinton said:

I think it's un-American. I think what he has promoted is not at all in keeping with American values. And I am going to take every opportunity to criticize him, to raise those issues. I'm not going to engage in the kind of language that he uses. I think we can make the case against him if he is the nominee, by pointing out what he has said. I think that's a better way. (Hains, 2016)

Clinton also took issue with Trump's proposal to construct a giant wall on the southern U.S. border, and highlighted the differences in their approaches to border security. For instance, she remarked, "First of all, as I understand him, he's talking about a very tall wall, a beautiful tall wall, the most beautiful tall wall, better than the Great Wall of China, that would run the entire border. He would somehow magically get the Mexican government to pay for it. It's just fantasy" (The Week, 2016). One could read this quote and think that Secretary Clinton's condescension and mockery were simply a campaign strategy to delegitimize the policy proposal of the opposing party nominee and make fun of the way he addressed issues. We maintain, however, that the comment was more telling than a simple campaign tactic. The condescension and mockery was there, but there was also a seriousness in her tone that seemed to indicate a deep level of concern. Comparing the proposed wall to the "Great Wall of China" and emphasizing the "fantasy" of Trump's plan, Secretary Clinton attempted to highlight her opponent's authoritarian and restrictionists elements as deviation from democratic norms and international decency, concepts she believed exemplify American values.

Trump's Authoritarian Ground Game

Although, in chapter 2, we reviewed psychological perspectives on authoritarianism and applied them to public attitudes toward immigration, the remainder of this book has focused primarily on authoritarian political culture—the words, phrases, symbols, and images found in news coverage, presidential rhetoric, and congressional hearings. Continuing this approach,

The Partisan Fear of Terrorism, the Polarization of Immigration Attitudes   137

we will remain agnostic on the psychological origins of Trump's behavior. There is abundant evidence, however, that much of Trump's rhetoric has been authoritarian. He was not the inventor of these tactics, nor the cultural foundation that allowed their success, but he proved to be a master of delivering them. As discussed in chapter 3, authoritarianism in the form of cultural elements involves the use of stereotypes or punitive categories in the discussion of outsiders, a stated willingness to reject outsiders, and arguments in favor of aggressively punishing outside threats and people who violate conventional values or traditions (Perrin, 2005). While some pundits argued that Trump's rhetoric was regularly "off message," he exhibited a disciplined adherence to the authoritarian script. The underlying logic of his campaign was to inflate people's fears of and grievances toward specific out-groups, while offering decisive, easy-to-understand plans for controlling these out-groups.

On the day of his presidential announcement, Trump began his campaign with a harsh, authoritarian statement about Mexican immigrants:

> When Mexico sends its people, they're not sending their best. They're not sending you. They're not sending you. They're sending people that have lots of problems, and they're bringing those problems with us. They're bringing drugs, They're bringing crime. They're rapists. And some, I assume, are good people. (Moreno, 2015)

This comment seemed to propel him to front-runner status, as the news media saturated him with free coverage, and offered him additional opportunities to offer (empirically unsupported) inflammatory statements about immigrants and other out-groups, as well as normalize acerbic racially biased rhetoric. For instance, he said: "What can be simpler or more accurately stated? The Mexican Government is forcing their most unwanted people into the United States. They are, in many cases, criminals, drug dealers, rapists" (Moody, 2015). He repeatedly embellished the number and rate of unauthorized immigrants entering the United States and referred to them as "killers" and "rapists" (Moreno, 2015).

Trump also laid out his now-famous, remarkably simplistic, yet seemingly persuasive plan to build a wall to keep people from crossing the U.S.-Mexican border illegally. It should be noted that fear appeals, such as referring to immigrants as killers and terrorists, are more effective when the source also articulates a clear plan for thwarting the danger. Trump described his plan as follows: "I would build a great wall, and nobody builds walls better than me. Believe me. And I'll build it very inexpensively. I'll build a great, great wall on our southern border and I will have Mexico pay for that wall. Mark my words" (Atkin, 2016). By all academic estimates, this wall, which he said would span the entire 1,954 mile southern U.S. border, would cost more than $10 billion, and some estimates were as high as $20 billion (Associated Press, 2016). Whether "the wall" was a physical structure or a metaphorical talking point was less important than the fact that it represented a symbol of security, which made his fear appeals about immigration more palatable and persuasive. The wall also symbolized Trump's clear distinction between the in-group and the out-group, between those who should be accepted and those who should be rejected. Trump drove home this point when he said that the wall would have a "big, beautiful door" in it, suggesting that only those deemed worthy will be allowed to enter the United States. In his first televised interview as President-Elect, Mr. Trump said that he did indeed intend to build a physical wall (Schultheis, 2016).

Trump also said that he would create a "deportation force" to round up all unauthorized immigrants and deport them back to their home countries. Aside from the fact that he grossly inflated the number of illegal immigrants, saying the number was close to 30 million, when in fact it was closer to 11 million, the infrastructure and system for such a force already existed under the Obama administration. In the first five years of his administration, Obama deported more than two million immigrants, significantly more than any other president and more than all other presidents combined up to 1997 (Golash-Boza, 2016). Using the national security state apparatus, the current laws, and the theory and philosophies of deportations from the Bush and Obama Administrations, Trump could have simply embraced the existing immigrant deportation structure (Golash-Boza and Hondagneu-Sotelo, 2013; Naber 2006; Chavez, 2013). Yet, he promised to move far beyond it by "viciously" removing all undocumented immigrants, and stressing, on multiple occasions, the need for a deportation force to handle what he described as a growing problem. Such comments were invariably intertwined with claims about the potential criminal or terrorist behaviors of unauthorized immigrants. For instance, in 2015, he stated: "We have a lot of bad dudes, as I said. We have a lot of really bad people here, I want to get the bad ones out. . . . And by the way, they're never coming back" (Diamond, 2015a). He went on to say, "We got to move 'em out, we're going to move 'em back in if they're really good people" (Diamond, 2015b). Even after securing the nomination and during the third presidential debate, Trump said, "We have some bad hombres here, and we're going to get them out (Earl, 2016)."

After winning the electoral college, President-Elect Trump gave an interview to CBS 60 minutes on Sunday November 13, 2016, wherein he said,

> What we are going to do is get the people that are criminal and have criminal records, gang members, drug dealers, where a lot of these people, probably two million, it could be even three million, we are getting them out of our country or we are going to incarcerate. But we're getting them out of our country, they're here illegally. (Schultheis, 2016)

This was a remarkable statement on the number of people who would be deported. As mentioned, it took President Obama nearly six years to deport this number of people. Consider for a moment that a 747 jet carries about 450 people, which means that Trump would need 6,667 jets just to physically remove that number of people. Whatever the timeframe of the deportation effort, the street-level resistance and protests to such an organizational endeavor would likely engender further authoritarian responses and justifications for such as policy. Directly after President-Elect Trump's first televised interview, the Republican Speaker of the House, Paul Ryan, said that the House and the Republican-controlled Congress were not planning to fund or support a deportation force to remove immigrants (Wootson, 2016).

Trump targeted other out-groups with a similar type of derogation, often fabricating crime statistics to make his point. For instance, he stated, "crime statistics show blacks kill 81 percent of white homicide victims" (Greenberg, 2015). "Sadly," he said, "the overwhelming amount of violent crime in our major cities is committed by blacks and Hispanics—a tough subject—must be discussed" (Moreno, 2015). Following a textbook authoritarian strategy, Trump regularly embellished the dangers posed by out-groups, while proposing reinforced security efforts and law and order:

> We need law and order. If we don't have it, we're not going to have a country, African Americans and Hispanics are living in hell. You walk down the street and you get shot. Gangs roaming the streets, African American communities are being decimated by crime. (Chan, 2016)

In addition to proposing a "great wall" to combat unauthorized immigration and taking a hardline stance on law and order to deal with the violent crimes of African Americans, he argued in favor of investigating mosques, creating a national register for Muslims, and banning Muslims from entering the country to curb terrorism. For instance, Trump told a raucous, approving crowd, "I want surveillance of certain mosques if that's OK. We've had it before" (Diamond, 2015). "I will absolutely take [a] database on the people coming in from Syria. If we can't stop it—but we are going to if I win—they're going back" (Diamond, 2015). Though he would receive criticism from his own party for this restrictionist stance, he proposed "a total and complete shutdown of Muslims entering the United States, until our country's representatives can figure out what the hell is going on" (Atkin, 2016).

As controversy swirled, he walked back his position on the Muslim ban and replaced it with "extreme vetting" for both Muslims and refugees entering the United States: "The time is overdue to develop a new screening test for the threats we face today. I call it extreme vetting. I call it extreme, extreme vetting" (Redden, 2016). He detailed his plan as follows:

140 *Chapter 6*

> In addition to screening out all members of the sympathizers of terrorist groups, we must also screen out any who have hostile attitudes toward our country or its principles or who believe that sharia law should supplant American law. Those who do not believe in our Constitution or who support bigotry and hatred will not be admitted for immigration into our country. Only those who we expect to flourish in our country and to embrace a tolerant American society should be issued visas. (Redden, 2016)

Trump's ideological test mirrors the philosophical approach to immigrants that President Theodore Roosevelt employed at the turn of the twentieth century. As immigration increased, as the rights and responsibilities of African Americans and Native Americans became a political concern, Roosevelt was challenged with substantively no good options (Dorsey, 2007). Yet, he took the most simplistic path, advocating that everyone can be an American if they just "embrace his concept of "American-ism," a belief that American identity revolved around a combination of physical strength, moral character, and the understanding that equality must be earned and not simply given" (Dorsey, 2007). Trump has similarly constructed an authoritarian "myth" of Americanism and national identity with his attempt to "ban" Muslims from entering the United States because they are "members or sympathizers of terrorist groups" and they have "hostile attitudes to our principles" (Park, 2016). Trump's authoritarian "myth" "promotes particular values-sacred principles-that distinguish it from other communities and justify its existence," as he expects all immigrants to acquiesce in exchange for their acceptance, citizenship, and "in-group" status (Dorsey, 2007).

Embracing authoritarian culture, Trump and the Republicans attempted to tap into the fears of the public, perhaps even to incite these fears, and thereby trigger authoritarian tendencies and bolster their authoritarian stances on immigration and other issues (Waldman, 2016; Turley, 2016). Trump often identified dangers in his opponent's supposed policy proposals. For instance, he claimed that Clinton favored open borders, saying:

> But she wants open borders. You saw that during the debate. WikiLeaks got her again. She never talked about open borders. She wants open borders. We could have 600 million people pour into our country. Think of it. Once you have open borders like that, you don't have a country anymore. . . . She wants to let people just pour in. You could have 650 million people pour in and we do nothing about it. Think of it. That's what could happen. You triple the size of our country in one week. (Deb, 2016)

During his 2016 campaign, Trump's statements about multiple out-groups—Mexican immigrants, African Americans, and Muslims—and his rhetoric on the risks of violent crime and terrorism went beyond the standard polarization that often characterizes presidential campaigns. Although the authoritarian script had already been written into American political culture, Trump was more devoted to a highly dramatized version of this script than any presidential candidate in the last decades. And this strategy, as revealed by the 2016 election results, was successful.

CONGRESSIONAL GRIDLOCK

The period prior to the 2016 presidential election was characterized by partisanship and polarization in the Congress as well. The typical high-stakes congressional politics were in play. Immigration experts, Democratic and Republican strategists, liberal and conservative intellectuals, and pundits of all stripes surmised that the Republicans would continue to lose national elections due to the shifting Hispanic demographic.[10] Members of the Congress regarded each potential vote on immigration reform as consequential to their long-term political prospects. Both the Republicans and Democrats want to be the party of immigration reform.

This type of political calculus was seen in previous periods as well. For example, President George W. Bush called for reform from 2001 through 2008, having majorities in the House and the Senate, but a comprehensive piece of legislation never materialized. President Obama had a filibuster-proof majority in the Senate and massive majorities in the House, yet could not push through reform legislation. Members of both parties wanted reform, called for reform, and would benefit from it. Yet, instead of compromise, the winner-takes-all atmosphere led to divisive political maneuvering that shaped the debate and precluded immigration reform legislation.

Since the terrorist attacks on 9/11, the parties have been close to a compromise on more than one occasion, with the only result being failure. The obvious question is, why? There are several different answers for each case of legislative derailment, but an underlying cause of congressional gridlock on immigration reform lies in the authoritarian and anti-authoritarian political cultures that were reinforced by a host of elite intermediaries after 9/11. Authoritarian language, and an anti-authoritarian response to it, has dominated the debate about immigration reform in congress since 9/11. When the two parties are close to compromise on an immigration reform bill, the group that is losing or unwilling to let the other group "win" and take ownership, has often defeated the bill by shifting the debate to either the dangers of immigration (border security, terrorism), or the need to rebuke authoritarian language on immigration and reject immoral restrictionist aspects of the legislation. In other words, the fate of immigration reform rests on an authoritarian versus anti-authoritarian fulcrum, where either side can tip the scale by reverting to the debate's most emotional and uncompromising elements. Yet,

142 *Chapter 6*

in most cases, "refocusing events" have pushed the debate and public opinion toward the authoritarian script on immigration (Wood, 2006).

For example, in 2016, as the presidential election loomed large, the United States was experiencing an increase in Syrian refugees. A civil war in Syria displaced about 11 million people and forced around 4 million to flee the country (Kelly, 2016). The Obama Administration wanted to allow 10,000 new refugees to enter the United States in 2016. Hillary Clinton, the Democratic Party nominee wanted to increase that number to 65,000, which amounted to a 550 percent increase. The Republican Party nominee, Donald Trump, exaggerated her request by saying she wanted 620,000 new refugees in her first term. He also said that Clinton wanted "$400 billion in terms of lifetime welfare and entitlement costs," which Politifact said was patently false (Valverde, 2016). Trump's blatant exaggerations created concerns about the long-term costs and the extent to which the refugees could be vetted for connections to terrorism.

These worries were mostly unfounded, per expert reports. A State Department study showed that since 2001, the United States allowed about 785,000 refugees to enter the country (Taxin, 2016). Of those refugees, only 20 have been proven to have ties to terrorism, which amounts to an infinitesimal threat (Taxin, 2016). Allowing refugees into the United States when their countries have been ravaged by war has been the traditional U.S. response since World War II (Rutledge, 1992; Simon, 1996; Kelly, 1986; Portes & Rumbaut, 2006; Current, 2008; Barber, 1997). In fact, annually, the United States typically allows around 70,000 to 85,000 refugees into the country (Taxin, 2016). However, in this period of polarization and authoritarian tendencies, controversies quickly arose when the war-torn countries in question were connected, even loosely, to acts of terrorism or sustained sponsorship of terrorist groups (Ahmed, 2010; Simon, 1996; Boot, 2001; Portes & Rumbaut, 2006; Barber, 1997).

In response to the concerns raised about the potential for terrorists to evade the extensive vetting process of the Department of State and enter the United States under the guise of a refugee, the Republican-controlled Congress drafted legislation in 2016 that would impose the most stringent vetting process that has ever existed for refugees to enter the United States. The bill required that the Secretary of Homeland Security, the FBI Director, and the Director of National Intelligence certify that each person admitted to the United States is not a terrorist. Such a requirement would effectively reduce the possibility for most refugees to enter the country. The House passed the bill by a large margin. The Senate, however, encountered the typical polarization and obstruction that leads to a filibuster. Because of the Democrats, the bill could not pass the filibuster threat. The bill failed on a 55 to 43 vote (Kelly, 2016). Even if it had passed, President Obama had threatened to veto it.

Further driving the polarization of the parties, the Democratic Party Minority Leader Harry Reid said that he would allow the bill to break the filibuster, giving the Republicans a victory, but in exchange, Reid demanded that the Republicans must allow a vote on a resolution condemning Donald Trump's comments regarding a complete ban on Muslims entering the United States (Kelly, 2016). The Republicans criticized the Minority Leader's attempt to bring the presidential election to the Senate floor. They probably understood that the vote had nothing to do with the refugee problem or the election, but rather it would give the Democratic Party an electoral win. The Democrats would be able to take the Senate vote to the American people in the 2016 election and say "even the Republicans in the Senate believe that Donald Trump's comments about this group are inappropriate and should be condemned." Once again, this case demonstrated how the immigration debate in Congress rested on a dialectical conflict between the authoritarian versus anti-authoritarian political cultures.

CONCLUSION

The events of 9/11 marked a psychological and cultural shift in American society. For the first time in history, the great majority of Americans were worried about being harmed by terrorists. This thesis bears out in numerous polls and academic studies. For instance, the Gallup organization has asked Americans to name "the most important problem facing the United States" since 1939. Before 9/11, terrorism never made the list. After 9/11, terrorism never left it. Numerous psychologists and social psychologists have shown that elevated feelings of perceived threat are positively associated with a range of negative attitudes and behaviors toward out-groups, such as minority ethnic groups or immigrants. In addition to the public's seemingly spontaneous reaction to the new danger, a host of elite intermediaries—news media, presidents, Congress, among others—offered a constant stream of frightening images and descriptions of the terrorist threat, and many also linked this threat to authoritarian policy prescriptions. Put differently, the post-9/11 discourse on terrorism operated in at least two ways: it produced direct and immediate effects on the thoughts and feelings of individuals, and long-term effects on social values and beliefs.

From this culture of fear, the age of authoritarian culture was born. With it came the interminable wars in Afghanistan and Iraq the long-term surge in defense spending, the PATRIOT Act, the increase in security measures everywhere, the tightening of immigration policies, the militarization of local law enforcement, the demonization of Islam, extraordinary rendition (interrogating suspects in places with less strict regulations), the prisoner abuses at Abu

144 Chapter 6

Ghraib, the unending detention of terrorism suspects at Gitmo, government-sponsored torture and assassinations, the drone war, the thousands of dead American soldiers and tens of thousands of civilian casualties (Woods, 2012).

This normalized state of fear persisted for more than 15 years, sometimes resting below the surface, sometimes animated by current events. In the more recent context, the perceived threat of terrorism transcended Arab and Muslim citizens to include any persons of color or differing ideologies. In the two years prior to the 2016 presidential election, nationalist attitudes and xenophobia were no longer subtle expressions tucked beneath the surface. In response to a few high-profile terrorist attacks at home and abroad, the fear of terrorism was once again on the rise during this period. The news media's response to the terrorist events, and the supposed link between terrorism and immigration, followed the patterns of the previous periods, but also reflected the growing polarization in public opinion, social media, presidential speech, and state and federal legislatures.

More so than any president in recent times, Donald Trump harnessed people's anxieties and grievances and generated public support during his presidential campaign. He advocated for the building of a wall, an ultimate signifier for separating "us" and "them." And the list went on for this candidate who prejudicially targeted and stereotyped several specific groups of people, and no group more so than immigrants. The polarization of public opinion, news media, presidential rhetoric, and congressional debate will likely continue in the years to come. But Donald Trump's victory in the 2016 presidential election revealed the tremendous appeal and persuasive power of authoritarian political culture in American society. As President Obama packed his bags in December 2016, the prospects for an anti-authoritarian culture to rise as an ideological counterbalance seemed low.

NOTES

1. See Pence's comments on Donald Trump Jr.'s Skittles reference during an interview with MSNBC in September 2016, at https://www.youtube.com/watch?v=98XRkXpoAM4.

2. See the "Quinnipiac University Poll of 960 Likely Voters Nationwide Conduced," September 8–13, 2016. Retrieved online on January 10, 2016, at http://www.pollingreport.com/terror.htm.

3. See the "Suffolk University/USA Today Poll of 1,000 Likely Voters Nationwide Conducted," June 26–29, 2016. Retrieved online on January 10, 2016, at http://www.pollingreport.com/terror.htm.

4. See the "ABC News/Washington Post Poll of 1,001 Adults Nationwide Conducted," June 20–23, 2016. Retrieved online on January 10, 2016, at http://www.pollingreport.com/terror.htm.

The Partisan Fear of Terrorism, the Polarization of Immigration Attitudes   145

5. See the "CBS News/New York Times Nationwide Poll of 1,358 Registered Voters Conducted," July 8–12, 2016. Retrieved online on January 10, 2016, at http://www.pollingreport.com/terror.htm.

6. See the "Quinnipiac University Nationwide Poll of 1,610 Registered Voters Conducted," June 21–27, 2016. Retrieved online on January 10, 2016, at http://www.pollingreport.com/terror.htm.

7. See the "CBS News Nationwide Poll of 1,011 Registered Voters Conducted," December 9–10. Retrieved online on January 10, 2016, at http://www.pollingreport.com/terror.htm.

8. See the "CBS News Nationwide Poll of 1,011 Registered Voters Conducted," December 9–10. Retrieved online on January 10, 2016, at http://www.pollingreport.com/terror.htm.

9. See "Fox News, The O'Reilly Factor," July 29, 2014, Juan Williams and Mary Katharine Ham on "Conservative Pundit George Will's Immigration Comments." Retrieved online on June 10, 2016, at https://www.youtube.com/watch?v=HQ9qFxwqKC4.

10. The Hispanic vote during the 2008 presidential election was crucial for Obama's victory (Preston, 2012). Senator Obama secured 67 percent of the Hispanic vote. In fact, there was a 25 percent increase in voter turnout from the 2004 presidential election. Hispanic voters increased their support for the Democratic Party by 14 percent from 2004. Nevertheless, according to Krogstad and Lopez (2014), 24.8 million Hispanic voters were eligible to vote in the 2014 midterm elections, which is 3.5 million more than the 2010 midterms. This makes them a little over 11 percent of all eligible voters. That number has increased by nearly 4 million for 2016. These numbers are even more complicated for both parties for battleground states like Florida. Currently, the Democratic Party is dominating the contest for Hispanic votes, winning this demographic by a 71 percent margin in the 2012 General Election, 62 percent in the 2014 Midterm Election, and 80 percent in the 2016 General Election.

Conclusion

As we all know, a young Orson Welles terrified the nation when his radio dramatization of the novel War of the Worlds hit the airwaves in 1938. For decades, teachers, journalists, history programs, and social media users have recounted, with fascination and dismay, the mass hysteria and errant reactions of millions of Americans who were duped into believing that Martians had landed on earth and were now using American citizens for target practice with their heat-ray guns. The hapless audience of Welles' radio show "fled their homes, jammed highways, overwhelmed telephone circuits, flocked to houses of worship, set about preparing defenses, and even contemplated suicide in the belief that the end of the world was at hand" (Campbell 2010, p. 27). In a 2013 episode of PBS's documentary series "American Experience," actors playing the roles of audience members offered vivid accounts of their reactions to the broadcast. The documentary suggested that Welles' program had led to suicides and panic-related deaths. Experts from the documentary claimed that the famous prank "unleashed the pent-up anxieties of a nation," "proved the power of propaganda," and "was such a key moment in the history of American emotional life in the 1930s: the atmosphere of fear and anxiety, the longing for reassurance, but the sense that at any moment destruction might come from the sky, from abroad, or from within the country."[1]

An episode of NPR's Radiolab offered a similar take on the hoax, reporting that "around twelve million people were listening. Most of them got the joke—it was Halloween after all—but if you consider that one in twelve people didn't get the joke . . . and some percentage of that one million ran out of their homes, towels over their faces, clutching children, tripping, breaking limbs—well, that constitutes a major freak out."[2]

The story of Americans' strong reactions to the War of the Worlds radio program is an interesting one, and many observers have used it as a

148   *Conclusion*

cautionary tale, warning of the powerful effects of media on people's emotions and behavior. The most interesting part of this story, however, is that it is largely untrue. The War of the Worlds program did air in 1938, and some Americans were indeed frightened by it. But the newspaper headlines of the day—"Radio Listeners in Panic, Taking War Drama as Fact," "Fake Radio War Stirs Terror through U.S.," "Thousands Terrified by Radio War Drama," "Radio Fake Scares Nation," "Radio Skit Causes Wave of Hysteria over Nation"—grossly exaggerated the intensity of people's behavioral responses (Campbell 2010, p. 28). At least two academic books (Campbell, 2010; Hayes, Battles & Hilton-Morrow, 2013) offer careful, detailed, empirically driven evaluations of the public's reactions, and both conclude that the news reports of what happened had very little in common with actual events. As Pooley and Socolow (2013) put it, "The supposed panic was so tiny as to be practically immeasurable on the night of the broadcast."

The streets of New York City were quiet just as War of the Worlds ended. Over the years, the projected number of people who were even listening to the program has far exceeded the actual number of people who had tuned in (Hayes, Battles & Hilton-Morrow, 2013). There is no evidence of people committing suicide or taking extreme actions, such as running into the streets to watch the Martian war, or packing up the family and escaping to the countryside. The surveys were taken not long after the program aired conflated people's reports of being "frightened" or disturbed" as being "panicked" (Chilton, 2016). The handful of aberrant reactions were exaggerated and overreported by newspapers. Although few academic studies have supported the panic thesis, the only one that did—Cantril, Gaudet, and Herzog's (1982) *The Invasion From Mars*—has been largely debunked by multiple scholars and journalists (Campbell, 2010; Hayes, Battles & Hilton-Morrow, 2013; Pooley & Socolow, 2013; Miller, 2013; Chilton, 2016; Hendley, 2016).

The main takeaway from the War of the Worlds case is not that media have the power to produce dramatic and immediate effects on people, but rather that media often amplify public concerns by establishing a cultural foundation for unfounded beliefs writ large. In this case, the amplified risk was not Martian invaders, but rather, the threat of irresponsible radio show producers who might incite the public and produce devastating individual and social outcomes. But why has the myth of the public's reaction persisted, despite scholarly efforts to debunk it? What is it about the threat from unscrupulous agents of mass media that continues to inform so many Americans? How was the threat constructed and why has it lasted so long in the American mind-set?

The aim of this book has been to answer a similar set of questions related to the myth of the immigrant threat. The answer in either case is complex. No one academic discipline can fully explain why aliens from Mexico freak Americans out, but Welles' aliens did not. Kasperson et al.'s (1988) "social amplification of risk" model provides the most complete model for understanding societal-based fears and perceived threats. As discussed in chapter 1, the approach is explicitly built on multiple academic traditions. Although it has been applied more frequently to public perceptions of environmental hazards, it can serve as a roadmap for explaining public reactions (or a lack thereof) to almost any danger.

The underlying assumption of the amplification framework is that few people have direct experiences with risk events. Dangerous interactions with immigrants, such as being physically attacked by a criminal or terrorist from a foreign land, are almost as rare as the number of people who witnessed others losing their minds in response to War of the Worlds. Following the amplification model, we know that the mediated images of the immigrant threat and the Wellesian hoax travel through "intermediaries" before reaching us, the "receivers." As this information passes through intermediaries, it is often filtered in a way that elevates people's concerns, reinforces stereotypes, facilitates attitude development, and, over time, establishes cultural beliefs among a vast segment of the population (Pidgeon, Kasperson & Slovic, 2003).

With its emphasis on large-scale organizations and institutional actors (intermediaries) who produce and distribute content from privileged social positions, as well as its focus on the cognitive and affective processes that shape how receivers understand these messages, the amplification of risk framework links micro and macros levels of analysis, and synthesizes theories of society and the individual. Put differently, many people believe that both Orson Welles and immigrants have threatened society because certain individuals and groups have the power to shape the news agenda and disseminate carefully crafted messages. These messages are also filtered through party identification, from trusted elites, which enables them to shorten what they process (Arthur, 2014; Wolf & Holian, 2006; Chong, 1996; Zaller, 1992). The success of these messages also depends on people's preexisting cultural scripts, schemas and values, and the conditions under which they receive the information.

Looking for the key intermediaries in the case of War of the Worlds, we see that news coverage of the public's reaction was not a random occurrence or the product of a few clever journalists who wanted to drum up readership with catchy headlines. Rather, we see a newspaper industry that wished to frame radio as irresponsible and dangerous and thereby decrease radio's attractiveness to advertisers. As Pooley and Socolow (2013) put it: "Radio had siphoned off advertising revenue from print during the Depression, badly damaging the newspaper industry. So, the papers seized the opportunity presented by Welles' program to discredit radio as a source of news." The fact that at least some people, however few, misunderstood the radio program allowed newspapers to castigate radio management, manufacture an irresistible story for consumers (then and now), and call for changes in radio broadcasting. The newspaper industry's attack on radio was, in a sense, an early repudiation of "fake news," coupled with a call for organizational change.

As one example, a *New York Times* editorial (1938) titled "Terror by Radio," published two days after the program aired, not only painted a vivid picture of the public's reaction—"a wave of mass hysteria"—and warned public officials of the potentially disastrous consequences of radio's irresponsible actions, but also called on radio to stop interweaving "news technique with fiction." Its critique mirrored a common complaint against social media and other new communication technologies of the early twenty-first century: "Radio is new but it has adult responsibilities. It has not mastered itself or the material it uses" (*New York Times* editorial, November 1, 1938). Given the ubiquity of the mass hysteria story and the legitimacy of those who told it, future institutional voices, including textbooks, teachers, and countless news articles, would accept and retell the story uncritically until it became a fixture in collective memory. In 2005, for instance, *New York Times* columnist Frank Rich (2005) repeated the hysteria claim and substantiated it with a reference to the 1938 *Times* editorial cited above.

A complete explanation of why the newspaper industry's messaging on the dangers of radio was so successful for so many years goes beyond the scope of this book. Such an analysis would require further research into the intermediaries that initially propagated the story, as well as those who perpetuated it over the decades. The characteristics of the most common or "dominant" news frames would need to be identified and unpacked. To properly apply the amplification framework, we would also need to determine how the dominant frames have shaped human consciousness (people's attitudes, beliefs, memories, and cultural values), as well as the behaviors of individuals, groups, and organizations (from conversations around the watercooler to government regulations of mass communication).

Popular beliefs about America's reaction to War of the Worlds are like many people's thoughts and feelings about immigration in the current age of terrorism, polarization, and President Trump. Despite the mobilization of numerous scholars, activists, journalists, and some politicians who have demonstrated, time and again, that immigrants do not pose a threat to American society, millions of people think they do. For many Americans, the notion that immigrants are more likely to harm people than non-immigrants is a "taken-for-granted" fact, just as many of us believe the mass hysteria myth of 1938. The two cases provide interesting and complex puzzles for social scientists to examine and solve.

Our attempt to solve the case of immigration began with a careful look at the evidence pertaining to the effects of immigrants on American society.

Conclusion 151

How many unauthorized immigrants reached the United States in the early twenty-first century? Has there been a dramatic rise in this population? Can this number be accurately framed as a "flood" or "tidal wave"? Careful scientific assessments conclude that the answer to the latter two questions is no. The number of unauthorized immigrants in the United States reached 12 million in 2007 and remained at roughly 11 to 12 million for the next decade. The task of counting this group is difficult, but the methods of analysis have improved over the decades and there is now a consensus on these numbers among researchers and policy analysts from diverse political and ideological backgrounds. Yet, many people, living in the age of terrorism, polarization, and President Trump, believe that the number has reached as high as 30 to 50 million.

Are immigrants more likely to commit crimes? Is the foreign-born population more prone to join ethnic gangs, sell drugs, and carryout heinous violence, such as rape and murder? Again, the answer to these questions is no. Whether researchers are comparing rates of crime, imprisonment, or recidivism, they have found that immigrants do not carry out more destructive acts on average than native-born individuals. Yet, the White House has created the Victims of Immigration Crime Engagement (VOICE) Office to "serve American victims" and provide "a voice to those who have been ignored by our media, and silenced by special interests"[3] and, at the same time, refuses to officially track gun deaths, which are known to be as high as 30,000 per year.[4] As for radicalized acts of violence or terrorism, the number of cases is so small that robust assessments of this threat are not possible. The perpetrators of the 9/11 attacks were foreign-born and this fact has overshadowed evidence showing that the radicalization of would-be terrorists is more likely to occur inside the United States than in foreign countries. In short, the small threat of terrorism that exists comes from inside and not outside U.S. borders. Nevertheless, recurrent media coverage has engendered an event schema of 9/11 (and other large-scale attacks) that has inflated public perceptions of the danger, and wrongly associated the threat with refugees and immigrants from the Middle East and Muslim countries.

Do immigrants hurt the U.S. economy? Do they take the jobs of the native-born and drive down wages? Are immigrants more likely to use and abuse the welfare system? Some scholarly debate characterizes the answers to these questions. Still, in the aggregate, a convincingly large number of studies have found that U.S. immigration brings neutral or positive economic outcomes, and restricting immigrants at the state-level hurts employment levels and reduces opportunities for people to grow businesses and stimulate the local economy. Yet, as Arthur and Woods (2017) found states continue to pass hundreds of restrictive immigration measures that limit immigrant participation in civic life.

152 *Conclusion*

Are new-wave immigrants from Mexico and Latin America less willing to assimilate than immigrants of the past? An expansive empirical literature says no. Immigrants of today are just as likely to adopt the language and customs of mainstream America as immigrants from earlier generations. Even the claim that immigration is changing the racial composition of the United States is not necessarily true, given the fact that race is a social construction that is constantly changing.

What explains the disconnect between empirical evidence and the growing concerns about immigration in the twenty-first century? We argued, starting in chapter 2, that the terrorist attacks on 9/11 fundamentally altered political culture in the United States. Shifts in the dominant repertoires on immigration and terrorism provided restrictionists with a new ideological tool for mobilizing American public opinion and policy in favor of anti-immigrant law enforcement practices and legislation. After the 9/11 disaster, the number of Americans who believed in and worried about the threat of terrorism reached a high-water mark. While terrorism-related deaths have been low compared to almost any other public health concern, terrorism has remained visible in the day-to-day news cycle and public mind-set for at least two decades. Reactions to terrorism always differ across individuals, and people have experienced the threat in different ways depending on the historical context. Still, in the first decades of the twenty-first century, very few Americans dismissed the threat completely or became strong critics of those political officials who promoted aggressive counterterrorism policies.

The public's terrorism concerns (latent or manifest) influenced a range of other attitudes, beliefs, and behaviors. In some respects, the threat of terrorism inspired pro-social behaviors. In the months after 9/11, Americans reached out to their neighbors, contributed more to charities, supported their communities, learned more about current events, and became more civically engaged. But the events of 9/11 also led to authoritarian sentiments and behaviors, such as support for war, assassination, and tougher law enforcement practices. Among the latter tendencies, which were generally more prominent and lasted longer, negative attitudes toward immigrants and immigration took hold among many Americans. At the individual level, the psychological reaction to danger is ephemeral. The argument here is not that the horrific images of 9/11 frightened Americans continually for two decades and led directly to anti-immigrant attitudes. But rather, 9/11 became a meaningful component of American culture and social cognition that many people used to make sense of international security matters. While some scholars refer to this pattern as an event schema and others as a facet of culture, millions of Americans, in either case, accepted the idea that foreigners can penetrate American borders and carryout atrocious attacks, and therefore a defensive posture against all immigrants seemed reasonable if not warranted. The myth

Conclusion 153

of the immigrant terrorist—along with other long-standing myths such as the immigrant as a job-taker, drug dealer, rapist, and cultural corruptor—would become a tool that tipped the balance in the immigration debate of the early twenty-first century.

As discussed in chapter 3, myths require maintenance. The connection between immigrants and terrorism, like the link between Orson Welles and mass panic, was punctuated by events (9/11 and the War of the Worlds program respectively) and reinforced, without interruption, for years by powerful intermediaries, including the news media, presidents, Congress, interest groups, and others. The post-9/11 authoritarian turn in political culture was seen in large-circulation newspapers. The most vivid foreign attack in U.S. history led to negative news coverage of immigrants and especially those whose skin color and culture differed most from the dominant Anglo norm. Backing conventional theories of authoritarianism, the negative shift in coverage was more pronounced in the conservative *Wall Street Journal* than in the liberal *New York Times*. In fact, the post-9/11 increase in negative framing was two times greater in the *Wall Street Journal*. The substantial increases in negative coverage of immigration was found in six out of the eight newspapers in our sample, indicating that the authoritarian turn was indeed a general culture shift, which included news outlets of different sizes, geographical locations, and ideologies.

Presidents, as discussed in chapter 4, also contributed to and were shaped by the dominant repertoires on immigration and terrorism. Although the lion's share of research and theorizing on presidential rhetoric treat the commander-in-chief as an active, independent agent, there is no doubt that presidents must also work within the current situational context. Chapter 4 showed how the president's take on immigration depended in part on several motivating conditions, including the events of 9/11. Based on many speeches made by presidents Clinton, Bush, and Obama, we concluded that presidents changed the level of negativity in their immigration rhetoric depending on when and where their speeches were given, and in response to externalities that they were mostly unable to control. The prevailing authoritarianism after 9/11 was especially prominent in the speeches of George W. Bush, who married the policy issues of immigration and terrorism. President Obama, in contrast, only rarely used the terrorism frame when discussing immigration, and appeared to part ways with the authoritarian stance in President Bush's rhetoric, especially during his second term. Yet, even President Obama, as well as Clinton, struggled at times to remain as positive and progressive as the positions stated in their party's platforms.

President Obama may have influenced the authoritarian turn in American culture, but he clearly did not transform it. After lying dormant in the last year of President Obama's second term, the immigration-terrorism nexus was reenergized during the 2016 presidential campaign and helped Donald Trump become president, as the candidate utilized rhetorical mechanisms and embraced an authoritarian approach to immigration and terrorism in an unprecedented fashion.

A harsh, emotional discourse on terrorism and immigration also flowed through Congress. In chapter 5, based on a study of Senate hearings pertaining to immigration, we found that 9/11 functioned as a shock to the immigration policy monopoly, expanding the authoritarian approach to immigration rhetoric to include terrorism and border security in the anti-immigration framing nexus. Competition for party ownership of the immigration issue led both Democrats and Republicans to connect immigration to border security without qualification. The dominance of border security in the discussion of immigration pushed aside progressive, inclusive, anti-authoritarian immigration narratives.

Finally, in chapter 6, we examined the ideological conditions in the run-up to the 2016 presidential election. Fueled by a few high-profile terrorist attacks at home and abroad, Donald Trump tapped the public's latent concerns about terrorism and immigration, generating support for his campaign. Hillary Clinton confronted Trump's tough stance on immigration directly, while remaining strong on anti-terrorism and national security issues. During this period, media portrayals, public opinion, congressional debate, and presidential rhetoric became increasingly polarized. Many Americans were becoming skeptical of the terrorist threat and more progressive on immigration just as many others were projecting their concerns about terrorism and their desire for tougher national security measures. More so than at any time after 9/11, a culturally imbued perception of threat was a powerful social force that divided Americans. Although this kind of polarization would persist for years after the 2016 election, Donald Trump's presidential victory clearly signaled a resurgence of authoritarian political culture in American society.

More than fifteen years have passed since the age of terrorism began on 9/11, and no major attacks by international terrorists have occurred on U.S. soil. Still, there is little doubt that the perceived threat of foreigners will continue to play an important role in the way millions of Americans make sense of today's most pressing social issues. To reverse the present course, our leaders would first need to reassure the public and begin chipping away at the culture of fear that undergirds authoritarian sentiment. In addition to political officials, we would need an army of courageous opinion leaders, professional naysayers, journalists, comedians, parents, educators, and voters to be more vocal in their support of leaders who discourage black-and-white thinking about terrorist groups, tame exaggerated estimates of the risk, situate the danger in historical context, decouple the threat from the immigration debate, and promote a culture of calm. An army of meaning makers has been constructing the immigrant threat for decades. Only an army of critical thinkers could tear it down.

NOTES

1. American Experience, "War of the Worlds." Retrieved from YouTube online at https://www.youtube.com/watch?v=M1iLFp6XyPY.

2. Radiolab, "War of the Worlds," Season 4, Episode 3. Retrieved online at http://www.radiolab.org/story/91622-war-of-the-worlds.

3. Kopan, Tal (2017). "What Is VOICE? Trump Highlights Crimes by Undocumented Immigrants." *CNN.* Accessed on March 30, 2017, from http://www.cnn.com/2017/02/28/politics/donald-trump-voice-victim-reporting/

4. Farley, Robert (2012). "Gun Rhetoric vs. Gun Facts We Offer Facts and Context as a National Gun-control Debate Intensifies." *Fact Check.* Accessed on March 30, 2017, from http://www.factcheck.org/2012/12/gun-rhetoric-vs-gun-facts/

References

9/11 by the numbers (2002). *New York Magazine,* September 16.

Abbott, Edith, and Alida C. Bowler (1931). National Commission on Law Observance and Enforcement Report on Crime and the Foreign Born. Report No. 10. Washington, DC: U.S. Government Printing Office.

Abbott, G. (1915). Immigration and Crime. *Journal of Criminal Law and Criminology,* 6: 522–532.

Abramson, Paul R., John H. Aldrich, Jill Rickershauser, and David W. Rohde (2007). Fear in the Voting Booth: The 2004 Presidential Election. *Political Behavior,* 29(2): 197–220.

Adorno, T. W., Frenkel-Brunswik, E., Levinson, D. J., and Sandford, N. (1950). *The Authoritarian Personality.* Oxford: Harpers Press.

A. H. Studenmund. (2010) *Using Econometrics: A Practical Guide, Sixth Edition. Addison-Wesley Series in Economics.* Pearson.

Ahmed, A. (2010). *Journey into America: The Challenge of Islam.* Brookings Institution Press.

Akins, Scott, Rubén Rumbaut, and Richard Stansfield. (2009). Immigration, Economic Disadvantage and Homicide: An Analysis of Communities in Austin, Texas. *Homicide Studies,* 13: 307–14.

Akresh, I. R. (2011). Wealth Accumulation among U.S. Immigrants: A Study of Assimilation and Differentials. *Social Science Research,* 40(5): 1390–1401.

Akresh, Ilana Redstone (2007). U.S. Immigrants' Labor Market Adjustment: Additional Human Capital Investment and Earnings Growth. *Demography,* 44: 865–881.

Alba R., Logan J., Lutz A., Stults B. (2002). Only English by the Third Generation? Loss and Preservation of the Mother Tongue among the Grandchildren of Contemporary Immigrants. *Demography,* 39: 467–84.

Alba, Richard (2016). The Likely Persistence of a White Majority. *The American Prospect,* Winter 2016: 67–71.

References

Alexseev, Mikhail A. (2006). *Immigration Phobia and the Security Dilemma: Russia, Europe, and the United States.* Cambridge: Cambridge University Press.

Allison, P. D. (2012, September 10). When Can You Safely Ignore Multicollinearity [Web blog post]. Retrieved from http://statisticalhorizons.com/blog.

Allison, P. D. (1999) Multiple Regression: A Primer (Sage).

Amuedo-Dorantes, Catalina, and Cynthia Bansak (2014). Employment Verification Mandates and the Labor Market of Likely Unauthorized and Native Workers. *Contemporary Economic Policy*, 32: 671–680.

Amuedo-Dorantes, Catalina, Cynthia Bansak, and Allan A. Zebedee (2015). The Impact of Mandated Employment Verification Systems on State-Level Employment by Foreign Affiliates. *Southern Economic Journal*, 81(4): 928–946.

Andreas, P. (2002). The Re-Bordering of America After 11 September. *Brown Journal of World Affairs,* VIII(2): 195–202.

Andreas, P. (2003). Redrawing the Line: Borders and Security in the Twenty-first Century. *International Security*, 28(2): 78–111.

Andreas, P. (2002). The Re-Bordering of America After 11 September. *Brown Journal of World Affairs,* VIII(2): 195–202.

Angling for the hopping mad (2016). *New York Times* (editorial), January 5.

Archibold, R. C. (1999). Schools Open to Face Maze of Problems. *New York Times,* September 10.

Arthur, C. D. (2014). *Economic Actors, Economic Behaviors, and Presidential Leadership: The Constrained Effects of Rhetoric.* Lexington Studies in Political Communication.

Arthur, C. D. and Woods, J. (2013). The Contextual Presidency: The Negative Shift in Presidential Immigration Rhetoric. *Presidential Studies Quarterly*, 43(3).

Arthur, C. D. and Woods, J. (2017). President Bush and Immigration Policy Rhetoric: The Effects of Negativity on the Political Landscape at the State Level. *White House Studies*, 14(1).

Associated Press. (2016). Unfinished US-Mexico Border Wall is a Costly Logistical Nightmare in Texas. *The Guardian.* Accessed on November 11, 2016, from https://www.theguardian.com/us-news/2016/jan/01/ unfinished-us-mexico-border-wall-texas-secure-fence-act.

Atkin, C. (2016). Donald Trump Quotes: The 10 Scariest Things the Presumptive Nominee Has Ever Said. *Independent.* Accessed on November 11, 2016, from http://www.independent.co.uk/us/donald-trump-quotes-the-10-scariest-things-the-presumptive-republican-nominee-has-ever-said-a7015236.html.

Ayers, J., Hofstetter, C., Schnakenberg, K., and Kolody, B. (2009). Is Immigration a Racial Issue? Anglo Attitudes on Immigration Policies in a Border County. *Social Science Quarterly*, 90(3): 593–610.

Baker, Bryan, and Rytina, Nancy (2012). Estimates of the Unauthorized Immigrant Population Residing in the United States: January 2012. Office of Immigration Statistics. Department of Homeland Security. Retrieved online January 7, 2016, at http://www.dhs.gov/sites/default/files/publications/ois_ill_pe_2012_2.pdf.

Baker, Susan Gonzalez (1990). *Cautious Welcome: The Legalization Programs of the Immigration Reform and Control Act.* Washington, DC: Urban Institute Press.

Barack Obama. Remarks at a Town Hall Meeting and a Question-and-Answer Session at Cross Campus in Santa Monica, California. October 9, 2014. Online by

Gerhard Peters and John T. Woolley, *The American Presidency Project.* http://www.presidency.ucsb.edu/ws/?pid=107787.

Barber, B. (1997). Feeding Refugees, or War-The Dilemma of Humanitarian Aid. *Foreign Affairs*, 76: 8.

Barrett, A. W. (2005). Going Public as a Legislative Weapon: Measuring Presidential Appeals Regarding Specific Legislation. *Presidential Studies Quarterly*, 35: 1–10.

Barrett, Andrew W. (2004). Gone Public: The Impact of Going Public on Presidential Legislative Success. *American Politics Research*, 32(3): 338–70.

Barrett A. W., and Eshbaugh-Soha M. (2007). Presidential Success on the Substance of Legislation. *Political Research Quarterly*, 60: 100–112.

Bar-Tal, Daniel, and Daniela Labin (2001). The Effect of a Major Event on Stereotyping: Terrorist Attacks in Israel and Israeli Adolescents' Perceptions of Palestinians, Jordanians and Arabs. *European Journal of Social Psychology*, 31(3): 265–280.

Baum, M. A. (2002). The Constituent Foundations of the Rally-Round-the-Flag Phenomenon. *International Studies Quarterly*, 46: 263–298.

Baumgartner, F., and Jones, B. (2009). *Agendas and Instability in American Politics*. Chicago: University of Chicago Press.

Baumgartner, F., and Jones, B. (1993). *Agendas and Instability in American Politics*. Chicago, IL: The University of Chicago Press.

Baumgartner, F. and Leech, B. (1998). *Basic Interests: The Importance of Groups in Politics and Political Science*. Princeton, NJ: Princeton University Press.

Bean, F. D., R. Corona, R. Tuirán, and K. Woodrow-Lafield (1998). The Quantification of Migration Between Mexico and the United States, pp. 1–90 in *Migration Between Mexico and the United States, Binational Study, Vol. 1,* Mexico City and Washington, DC: Mexico Ministry of Foreign Affairs and U.S. Commission on Immigration Reform.

Bean, F. D., Stevens G. (2003). *America's Newcomers and the Dynamics of Diversity*. New York: Russell Sage Foundation.

Bean, Frank D., Allan G. King, and Jeffrey S. Passel (1983). The Number of Illegal Migrants of Mexican Origin in the United States: Sex Ratio-Based Estimates for 1980. *Demography*, 20(1, February): 99–109.

Bean, Frank D., Rodolfo Corona, Rodolfo Tuiran, Karen A. Woodrow-Lafield, and Jennifer van Hook (2001). Circular, Invisible, and Ambiguous Migrants: Components of Difference in Estimates of the Number of Unauthorized Mexican Migrants in the United States. *Demography*, 38(3). Springer: 411–22.

Beasley, V. B. (2011). *You, the People: American National Identity in Presidential Rhetoric* (No. 10). Texas A&M University Press.

Beasley, V. B. (2006). *Who Belongs in America? Presidents, Rhetoric, and Immigration*. College Station, TX: Texas A&M University Press.

Bell, Alistair (2014). Americans Worry that Illegal Migrants Threaten Way of Life, Economy. August 7. Retrieved online April 2016, at http://www.reuters.com/article/us-usa-immigration-worries-idUSKBN0G70BE20140807.

Bell, G. (2001). Ashcroft Is Right to Detain Suspects in Terror Probe. *Wall Street Journal*, December 17.

Benford, Robert D., and David A. Snow (2000). Framing Processes and Social Movements: An Overview and Assessment. *Annual Review of Sociology*, 26: 611–639.

Bennett, L. W. (1990). Toward a Theory of Press-State Relations in the United States. *Journal of Communication*, 40(2): 103–25.

Benson, R. (2009). What Makes News More Multiperspectival? A Field Analysis. *Poetics*, 37(5–6): 402–418.

Benson, R. and Saguy, A. C. (2005). Constructing Social Problems in an Age of Globalization: A French-American Comparison. *American Sociological Review*, 70: 233–259.

Bernstein, N. (2004). 2 Men Charge Abuse in Arrests After 9/11 Terror Attack. *New York Times*, May 3.

Best, Samuel J., Brian S. Krueger, and Jeffrey Ladewig (2006). Privacy in the Information Age. *Public Opinion Quarterly*, 70(3): 375–401.

Birkland, T. A. (1998). Focusing Events, Mobilization, and Agenda Setting. *Journal of Public Policy*, 18(01): 53–74.

Bizarre responses to a plea for reason. (2015). *New York Times* (editorial), December 8.

Bobic, I. (2014). Rob Portman: Obama Will Face "Lawsuits" If He Acts Alone on Immigration. Politics, *Huffington Post*. Accessed on November 2, 2016, from http://www.huffingtonpost.com/2014/11/19/rob-portman-lawsuits-immigration-obama_n_6184822.html.

Bogart, L. (1989). *Press and Public: Who Reads What, When, Where, and Why in American Newspapers*. Hillsdale, NY: Erlbaum.

Bohn, Sarah, Magnus Lofstrom, and Steven Raphael (2015). Do E-Verify Mandates Improve Labor Market Outcomes of Low-Skilled Native and Legal Immigrant Workers? *Southern Economic Journal*, 81: 960–979.

Boot, M. (2001). The Case for American Empire. The Most Realistic Response to Terrorism is for America to Embrace its Imperial Role. *The Weekly Standard*, 15.

Borjas, George (2015). The Wage Impact of the Marielitos: A Reappraisal. *NBER Working Paper* No. 21588. Issued September 2015.

Borjas, George (2016). The Wage Impact of the Marielitos: Additional Evidence. *NBER Working Paper* No. 21850. Issued January 2016.

Bourdieu, P. (1990). *The Logic of Practice*. Stanford University Press.

Brace, P. and Hinckley, B. (1992). *Follow the Leader: Opinion Polls and the Modern Presidents*. New York, NY: Basic Book Publishing.

Brader, T., Valentino, N. A., and Suhay, E. (2008). What Triggers Public Opposition to Immigration? Anxiety, Group Cues, and Immigration Threat. *American Journal of Political Science*, 52(4): 959–978.

Bradner, E. (2016). 7 Lines that Defined Trump's Immigration Speech. CNN. Accessed on November 11, 2016, from http://www.cnn.com/2016/08/31/politics/donald-trump-immigration-top-lines/.

Bram, Jason, James Orr, and Carol Rapaport (2002). Measuring the Effects of the September 11 Attack on New York City. *FRBNY Economic Policy Review*, 8(2): 5–20.

Branton, R. and Dunaway, J. (2009a). Spatial Proximity to the U.S.-Mexico Border and Newspaper Coverage of Immigration Issues. *Political Research Quarterly*, 62(2): 289–302.

Branton, R. and Dunaway, J. (2009b). Slanted Newspaper Coverage of Immigration: The Importance of Economics and Geography. *The Policy Studies Journal*, 37(2).

References

Branton, R., and Dunaway, J. (2008). English- and Spanish-Language Media Coverage of Immigration: A Comparative Analysis. *Social Science Quarterly*, 89(4): 1006–1022.

Brinkley, J. (1999). New Protection for Refugees From Right-Wing Oppression. *New York Times*, May 21.

Brodkin, Karen (1998). *How Jews Became White Folks and What that Says About Race in America*. New Brunswick, NJ: Rutgers University Press.

Brotherton, D. C. and Kretsedemas, P. (2008). *Keeping Out the Other: A Critical Introduction to Immigration Enforcement Today*. New York: Columbia University Press.

Burke, Ronald J. (2005). Effects of 9/11 on Individuals and Organizations: Down but Not Out! *Disaster Prevention and Management: An International Journal*, 14(5): 629–638.

Bush, George W. (2001). Homeland Security Presidential Directive 2: Combating Terrorism Through Immigration Policies. Washington: The White House, available at: http://www.dm.usda.gov/physicalsecurity/hspd.pdf

Bush, George W. (2003). *Public Papers of the Presidents of the United States. Book II—July 1 to December 31, 2001*. Washington, DC: United States Government Printing Office.

Bush, George W. (2001). Remarks to Federal Bureau of Investigation Employees, September 25, 2001. Online by Gerhard Peters and John T. Woolley, *The American Presidency Project*. http://www.presidency.ucsb.edu/ws/?pid=65083

Bush, George W. (2001). Homeland Security Presidential Directive-2—Combating Terrorism Through Immigration Policies, October 29, 2001. Online by Gerhard Peters and John T. Woolley, *The American Presidency Project*. http://www.presidency.ucsb.edu/ws/?pid=73446

Bush, George W. (2001). Executive Order 13228—Establishing the Office of Homeland Security and the Homeland Security Council, October 8, 2001. Online by Gerhard Peters and John T. Woolley, *The American Presidency Project*. http://www.presidency.ucsb.edu/ws/?pid=61509

Bush, George W. (2001). Interview with Telemundo, March 20, 2002. Online by Gerhard Peters and John T. Woolley, *The American Presidency Project*. http://www.presidency.ucsb.edu/ws/?pid=62895

Butcher, K. F., & Piehl, A. M. (1998). Cross-City Evidence on the Relationship Between Immigration and Crime. *Journal of Policy Analysis and Management*, 17(3): 457–493.

Byers, Bryan, and James Jones (2007). The Impact of the Terrorist Attacks of 9/11 on Anti-Islamic Hate Crime. *Journal of Ethnicity in Criminal Justice*, 5(1): 43–56.

Cab Drivers and Guards Detained in a Three-Month Immigration Sweep. (2003). *New York Times*, January 25.

Campbell, W. J. (2010). *Getting It Wrong: Ten of the Greatest Misreported Stories in American Journalism*. Berkeley: University of California Press.

Cameron, C. (2000). *Veto Bargaining: Presidents and the Politics of Negative Power*. New York, NY: Cambridge University Press.

Canes-Wrone, B. (2006). *Who Leads Whom? Presidents, Policy, and the Public*. Chicago: University of Chicago Press.

References

Canes-Wrone, B. (2004). The Public Presidency, Personal Approval Ratings, and Policy Making. *Presidential Studies Quarterly*, 34(3): 477–490.

Canes-Wrone, B. and Shotts, K.W. (2004). The Conditional Nature of Presidential Responsiveness to Public Opinion. *American Journal of Political Science*, 48(4): 690–706.

Canes-Wrone, B. and de Marchi, S. (2002). Presidential Approval and Legislative Success. *Journal of Politics*, 64(2): 491–509.

Cantril, H., Gaudet, H., and Herzog, H. (1982). *The Invasion from Mars: A Study in the Psychology of Panic*. Princeton, NJ: Princeton University Press.

Caplan, Bryan (2002). Systematically Biased Beliefs about Economics: Robust Evidence of Judgemental Anomalies from the Survey of Americans and Economists on the Economy. *The Economic Journal*, 112(479): 433–458.

Caplan, Bryan (2002). Systematically Biased Beliefs about Economics: Robust Evidence of Judgemental Anomalies from the Survey of Americans and Economists on the Economy. *The Economic Journal*, 112(479): 433–458.

Capps, Randolph, Leighton Ku, Michael E. Fix, Chris Furgiuele, Jeffrey S. Passel, Rajeev Ramchand, Scott McNiven, and Dan Perez-Lopez (2002). *How Are Immigrants Faring After Welfare Reform? Preliminary Evidence from Los Angeles and New York City—Final Report*. Washington, DC: Urban Institute, March. Retrieved online at http://www.urban.org/research/publication/how-are-immigrants-faring-after-welfare-reform.

Card, David (1990). The Impact of the Mariel Boatlift on the Miami Labor Market. *Industrial and Labor Relations Review*, 43(2): 245–257.

Card, David (2005). Is the New immigration Really so Bad? *Economic Journal*, 115(506): 300–323.

Carty, Thomas (2004). *A Catholic in the White House?: Religion, Politics, and John F. Kennedy's Presidential Campaign*. New York: Palgrave Macmillan.

Chan, M. (2016). Donald Trump Claims Black and Hispanic People Are "Living in Hell." *Fortune*. Accessed on November 11, 2016, from http://fortune.com/2016/09/26/presidential-debate-donald-trump-living-in-hell-black-people/.

Chavez, Leo. (2013). *The Latino Threat: Constructing Immigrants, Citizens, and the Nation*. Palo Alto, CA: Stanford University Press.

Chavez, L. R. (2008). *The Latino Threat: Constructing Immigrants, Citizens, and the Nation*. Stanford, CA: Stanford University Press.

Chilton, Martin (2016). The War of the Worlds Panic Was a Myth. *The Telegraph*, May 6. Retrieved online March 15, 2017, at http://www.telegraph.co.uk/radio/what-to-listen-to/the-war-of-the-worlds-panic-was-a-myth/.

Chiswick, Barry R. (1978). The Effect of Americanization on the Earnings of Foreign-Born Men. *Journal of Political Economy*, 86: 897–921.

Chiswick, Barry R. (1983). An Analysis of the Earnings and Employment of Asian American men. *Journal of Labor Economics*, 1: 197–214.

Chock, P. P. (1991). "Illegal Aliens" and "Opportunity": Myth-Making in Congressional Testimony. *American Ethnologist*, 18(2): 279–294.

Chong, D. (1996). Creating Common Frames of Reference on Political Issues. In *Political Persuasion and Attitude Change*, edited by Mutz, D. C., Sniderman, P. M., and Brody, R. A. Ann Arbor, MI: The University of Michigan Press.

References

Cisneros, J. D. (2014). *The Border Crossed Us: Rhetorics of Borders, Citizenship, and Latina/o Identity*. Tuscaloosa: University Alabama Press.

Cisneros, J. D. (2011). (Re)Bordering the Civic Imaginary: Rhetoric, Hybridity, and Citizenship in La Gran Marcha. *Quarterly Journal Of Speech*, 97(1): 26–49. doi:1 0.1080/00335630.2010.536564.

Cisneros, D. (2008). Contaminated Communities: The Metaphor of "Immigrant as Pollutant" in Media Representations of Immigration. *Rhetoric & Public Affairs*, 11(4): 569–601.

Clinton, William J. (1993). Remarks and an Exchange with Reporters on Immigration Policy, July 27, 1993. Online by Gerhard Peters and John T. Woolley, *The American Presidency Project*. http://www.presidency.ucsb.edu/ws/?pid=46906.

Clinton, William J. (1993). Interview with the California Media, July 30, 1993. Online by Gerhard Peters and John T. Woolley, *The American Presidency Project*. http://www.presidency.ucsb.edu/ws/?pid=46934.

Clinton, William J. (1996). Statement on Signing the Antiterrorism and Effective Death Penalty Act of 1996, April 24, 1996. Online by Gerhard Peters and John T. Woolley, *The American Presidency Project*. http://www.presidency.ucsb.edu/ws/?pid=52713.

Cohen, F., S. Solomon, M. Maxfield, T. Pyszczynsk and J. Greenberg (2004). Fatal Attraction. The Effects of Mortality Salience on Evaluations of Charismatic, Task-Oriented, and Relationship-Oriented Leaders. *Psychological Science*, 15(12): 846–851.

Cohen, J. (2010). *Going Local: Presidential Leadership in the Post-Broadcast Age*. New York, NY: Cambridge University Press.

Cohen, J. (2008). *The Presidency in the Era of 24-Hour News*. Princeton, NJ: Princeton University Press.

Cohen, J. (1995). Presidential Rhetoric and the Public Agenda. *American Journal of Political Science* 39 (February): 87–107.

Cohen, Joseph. (1931). Report on Crime and the Foreign Born. *Michigan Law Review*, 30: 99–104.

Cohrs, J. C., and Stelzl, M. (2010). Right Wing Authoritarianism and Social Dominance Orientation as Predictors of Host Society Member's Attitudes Toward Immigrants: Toward Understanding Cross-National Differences. *Journal of Social Issues*, 66: 673–694.

Colby, S. L., and Ortman, J. M. (2014). *Projections of the Size and Composition of the U.S. Population: 2014 to 2060*. Washington, DC: US Census Bureau.

Cook, F. L., Barabas, J., and Page, B. I. (2002). Invoking Public Opinion: Policy Elites and Social Security. *Public Opinion Quarterly*, 66(2): 235–264.

Cook, C. (2002). "The Contemporary Presidency": The Permanence of the "Permanent Campaign": George W. Bush's Public Presidency. *Presidential Studies Quarterly*, 32(4): 753–764.

Corwin, A. F. (1982). The Numbers Game: Estimates of Illegal Aliens in the United States, 1970–1981. *Law and Contemporary Problems*, 45(2): 223–297.

Coser, Lewis A. (1964). *The Functions of Social Conflict*. New York: Free Press of Glencoe. Council.

Covello, V. T. (1992). Risk Communication: An Emerging Area of Health Communication Research. In *Communication Yearbook*, ed. S. Deetz, 15th Edition. Newbury Park: Sage Publications.

Crenshaw, K. (1991). Mapping the Margins: Intersectionality, Identity Politics, and Violence against Women of Color. *Stanford Law Review*, 43(6): 1241–1299.

Cress, D. M., and D. A. Snow (2000). The Outcomes of Homeless Mobilization: The Influence of Organization, Disruption, Political Mediation, and Framing. *American Journal of Sociology*, 105: 1063–1104.

Crowson, H. M., T. K. Debacker, and S. J. Thoma (2006). The Role of Authoritarianism, Perceived Threat and Need for Closure or Structure in Predicting Post-9/11 Attitudes and Beliefs. *Journal of Social Psychology*, 146(6): 733–50.

Current, C. B. (2008). Normalizing Cuban Refugees Representations of Whiteness and Anti-communism in the USA During the Cold War. *Ethnicities*, 8(1): 42–66.

D'Appollonia, A. C. (2012). *Frontiers of Fear: Immigration and Insecurity in the United States and Europe*. Cornell University Press.

Davies, G., and Fagan, J. (2012). Crime and Enforcement in Immigrant Neighborhoods: Evidence from New York City. *The Annals of the American Academy of Political and Social Science*, 641: 99–124.

Davis, M. (2011). How September 11 Affected The U.S. Stock Market. *Investopedia*. September 9, 2011. Accessed on October 2, 2016, from http://www.investopedia. com/financial-edge/0911/how-september-11-affected-the-u.s.-stock-market.aspx.

Davis, Darren (2007). *Negative Liberty: Public Opinion and the Terrorist Attacks on America*. New York: Russell Sage Foundation.

Deb, S. (2016). Trump Says Clinton could let 650 Million New Immigrants into U.S." CBS News. Accessed on November 2, 2016, from http://www.cbsnews.com/news/ donald-trump-says-hillary-clinton-could-let-650-million-new-immigrants-into-u-s/.

Democratic Party Platform. 2016. Democratic Party Platform, July 21, 2016. Online by Gerhard Peters and John T. Woolley, *The American Presidency Project*. http:// www.presidency.ucsb.edu/papers_pdf/117717.pdf.

DeParle, J. (2011). The Anti-Immigration Crusader. *New York Times*, April 17.

Desmond, Scott and Charis Kubrin. (2009). The Power of Place: Immigrant Communities and Adolescent Violence. *Sociological Quarterly*, 50: 581–607.

Dewey, M. M. and L. Barr (1964). A Study of the Structure and Distribution of the Nexus. *The Journal of Cell Biology*, 23: 553–585.

Diamond, J. (2015a). Trump's Immigration Plan: Deport the Undocumented, "Legal Status" for Some. CNN. Accessed on November 11, 2016, from http://www.cnn. com/2015/07/29/politics/donald-trump-immigration-plan-healthcare-flip-flop/.

Diamond, J. (2015b). Trump: "I want Surveillance of Certain Mosques." CNN. Accessed on November 11, 2016, from http://www.cnn.com/2015/11/21/politics/ trump-muslims-surveillance/.

Díaz, Jr., J. (2011). Immigration Policy, Criminalization and the Growth of the Immigration Industrial Complex: Restriction, Expulsion, and Eradication of Undocumented in the U.S. *Western Criminology Review*, 12(2): 35–54.

Diermeier, D., and Feddersen, T. J. (2000). Information and Congressional Hearings. *American Journal of Political Science*, 51–65.

Doherty, Carroll (2016). 5 Facts About Trump Supporters' Views of Immigration. Pew Research Center, August 25.

References

165

Doherty, B. J. (2007). Elections: The Politics of the Permanent Campaign: Presidential Travel and the Electoral College, 1977–2004. *Presidential Studies Quarterly*, 37(4): 749–773.

Dolan, C., Frendreis. J., and Tatalovich, R. (2008). *The Presidency and Economic Policy*. New York, NY: Rowman & Littlefield.

Doosje, Bertjan, Anja Zimmermann, Beate Küpper, Andreas Zick, and Roel Meertens (2009). Terrorist Threat and Perceived Islamic Support for Terrorist Attacks as Predictors of Personal and Institutional Out-Group Discrimination and Support for Anti-Immigration Policies—Evidence from 9 European Countries. *Revue Internationale de Psychologie Sociale*, 22(3–4): 203–234.

Dorsey, L. G. (2007). *We Are All Americans, Pure and Simple: Theodore Roosevelt and the Myth of Americanism*. Tuscaloosa: University Alabama Press.

Doty, R. M., Peterson, B. E., and Winter, D. G. (1991). Threat and Authoritarianism in the United States, 1978–1987. *Journal of Personality and Social Psychology*, 61: 629–640.

Dovidio, J. F., and Esses, V. M. (2001). Immigrants and Immigration: Advancing the Psychological Perspective. *Journal of Social Issues*, 57: 375–388.

Dowling, Julie A., Ellison, Christopher G., Leal, David L. (2012). Who Doesn't Value English? Debunking Myths About Mexican Immigrants' Attitudes Toward the English Language. *Social Science Quarterly*, 93(2): 356–378.

Downs, A. (1996). 2.1. Up and Down with Ecology: The Issue-Attention Cycle. *The Politics of American Economic Policy Making*, 48.

Druckman, J. N. and Holmes, J. W. (2004). Does Presidential Rhetoric matter? Priming and Presidential Approval. *Presidential Studies Quarterly*, 34: 755–777.

Duleep, Harriet Orcutt, and Daniel J. Dowhan (2002). Insights from Longitudinal Data on the Earnings Growth of U.S. Foreign-born Men. *Demography*, 39: 485–506.

Dustmann, C., and Preston, I. P. (2007). Racial and Economic Factors in Attitudes to Immigration. *The B.E. Journal of Economic Analysis & Policy*, 7(1), Article 62.

Earl, Jennifer. (2016). Donald Trump's "Bad Hombres" Comment Causes Confusion. *CBS News*. October 19, 2016. Accessed on April 2, 2017, from http://www.cbsnews.com/news/donald-trumps-bad-hombres-comment-causes-confusion/.

Echebarria-Echabe, A., and Fernández-Guede, E. (2006). Effects of Terrorism on Attitudes and Ideological Orientation. *European Journal of Social Psychology*, 36(2): 259–265.

Edwards, Jason A. (2014). The Good Citizen: Presidential Rhetoric, Naturalization Ceremonies, and Immigrants. *The American Communication Journal*, 16(2): 43–51.

Economist, The. (2016). Special Report. Artificial Intelligence: The Impact on Jobs. Automation and Anxiety: Will Smarter Machines Cause Mass Unemployment. *The Economist*. June 25, 2016. Accessed on April 3, 2017, from http://www.economist.com/news/special-report/21700758-will-smarter-machines-cause-mass-unemployment-automation-and-anxiety.

Edwards, Jason A. and Richard Herder (2012). Melding a New Immigration Narrative? President George W. Bush and the Immigration Debate. *Howard Journal of Communications*, 23(1): 40–65, DOI: 10.1080/10646175.2012.641878.

Edwards, G., and Wayne, S. (1985). *Presidential Leadership: Politics and Policy Making*. New York, NY: St. Martin's Press Inc.

Edwards III, G., and Wood, D. (1999). Who Influences Whom? The President, Congress, and the Media. *American Political Science Review*, 93(2): 327–344.

Edwards, G. C., III. (2003). *On Deaf Ears: The Limits of the Bully Pulpit*. New Haven, CT: Yale University Press.

Egan, Patrick J. (2013). Partisan Priorities: How Issue Ownership Drives and Distorts American Politics. Cambridge University Press.

Ehrenfreund, M. (2014). Your Complete Guide to Obama's Immigration Executive Action. *Washington Post*. Accessed on November 2, 2016, from https://www.washingtonpost.com/news/wonk/wp/2014/11/19/your-complete-guide-to-obamas-immigration-order/.

Eilperin, J. (2007). *Fight Club Politics: How Partisanship is Poisoning the House of Representatives*. Rowman & Littlefield.

Elliot, J. (2011). Debunking the Latest Sharia Scare. *Salon,* April 2.

Engle, P. (2015). "DONALD TRUMP: 'I Would Bomb the s--- out of' ISIS" *Business Insider*. Accessed on November 11, 2016, from http://www.businessinsider.com/donald-trump-bomb-isis-2015–11.

Entman, R. M. (2003). Cascading Activation: Contesting the White House's Frame After 9/11. *Political Communication*, 20(4): 415–432.

Eshbaugh-Soha, M. (2008). Local Newspaper Coverage of the Presidency. *International Journal of Press/Politics*, 13: 103–119.

Eshbaugh-Soha, M., and Peake, J. (2008). The Presidency and Local Media: Local Newspaper Coverage of President George W. Bush. *Presidential Studies Quarterly*, 38(4): 609–631.

Eshbaugh-Soha, M., and Peake, J. S. (2006). The Contemporary Presidency: "Going Local" to Reform Social Security. *Presidential Studies Quarterly*, 36: 689–704.

Espenshade, Thomas J. (1995). Unauthorized Immigration to the United States. *Annual Review of Sociology*, 21: 195–216.

Esses, V. M., Dovidio, J. F., and Hodson, G. (2002). Public Attitudes Toward Immigration in the United States and Canada in Response to the September 11, 2001, "Attack on America." *Analysis of Social Issues and Public Policy*, 2(1): 69–85.

Falk, Erika, and Kate Kenski (2006). Issue Saliency and Gender Stereotypes: Support for Women as Presidents in Times of War and Terrorism. *Social Science Quarterly*, 87(1): 1–18.

Farley, R., Kiely, E., and Gore, D. (2014). "Obama's Actions 'Same' as Past Presidents?" The Wire. Accessed on November 2, 2016, from http://www.factcheck.org/2014/11/obamas-actions-same-as-past-presidents/.

FBI. (2008). FBI 100 First Strike: Global Terror in America. *FBI News Stories*. Accessed on February 2008 from https://archives.fbi.gov/archives/news/stories/2008/february/tradebom_022608.

Feldman, S. (2003). Enforcing Social Conformity: A Theory of Authoritarianism. *Political Psychology*, 24(1): 41–74.

Feldman, S., and Stenner, K. (1997). Perceived Threat and Authoritarianism. *Political Psychology*, 18(4): 741–770.

References

Feldmeyer, Ben. (2009). Immigration and Violence: The Offsetting Effects of Immigrant Concentration on Latino Violence. *Social Science Research*, 38: 717–31.

Fenno, R. F., and Fenno Jr, R. F. (1978). *Home Style: House Members in Their Districts*. HarperCollins.

Fernandes, D. (2007). *Targeted: National Security and the Business of Immigration*. St. Paul, MN: Seven Stories Press.

Fetzer, J. S. (2000). *Public Attitudes toward Immigration in the United States, France, and Germany*. New York: Cambridge University Press.

Finocchiaro, C. J., and Rohde, D. W. (2008). War for the Floor: Partisan Theory and Agenda Control in the US House of Representatives. *Legislative Studies Quarterly*, 33(1): 35–61.

Fischhoff, B., P. Slovic, S. Lichtenstein, S. Read, and B. Combs (1978). How Safe is Safe Enough? A Psychometric Study of Attitudes towards Technological Risks and Benefits. *Policy Sciences*, 9: 127–152.

Flores, L. A. (2003). Constructing Rhetorical Borders: Peons, Illegal Aliens, and Competing Narratives of Immigration. *Critical Studies in Media Communication*, 20(4): 362–387.

Foley, E. (2014). John Boehner: Eric Cantor Loss Didn't Kill Immigration Reform, Obama Did. Politics, *Huffington Post*. Accessed on November 4, 2016, from http://www.huffingtonpost.com/2014/06/12/john-boehner-immigration_n_5488587.html.

Franklin, Benjamin (1753). Letter to Peter Collinson, May 9, 1753. Retrieved online May 2016 at http://founders.archives.gov/documents/Franklin/01–04–02–0173.

Frum, D., and Friedersdorf, C. (2017). Debating Immigration Policy at a Populist Moment as Right-wing Parties across the West Indulge Fascist Impulses, should the United States Pursue a Relatively Restrictionist or Libertarian Policy? *The Atlantic Monthly*. March 9

Fryberg, S. A., Stephens, N. M., Covarrubias, R., Markus, H. R., Carter, E. D., Laiduc, G. A., and Salido, A. J. (2011). How the Media Frames the Immigration Debate: The Critical Role of Location and Politics. *Analyses of Social Issues and Public Policy*, 0: 1–17.

Fujiwara, L. H. (2005). Immigrant Rights Are Human Rights: The Reframing of Immigrant Entitlement and Welfare. *Social Problems*, 52(1): 79–101.

Gailliot, M. T., B. J. Schmeichel, and R. F. Baumeister (2006). Self-Regulatory Processes Defend Against the Threat of Death: Effects of Self-Control Depletion and Trait Self-Control on Thoughts and Fears of Dying. *Journal of Personality and Social Psychology*, 91: 49–62.

Gaines, B. J. (2002). Where's the Rally? Approval and Trust of the President, Cabinet, Congress, and Government Since September 11. *PS: Political Science and Politics*, 35(3): 530–536.

Gallup Center for Muslim Studies. (2010). In U.S., Religious Prejudice Stronger Against Muslims. *Gallup News Service*, January 21.

Gallup. (2014). No Dominant Issue Leading into Midterm Elections. Polls. *Washington Post*. Accessed on November 4, 2016, from http://apps.washingtonpost.com/g/page/national/no-dominant-issue-leading-into-midterm-elections/1243/.

168 *References*

Gallup Organization. (2001). War on Terrorism, *Gallup News Service*, November 26–27.

Gallup Organization. (2007). Gallup's Pulse of Democracy: Immigration. Accessed on October 5, 2007, from www.galluppoll.com.

Gamson, W. (1992). *Talking Politics*. New York: Cambridge University Press.

Gamson, W., D. Croteau, W. Hoynes, and T. Sasson (1992). Media Images and the Social Construction of Reality. *Annual Review of Sociology*, 18: 373–393.

Gans, H. J. (1979). *Deciding What's News: A Study of CBS Evening News, NBC Nightly News, Newsweek, and Time*. New York: Pantheon.

Garand, J. C. (2010). Income Inequality, Party Polarization, and Roll-call Voting in the US Senate. *The Journal of Politics*, 72(04): 1109–1128.

Gaynor, Tim, and David Schwartz (2010). Arizona Passes Tough Illegal Immigration Law, *Reuters*, April 19.

Gentzkow, M., and Shapiro, J. (2010). What Drives Media Slant? Evidence from U.S. Daily Newspapers. *Econometrica*, 78(1): 35–71.

Gentzkow, M.A., and Shapiro, J. M. (2006). What Drives Media Slant? Evidence from U.S. Daily Newspapers (November 13). Available at SSRN: http://ssrn.com/abstract=947640.

German Marshall Fund. (2002). *A World Transformed: Foreign Policy Attitudes of the U.S. Public After September 11th*, September 4. Retrieved online at http://www.worldviews.org/docs/U.S.9–11v2.pdf.

Gitlin, T. (1980). *The Whole World Is Watching: Mass Media in the Making & Unmaking of the New Left*. Berkeley: University of California Press.

Golash-Boza, T. (2016). The Parallels between Mass Incarceration and Mass Deportation: An Intersectional Analysis of State Repression. *Journal of World-Systems Research*, 22(2): 484–509. doi:http://dx.doi.org/10.5195/jwsr.2016.616.

Golash-Boza, T. (2015). *Deported: Immigrant Policing, Disposable Labor and Global Capitalism*. New York: New York University Press.

Golash-Boza, T. (2012). *Due Process Denied: Detentions and Deportations in the 21st Century*. New York: Routledge.

Golash-Boza, T. (2012). *Immigration Nation: Raids, Detentions and Deportations in Post-911 America*. Boulder, CO: Paradigm Publishers. (Release date: September 2011).

Golash-Boza, T. (2009). The Immigration Industrial Complex: Why We Enforce Immigration Policies Destined to Fail. *Sociology Compass*, 3(2): 295–309.

Golash-Boza, Tanya, and Pierrette Hondagneu-Sotelo. (2013). Latino Immigrant Men and the Deportation Crisis: A Gendered Racial Removal Program. Latino Studies, 11(3): 271–292.

Gordijn, Ernestine H., and Diederik A. Stapel (2006). When Controversial Leaders with Charisma are Effective: The Influence of Terror on the Need for Vision and Impact of Mixed Attitudinal Messages. *European Journal of Social Psychology*, 38(3): 389–411.

Gottschalk, M. (2014). *Caught: The Prison State and the Lockdown of American Politics*. Princeton, NJ: Princeton University Press.

Graber, D. (2009). *Mass Media and American Politics*. Washington, DC: Congressional Quarterly Press.

References 169

Graber, D. (1988). *Processing the News: How People Tame the Information Tide.* New York, NY: Longman.

Graham, Matt (2013). Border Security Assets. Bipartisan Policy Center, Washington, DC. Retrieved online September 12, 2016, at http://bipartisanpolicy.org.

Greenberg, J. (2015). Trump's Pants on Fire Tweet that Blacks Killed 81% of White Homicide Victims. Politifact. Accessed on November 11, 2016, from http://www.politifact.com/truth-o-meter/statements/2015/nov/23/donald-trump/trump-tweet-blacks-white-homicide-victims/.

Greenberg, J. (2014). Economist: Immigrants Have Taken All New Jobs Created since 2000. Politifact. Accessed on November 2, 2016, from http://www.politifact.com/punditfact/statements/2014/dec/02/peter-morici/economist-immigrants-have-taken-all-new-jobs-creat/.

Greenberg, J., Pyszczynski, T., Solomon, S., Rosenblatt, A., Veeder, M., Kirkland, S., and Lyon, D. (1990). Evidence for Terror Management Theory II: The Effects of Mortality Salience on Reactions to those who Threaten or Bolster the Cultural Worldview. *Journal of Personality and Social Psychology*, 58: 308–318.

Greenberg, Jeff, Sheldon Solomon, and Tom Pyszczynski (1997). Terror Management Theory of Self-Esteem and Cultural Worldviews: Empirical Assessments and Conceptual Refinements. In *Advances in Experimental Social Psychology*, Vol. 29, ed. M. P. Zanna (San Diego, CA: Academic Press. 1997), 61–139.

Greenberg, M., P. Craighill, and A. Greenberg (2004). Trying to Understand Behavioral Responses to Terrorism: Personal Civil Liberties, Environmental Hazards, and U.S. Resident Reactions to the September 11, 2001 Attacks. *Human Ecology Review*, 11(2): 165–176.

Griswold, Eliza (2016). Why Is It So Difficult for Syrian Refugees to Get Into the U.S.? *New York Times Magazine*, January 20.

Groseclose, T., and Milyo, J. (2005). A Measure of Media Bias. *Quarterly Journal of Economics*, 120(4): 1191–1237.

Guglielmo, Jennifer, and Salvatore Salerno (2003). *Are Italians White? How Race is Made in America.* New York: Routledge.

Hagan, J., and Palloni, A. (1999). Sociological Criminology and the Mythology of Hispanic Immigration and Crime. *Social Problems*, 46(4): 617–632.

Hagan, John, and Alberto Palloni (1998). Immigration and Crime in the United States. Pp. 367–87. In *The Immigration Debate: Studies on the Economic, Demographic, and Fiscal Effects of Immigration*, edited by J. P. Smith and B. Edmonston. Washington, DC: National Academy Press.

Hagan, John, and Alberto Palloni. (1998). Immigration and Crime in the United States. In *The immigration debate*, edited by J. P. Smith and B. Edmonston. Washington, DC: National Academy Press.

Hains, T. (2016). Hillary Clinton: Donald Trump Is "Trafficking in Prejudice and Paranoia," He Is "Un-American." *RealClear Politics*. Accessed on November 16, 2016, from http://www.realclearpolitics.com/video/2016/03/09/clinton_trump_is_trafficking_in_prejudice_and_paranoia_un-american html.

Hamilton, Alexander, James Madison, and John Jay (1788). *The Federalist: On the New Constitution.* New York: George F. Hopkins.

170 *References*

Hammond, J. (2011). Immigration Control as a (False) Security Measure. *Critical Sociology*, 37(6): 739–761.

Hart, R. P. (1987). *The Sound of Leadership: Presidential Communication in the Modern Age*. Chicago, IL: University of Chicago Press.

Hastings, B. M., and B. A. Shaffer (2005). Authoritarianism and Sociopolitical Attitudes in Response to Threats of Terror. *Psychological Reports*, 97(2): 623–630.

Hayes, Joy E., Kathleen Battles, and Wendy Hilton-Morrow (eds.) (2013). *War of the Worlds to Social Media: Mediated Communication in Times of Crisis*. New York: Peter Lang.

Heer, David M., and Jeffrey S. Passel. (1987). Comparison of Two Methods for Estimating the Number of Undocumented Mexican Adults in Los Angeles County. *The International Migration Review*, 21(4): 1446–1473.

Hendley, Nate (2016). *The Big Con: Great Hoaxes, Frauds, Grifts, and Swindles in American History*. Santa Barbara, CA: ABC-CLIO.

Hertog, J. K. (2000). Elite Press Coverage of the 1986 U.S.–Libya Conflict: A Case Study of Tactical and Strategic Critique. *Journalism & Mass Communication Quarterly*, 77(3): 612–27.

Hetherington, Marc J., and Jonathan D. Weiler (2009). *Authoritarianism and Polarization in American Politics*. New York: Cambridge University Press.

Hillary's Trump card. (2015). *Wall Street Journal* (editorial), July 10.

Hobbes, T. (1950). *Leviathan*. New York: Dutton.

Hood III, M. V., and Morris, I. L. (1997). ¿Amigo o Enemigo?: Context, Attitudes, and Anglo Public Opinion toward Immigration. *Social Science Quarterly*, 78(2): 309–323.

Hood III, M. V., and Morris, I. L. (1998). Give Us Your Tired, Your Poor . . . But Make Sure They Have a Green Card: The Effects of Documented and Undocumented Migrant Context on Anglo Opinions Toward Immigration. *Political Behavior*, 21(1): 1–15.

Hopkins, Daniel J. (2010). Explaining Where and When Immigrants Provoke Local Opposition. *The American Political Science Review*, 104(1): 40–60.

Hopkins, D. J. and King, G. (2010). Automated Nonparametric Content Analysis for Social Science. *American Journal of Political Science*, 54(1): 229–247.

Horvit, B. (2003). Combat, Political Violence Tops International News Categories. *Newspaper Research Journal*, 24(2): 22–35.

Hourwich, I. A. (1912). Immigration and Crime. *American Journal of Sociology*, 17(4): 478–490.

Huddy, Leoni, Nadia Khatib, and Theresa Capelos (2002). Trends: Reactions to the Terrorist Attacks of September 11, 2001. *Public Opinion Quarterly*, 66(3): 418–450.

Huddy, Leonie, Stanley Feldman, Charles Tabar, and Gallya Lahav (2005). Threat, Anxiety, and Support of Antiterrorism Policies. *American Journal of Political Science*, 49(3): 593–608.

Hunt, V. (2002). The Multiple and Changing Goals of Immigration Reform: A Comparison of House and Senate Activity, 1947–1993. In Baumgartner, F. R., and Jones, B. D. (2002). *Policy Dynamics*. University of Chicago Press.

References 171

Hunt, Jennifer, and Marjolaine Gauthier-Loiselle (2008). How Much Does Immigration Boost Innovation? *NBER Working Paper*, No. 14312, Issued in September.

Hyman, L., and Iskander, N. (2016). What the Mass Deportation of Immigrants Might Look Like: Operation Wetback didn't merely enforce immigration law—it enforced the idea that American citizens are white. *Slate*. History—Then, Again. Accessed on April 3, 2017, from http://www.slate.com/articles/business/metropolis/2017/04/the_last_thing_america_needs_from_trump_s_infrastructure_plan_is_more_roads.html.

Inglehart, R., and Baker, W. (2000). Modernization, Cultural Change, and the Persistence of Traditional Values. *American Sociological Review*, 65(1): 19–51.

Ingraham, H., and Fraser, L. (2006). Path Dependency and Adroit Innovation. in Robert Repetto, ed. *Punctuated Equilibrium and the Dynamics of US Environmental Policy*. Yale University Press.

Iyengar, Shanto (1991). *Is Anyone Responsible?* Chicago: University of Chicago Press.

Jackson, L. M., and Esses, V. M. (2000). Effects of Perceived Economic Competition on People's Willingness to Help Empower Immigrants. *Group Processes & Intergroup Relations*, 3(4): 419–435.

Jacobs, L. R. and Shapiro, R. Y. (2000). *Politicians Don't Pander: Political Manipulation and the Loss of Democratic Responsiveness*. Chicago, IL: The University of Chicago Press.

Jamieson, Kathleen Hall, and Cappella, Joseph N. (2008). *Echo Chamber: Rush Limbaugh and the Conservative Media Establishment*. New York: Oxford University Press.

Jarymowicz, Maria, and Daniel Bar-Tal (2006). The Dominance of Fear Over Hope in the Life of Individuals and Collectives. *European Journal of Social Psychology*, 36(3): 367–392.

Jasny, Lorien, Waggle, Joseph, and Fisher, Dana R. (2015). An Empirical Examination of Echo Chambers in US Climate Policy Networks. *Nature Climate Change*, 5: 782–786.

Jones, Bradley (2016). Americans' Views of Immigrants Marked by Widening Partisan, Generational Divides, Gallup Organization, April 15. Retrieved online at http://www.pewresearch.org/fact-tank/2016/04/15/americans-views-of-immigrants-marked-by-widening-partisan-generational-divides/.

Jones, B. D. (1994). *Reconceiving Decision-making in Democratic Politics: Attention, Choice, and Public Policy*. University of Chicago Press.

Jones, Jeffrey M. (2016). Republicans, Democrats Interpret Orlando Incident Differently, *Gallup Organization*, June 17. Retrieved online October 2, 2016, at http://www.gallup.com/poll/192842/republicans-democrats-interpret-orlando-incident-differently.aspx?g_source=terrorism&g_medium=search&g_campaign=tiles.

Jones, J. M. (2007). Only 4 in 10 Americans Satisfied With Treatment of Immigrants. *Gallup News Service*, August 15.

Jones, Seth G. (2015). The Terrorism Threat to the United States and Implications for Refugees. Rand Corporation Testimony. House Committee on Homeland Security: Subcommittee on Counterterrorism and Intelligence. Retrieved online August 18, 2016, at http://www.rand.org/pubs/testimonies/CT443.html.

172 *References*

Kam, C. D., and Kinder, D. R. (2007). Terror and Ethnocentrism: Foundations of American Support for the War on Terrorism. *Journal Of Politics*, 69(2): 320–338.

Kasperson, R. E., Renn, O., Slovic, P., Brown, H. S., Emel, J., Goble, R., Kasperson, J. X., and Ratick, S. (1988). The Social Amplification of Risk: A Conceptual Framework. *Risk Analysis*, 8: 177–187.

Kelly, Charles B. (1977). Counting the Uncountable: Estimates of Undocumented Aliens in the United States. *Population and Development Review*, 3(4): 473–481.

Kelly, E. (2016). Senate Democrats Block Bill to Restrict Syrian Refugees from Entering U.S. USA Today. Accessed on November 14, 2016, from http://www.usatoday.com/story/news/2016/01/20/senate-democrats-block-bill-restrict-syrian-refugees-entering-us/79063266/.

Kelly, G. P. (1986). Coping with America: Refugees from Vietnam, Cambodia, and Laos in the 1970s and 1980s. *The Annals of the American Academy of Political and Social Science*, 138–149.

Kelsey, C. (1926). Immigration and Crime. *The Annals of the American Academy of Political and Social Science*, 125: 165–174.

Keogan, K. (2002). A Sense of Place: The Politics of Immigration and the Symbolic Construction of Identity in Southern California and the New York Metropolitan Area. *Sociological Forum*, 17(2): 223–253.

Kernell, Samuel. (2007). *Going Public: New Strategies of Presidential Leadership*. 4th ed. Washington, DC: Congressional Quarterly Press.

Kersh, R. (2006). The Well-Informed Lobbyist: Information and Interest Group Lobbying. In Cigler and Loomis *Interest Group Politics*. Washington, DC: Congressional Quarterly Press.

King, D. (1994). The Nature of Congressional Committee Jurisdictions. *APSR*, 88: 48–62.

King G., and Roberts, M. (2014). How Robust Standard Errors Expose Methodological Problems They Do Not Fix, and What to Do About It. *Political Analysis*, (2015) 23: 159–179.

Kolankiewicz, Leon (2000). Immigration, Population, and the New Census Bureau Projections. Center for Immigration Studies, June. Retrieved in May 2016 at http://cis.org/CensusBureauProjections-Immigration%2526Population.

Kingdon, J. W. (1995). *Agendas, Alternatives, and Public Policies*. Longman Pub Group.

Kossoudji, Sherrie A. (1988). English Language Ability and the Labor Market Opportunities of Hispanic and East Asian Immigrant Men. *Journal of Labor Economics*, 6: 205–228.

Kossoudji, Sherrie A. (1989). Immigrant Worker Assimilation: Is It a Labor Market Phenomenon? *Journal of Human Resources*, 24: 494–527.

Krippendorff, K. (1978). Reliability of Binary Attribute Data. *Biometrics*, 34(1): 142–144.

Krogstad, Jens Manuel, Renee Stepler, and Mark Hugo Lopez (2015). English Proficiency on the Rise Among Latinos U.S. Born Driving Language Changes, May 12. Retrieved online in May 2016 at http://www.pewhispanic.org/2015/05/12/english-proficiency-on-the-rise-among-latinos/.

Krogstad, J. M., and Lopez, M. H. (2014). Hispanic Nativity Shift. *Pew Research Center*, 29.

References   173

Kubrin, Chans E. and Hiromi Ishizawa (2012). Why Some Immigrant Neighborhoods Are Safer than Others: Divergent Findings from Los Angeles and Chicago. *Annals of the American Academy of Political and Social Science*, 641: 148–73.

Kubrin, Charis E., Marjorie S. Zatz, and Ramiro Martinez (eds.) (2012). *Punishing Immigrants: Policy, Politics, and Injustice*. New York: New York University Press.

Lahav, Gallya, and Marie Courtemanche (2012). The Ideological Effects of Framing Threat on Immigration and Civil Liberties. *Political Behavior*, 34(3): 477–505.

Lamont, M., and Laurent, T. (eds). 2000. *Rethinking Comparative Cultural Sociology: Repertoires of Evaluation in France and the United States*. Cambridge, UK: Cambridge University Press.

Landau, M. J., S. Solomon, J. Greenberg, F. Cohen. T. Pyszczynski, J. Arndt, C. H. Miller, D. M. Ogilvie, and A. Cook (2004). Deliver Us from Evil: The Effects of Mortality Salience and Reminders of 9/11 on Support for President George W. Bush. *Personality and Social Psychology Bulletin*, 30: 1136–1150.

Lavine, H., Lodge, M., and Freitas, K. (2005). Threat, Authoritarianism, and Selective Exposure to Information. *Political Psychology*, 26(2): 219–244.

Lawless, Jennifer L. (2004). Women, War, and Winning Elections: Gender Stereotyping in the Post-September 11th Era. *Political Research Quarterly*, 57(3): 479–490.

Lazar, A. (2014). Governor Says Immigrant Children Could Have Measles, But that Claim's Been Disputed. Politics, Huffington Post. Accessed on November 4, 2016, from http://www.huffingtonpost.com/2014/07/18/tom-corbett-immigration_n_5600744.html.

Lee, F. E. (2008). Agreeing to Disagree: Agenda Content and Senate Partisanship, 1981–2004. *Legislative Studies Quarterly*, 33(2): 199–222.

Lee, J., and F.D. Bean (2004). America's Changing Color Lines: Immigration, Race/Ethnicity, and Multiracial Identification. *Annual Review of Sociology*, 30: 221–42.

Lee, M. T., and Martinez, R. (2009). Immigration Reduces Crime: An Emerging Scholarly Consensus. *Sociology of Crime, Law and Deviance*, 13: 3–16.

Lee, M. T., Martinez, R., and Rosenfeld, R.. (2001). Does Immigration Increase Homicide? Negative Evidence from Three Border Cities. *The Sociological Quarterly*, 42(4): 559–580.

Lee, Matthew T. (2003). *Crime on the Border: Immigration and Homicide in Urban Communities*. New York: LFB Scholarly Publishing.

Lee, Michelle Ye Hee (2015). The Viral Claim that "Not One" Refugee Resettled since 9/11 Has Been Arrested on Domestic Terrorism Charges. *Washington Post*, November 19.

Legewie, Joscha (2013). Terrorist Events and Attitudes Toward Immigrants: A Natural Experiment. *American Journal of Sociology*, 118(5): 1199–1245.

Levendusky, M. S. (2013). Why Do Partisan Media Polarize Viewers? *American Journal of Political Science*, 57(3): 611–623.

Lewis, Carol (2005). The Clash between Security and Liberty in the U.S. Response to Terror. *Public Administration Review*, 65(1): 18–30.

Leyden, K. M. (1995). Interest Group Resources and Testimony at Congressional Hearings. *Legislative Studies Quarterly*, 431–439.

Light, P. (1999). *The President's Agenda: Domestic Policy Choice from Kennedy to Clinton*. Baltimore, MD: The Johns Hopkins University Press.

174 *References*

Lind, Andrew W. (1930). Some Ecological Patterns of Community Disorganization in Honolulu. *American Journal of Sociology*, 36: 206–220.

LoBianco, T. (2015). Donald Trump Promises "Deportation Force" to Remove 11 Million. CNN. Accessed on November 11, 2016, from http://www.cnn.com/2015/11/11/politics/donald-trump-deportation-force-debate-immigration/.

Lohr, S. (2010). *Sampling: Design and Analysis*. Boston, MA: Brooks/Cole Cengage Learning.

Longhi, S, Nijkamp, P, and Poot, J. (2005). A Meta-analytic Assessment of the Effect of Immigration on Wages. *Journal of Economic Surveys*, 19(3): 451–477.

Longhi, S., Nijkamp, P., and Poot, J. (2010). Joint Impacts of Immigration on Wages and Employment: Review and Meta-analysis. *Journal of Geographical Systems*, 12(4): 355–387.

Lost in the immigration frenzy. (2015). *New York Times* (editorial), July 13.

Loveman, B., and Hofstetter, C. (1984). American Perceptions of Undocumented Immigrants: Political Implications. *New Scholar*, 9: 111–18.

Lutz, H., Maria Teresa Herrera Vivar, and Supik, L. (eds.) (2011). *Framing Intersectionality: Debates on a Multi-Faceted Concept in Gender Studies*. Burlington, VT: Ashgate.

Lyons, C. J., Vélez, M. B., and Santoro, W. A. (2013). Neighborhood Immigration, Violence, and City-Level Immigrant Political Opportunities. *American Sociological Review*, 78(4): 604–632.

Macdonald, John M., and Robert Sampson (2012). Don't Shut the Golden Door: The Beneficial Impact of Immigration. *New York Times*, April 5.

MacDonald, John, and Jessica Saunders (2012). Are Immigrant Youth Less Violent? Specifying the Reasons and Mechanisms. *The Annals of the American Academy of Political and Social Science*, 641: 125–147.

MacDonald, John, and Robert J. Sampson (2012). The World in a City: Immigration and America's Changing Social Fabric. *The ANNALS of the American Academy of Political and Social Science May*, 641: 6–15.

Machiavelli, N. (1999/1513). *The Prince*. London and New York: Penguin Classics.

Maney, G., Woehrle, L.,and Coy, P. (2005). *Harnessing and Challenging Hegemony*: The *U.S. Peace Movement after 9/11*. *Sociological Perspectives*, 48(3): 357–381.

Marcus, G. E., Neuman, W. R., and MacKuen, M. (2000). *Affective Intelligence and Political Judgment*. Chicago: University of Chicago Press.

Martinez, Ramiro, Jr., and Jacob I. Stowell. (2012). Extending Immigration and Crime Studies: National Implications and Local Settings. *The Annals of the American Academy of Political and Social Science*, 641(1): 174–192.

Martinez, Ramiro, Jr., Jacob I. Stowell, and Matthew T. Lee (2010). Immigration and Crime in an Era of Transformation: A Longitudinal Analysis of Homicides in San Diego Neighborhoods, 1980–2000. *Criminology*, 48(3): 797–830.

Martinez, R., and Lee, M. T. (2000). Comparing the Context of Immigrant Homicides in Miami: Haitians, Jamaicans and Mariels. *The International Migration Review*, 34(3): 794–812.

Martinez, Ramiro, Jr., and Abel Valenzuela Jr. (eds.) (2006). *Immigration and Crime: Race, Ethnicity, and Violence*. New York: New York University Press, 2006.

References 175

Martínez, Ramiro, Jr., and Matthew T. Lee (2000). On Immigration and Crime, in National Institute of Justice, *Criminal Justice 2000: The Nature of Crime, vol. 1* (NCJ 182408). Washington, DC: U.S. Department of Justice, Office of Justice Programs, 485–524.

Massey D. (1985). Ethnic Residential Segregation: A Theoretical Synthesis and Empirical Review. *Sociology and Social Research*, 69: 315–50.

Massey D. S. (1981). Dimensions of the New Immigration to the United States and Prospects for Assimilation. *Annual Review of Sociology*, 7: 57–85.

Massey, Douglas S. (1987). Do Undocumented Migrants Earn Lower Wages than Illegal Immigrants? New Evidence from Mexico. *International Migration Review*, 21: 236–274.

Massey, Douglas S., and Audrey Singer (1995). New Estimates of Undocumented Mexican Migration and the Probability of Apprehension. *Demography*, 32: 203–213.

Mataconis, D. (2014). If Obama Takes Executive Action on Immigration, GOP has Limited Options. *Politics Voices. Christian Science Monitor.* Accessed on November 2, 2016, from http://www.csmonitor.com/USA/Politics/Politics-Voices/2014/1114/If-Obama-takes-executive-action-on-immigration-GOP-has-limited-options.

McCord, Joan. (1995). Ethnicity, Acculturation, and Opportunities: A Study of Two Generations. In *Ethnicity, Race, and Crime*, edited by D. F. Hawkins. Albany: State University of New York Press.

McTague, J., and Pearson-Merkowitz, S. (2013). Voting from the Pew: The Effect of Senators' Religious Identities on Partisan Polarization in the US Senate. *Legislative Studies Quarterly*, 38(3): 405–430.

Mayhew, D. (1989). Does it Make a Difference Whether Party Control of the American National Government is Unified or Divided?. Paper presented at the annual meeting of the American Political Science Association, Atlanta, GA.

Mikulincer, Mario, Victor Florian, and Gilad Hirschberger (2003). The Existential Function of Close Relationships: Introducing Death Into the Science of Love. *Personality and Social Psychology Review*, 7(1): 20–40.

Milkis, S., Rhodoes, J., and Charnock, E. (2012). What Happened to Post-Partisanship? Barack Obama and the New American Party System. *Perspectives on Politics*, 10(1). doi:10.1017/S1537592711004907.

Miller, David L. (2013). *Introduction to Collective Behavior and Collective Action*. Long Grove, IL: Waveland Press.

Miroff, B. (2003). Entrepreneurship and Leadership. *Studies in American Political Development*, 17(Fall): 204–211.

Mitchell, A. (2001). Ridge Is Opening a Center to Analyze and Share Data. *New York Times*, December 24.

Mitchell, Amy, Jeffrey Gottfried, Jocelyn Kiley, and Katerina Matsa (2014). Political Polarization & Media Habits, Pew Research Center, October 21. Retrieved online October 6, 2016, at http://www.journalism.org/2014/10/21/political-polarization-media-habits/.

Montalvo, D., and Torres, J. (2005). *Network Brownout Report: The Portrayal of Latinos and Latino Issues on Network Television News*. Washington, DC: National Association of Hispanic Journalists.

Moody, C. (2015). Donald Trump Digs in on Immigration. CNN. Accessed on November 11, 2016, from http://www.cnn.com/2015/07/07/politics/trump-immigration-rapists-mexicans-clinton/.

Moore, K. M. (2002). "United We Stand": American Attitudes toward (Muslim) Immigration Post-September 11th. *The Muslim World*, 92(1–2): 39–57.

Morin, D. T., and Flynn, M. A. (2014). We Are the Tea Party!: The Use of Facebook as an Online Political Forum for the Construction and Maintenance of in-Group Identification during the "GOTV" Weekend. *Communication Quarterly*, 62(1): 115–133.

Moreno, C. (2015). 9 Outrageous Things Donald Trump Has Said About Latinos. *Huffington Post*. Accessed on November 11, 2016, from http://www.huffingtonpost.com/entry/9-outrageous-things-donald-trump-has-said-about-latinos_us_55e483a1e4b0c818f618904b.

Morning Joe (2016). Donald Trump Rounds out the Week on Morning Joe, Morning Joe, July 24. Retrieved online January 2, 2016, at http://www.msnbc.com/morning-joe/watch/donald-trump-rounds-out-the-week-on-morning-joe-490679363866.

Muste, Christopher P. (2013). The Dynamics of Immigration Opinion in the United States, 1992–2012. *Public Opinion Quarterly*, April 77, (1): 398–416.

Naber, Nadine. (2006). The Rules of Forced Engagement Race, Gender, and the Culture of Fear among Arab Immigrants in San Francisco Post-9/11. *Cultural Dynamics*, 18(3): 235–267.

Nadadur, Ramanujan (2009). Illegal Immigration: A Positive Economic Contribution to the United States. *Journal of Ethnic and Migration Studies*, 35(6): 1037–1052.

Nagel, C. R. (2002). Geopolitics by Another Name: Immigration and the Politics of Assimilation. *Political Geography*, 21(8): 971–987.

Nagel, J. (1994). Constructing Ethnicity: Creating and Recreating Ethnic Identity and Culture. *Social Problems*, 41: 152–76.

Nakamura, D. (2016). Clinton's Stance on Immigration is a Major Break from Obama. Politics, *Washington Post*. Accessed on November 16, 2016, from https://www.washingtonpost.com/politics/clintons-stance-on-immigration-is-a-major-break-from-obama/2016/03/10/6388a1f8-e700–11e5-a6f3–21ccdbc5f74e_story.html.

National Archives. (2017). President Franklin Delano Roosevelt's Executive Order 9066 Authorizing the Military Detention of Anyone Deemed a Threat to National Security. Accessed on April 4, 2017, from https://www.archives.gov/files/historical-docs/doc-content/images/japanese-relocation-order.pdf.

Neustadt, R. (1991). *Presidential Power and the Modern Presidents: The Politics of Leadership from Roosevelt to Reagan*. New York, NY: The Free Press.

Newland, Kathleen (2015). The U.S. Record Shows Refugees Are Not a Threat By Kathleen Newland. Migration Policy Institute. Retrieved online August 18, 2016, at http://www.migrationpolicy.org/news/us-record-shows-refugees-are-not-threat.

Newport, Frank (2007). Americans Have Become More Negative on Impact of Immigrants. *Gallup News Service*, July 13.

Newport, Frank (2009). Americans Still Say Muslims Have Negative View of U.S. *Gallup News Service*, June 3.

Nielsen, Amie L., and Ramiro Martínez Jr. (2011). Nationality, Immigrant Groups, and Arrest: Examining the Diversity of Arrestees for Urban Violent Crime. *Journal of Contemporary Criminal Justice*, 27(3): 342–360.

Nielsen, Amie L., Matthew T. Lee, and Ramiro Martinez Jr. (2005). Integrating Race, Place, and Motive in Social Disorganization Theory: Lessons from a Comparison of Black and Latino Homicide Types in Two Immigrant Destination Cities. *Criminology*, 43: 837–872.

Norman, Jim (2016). Majority in U.S. Now Dissatisfied With Security from Terrorism. Gallup Organization, January 18. Retrieved online September 24, 2016, at http://www.gallup.com/poll/188402/majority-dissatisfied-security-terrorism.aspx?g_source=terrorism&g_medium=search&g_campaign=tiles.

Noy, Darren (2009). The Contradictions of Public Sociology: A View from a Graduate Student at Berkeley. *The American Sociologist*, 40(4): 235–248.

Office of the Press Secretary. (2002). *Securing America's Borders Fact Sheet: Border Security*. Retrieved online January 29, 2014, at http://georgewbush-whitehouse.archives.gov/news/releases/2002/01/20020125.html.

Olivas, M. A. (2013). Empirical Data on Immigration. In *Those Damned Immigrants: Americas Hysteria over Undocumented Immigration* (pp. 43–84). NYU Press.

Olivas-Luján, Miguel R., Anne-Wil Harzing, and Scott McCoy (2004). September 11, 2001: Two Quasi-Experiments on the Influence of Threats on Cultural Values and Cosmopolitanism. *International Journal of Cross Cultural Management*, 4(2): 211–228.

Orrenius, Pia M., and Madeline Zavodny (2015). The Impact of E-Verify Mandates on Labor Market Outcomes. *Southern Economic Journal*, 81: 947–959.

Ortman, J. M., Velkoff V. A., and Hogan H. (2014). An Aging Nation: The Older Population in the United States. Washington, DC: U.S. Census Bureau; 2014. Report No.: Current Population Reports, P25–114C.

Ottaviano, G., and Peri G. (2008). *Immigration and National Wages: Clarifying the Theory and Empirics*, NBER Working Paper No. 14188.

Ottaviano, G., and Peri, G. (2011). Rethinking the Effects of Immigration on Wages. *Journal of the European Economic Association*, 10(1): 1542–4774.

Ousey, Graham C., and Charis E. Kubrin (2009). Exploring the Connection between Immigration and Violent Crime Rates in U.S. Cities, 1980–2000. *Social Problems*, 56(3): 447–473.

Page, B. (1996). *Who Deliberates? Mass Media in Modern Democracy*. Chicago: University of Chicago Press.

Panagopoulos, Costas (2006). The Polls-Trends. Arab and Muslim Americans and Islam in the Aftermath of 9/11. *Public Opinion Quarterly*, 70(4): 608–624.

Papacharissi, Zizi, and Maria de Fatima Oliveira (2008). News Frames Terrorism: A Comparative Analysis of Frames Employed in Terrorism Coverage in U.S. and U.K. Newspapers. *The International Journal of Press/Politics*, 13: 52–74.

Pariser, Eli. (2011). *The Filter Bubble: What the Internet is Hiding from You*. London: Viking/Penguin Press.

Park, H. (2016). Millions Could be Blocked from Entering the U.S. Depending on How Trump Would Enforce a Ban on Muslim Immigration. *The New York Times*. December 22, 2016. Accessed on April 3, 2017, from https://www.nytimes.com/interactive/2016/07/22/us/politics/trump-immigration-ban-how-could-it-work.html?_r=0.

Park, H. (2014). Q. and A.Children at the Border. *New York Times*. Accessed on November 4, 2016, from http://www.nytimes com/interactive/2014/07/15/us/100000003001471.mobile.html.

178 *References*

Parkinson, John (2014). DHS Rebuffs Congressman's Claim ISIS Infiltrating Southern Border. *ABC News*, October 8. Accessed on August 17, 2016, from http://abcnews.go.com/Politics/dhs-rebuffs-congressmans-claim-isis-infiltrating-southern-border/story?id=26043280.

Parrado, E. A. (2012). Immigration Enforcement Policies, the Economic Recession, and the Size of Local Mexican Immigrant Populations. *The Annals of the American Academy of Political and Social Science*, 641: 16–37.

Partlow, Joshua, Sean Sullivan, and Jose A. DelReal (2016) After subdued trip to Mexico, Trump talks tough on immigration in Phoenix. *Washington Post*, August 31.

Passel, J. (2007). Unauthorized Migrants in the United States: Estimates, Methods, and Characteristics. *OECD Social, Employment and Migration Working Papers*, No. 57, OECD Publishing. Retrieved online at http://www.oecd-ilibrary.org/social-issues-migration-health/unauthorized-migrants-in-the-united-states_110780068151.

Passel, Jeffrey S., and Karen A. Woodrow. (1984). Geographic Distribution of Undocumented Immigrants: Estimates of Undocumented Aliens Counted in the 1980 Census by State. *The International Migration Review*, 18(3). [Center for Migration Studies of New York, Inc., Wiley]: 642–71.

Passel, Jeffrey S., and Karen A. Woodrow. (1987). Change in the Undocumented Alien Population in the United States, 1979–1983. *The International Migration Review*, 21(4). [Center for Migration Studies of New York, Inc., Wiley]: 1304–34.

Passel, Jeffrey S., D'Vera Cohn, Jens Manuel Krogstad, and Ana Gonzalez-Barrera (2014). As Growth Stalls, Unauthorized Immigrant Population Becomes More Settled. Published on Pew Research Center web site September 3. Retrieved online January 7, 2016, at http://www.pewhispanic.org/files/2014/09/2014–09–03_Unauthorized-Final.pdf.

Penner, L., Michael T. Brannick, Shannon Webb, and Patrick Connell (2005). Effects on Volunteering of the September 11, 2001, Attacks: An Archival Analysis. *Journal of Applied Social Psychology*, 35(7): 1333–1360.

Peri, Giovanni, and Vasil Yasenov (2015). The Labor Market Effects of a Refugee Wave: Applying the Synthetic Control Method to the Mariel Boatlift. *NBER Working Paper*, No. 21801, issued December 2015.

Perlmann, J., M. C. Waters (2004). Intermarriage then and Now: Race, Generation and the Changing Meaning of Marriage. In *Not Just Black and White: Immigration, Race and Ethnicity, Then to Now*, ed. N. Foner, and G. Frederickson, pp. 262–77. New York: Russell Sage Foundation.

Perrin, A. J. (2005). National Threat and Political Culture: Authoritarianism, Antiauthoritarianism, and the September 11 Attacks. *Political Psychology*, 26: 167–194.

Peterson, D., and Djupe, P. (2005). When Primary Campaigns Go Negative: The Determinants of Campaign Negativity. *Political Research Quarterly*, 58(1): 45–54.

Peterson, C., and Martin E. P. Seligman (2003). Character Strengths Before and After September 11. *Psychological Science*, 14(4): 381–384.

References

Peterson, M. A. (1990). *Legislating Together: The White House and Capitol Hill from Eisenhower to Reagan*. Cambridge, MA: Harvard University Press.

Pew Research Center. (2015a). Modern Immigration Wave Brings 59 Million to U.S., Driving Population Growth and Change Through 2065: Views of Immigration's Impact on U.S. Society Mixed. Washington, DC: September.

Pew Research Center. (2015b). Views of Government's Handling of Terrorism Fall to Post-9/11 Low. Little change in views of relationship between Islam and violence. December 15. Retrieved online September 29, 2016, at http://www.people-press. org/2015/12/15/views-of-governments-handling-of-terrorism-fall-to-post-911-low/.

Pew Research Center. (2016). 15 Years After 9/11, a Sharp Partisan Divide on Ability of Terrorists to Strike U.S., September 7. Retrieved online September 29, 2016, at http://www.people-press.org/2016/09/07/15-years-after-911-a-sharp-partisan-divide-on-ability-of-terrorists-to-strike-u-s/.

Pew Research Center. (2016b). On Immigration Policy, Partisan Differences but Also Some Common Ground, August 25. Retrieved online October 2, 2016, at http://www.people-press.crg/2016/08/25/on-immigration-policy-partisan-differences-but-also-some-common-ground/.

Pew Research Center. (2014). Political Polarization in the American Public How Increasing Ideological Uniformity and Partisan Antipathy Affect Politics, Compromise and Everyday Life, June 12. Retrieved online October 8, 2016, at http://www.people-press.org/2014/06/12/political-polarization-in-the-american-public/.

Pew Research Center. (2010). Americans Spending More Time Following the News. September 12, 2010. Retrieved December 18, 2013, at http://www.people-press.org/files/legacy-pdf/652.pdf.

Pew Research Center. (2006). No Consensus on Immigration Problem or Proposed Fixes, March 30. Retrieved online at http://people-press.org.

Pham, Huyen, and Pham Hoang Van (2010). Economic Impact of Local Immigration Regulation: An Empirical Analysis. *Cardozo Law Review*, 32(2): 485–518.

Phillips, A. (2016). A House Republican Already Wants to Impeach Hillary Clinton. *Washington Post*. Accessed on November 2, 2016, from https://www.washingtonpost.com/news/the-fix/wp/2016/09/09/a-house-republican-already-wants-to-impeach-hillary-clinton/.

Pidgeon, Nick F., Roger E. Kasperson, and Paul Slovic (2003). *The Social Amplification of Risk*. Cambridge: Cambridge University Press.

Pilkington, Ed (2011). Alabama Immigration: Crops Rot as Workers Vanish to Avoid Crackdown. *The Guardian*, October 14.

Poole, K. T., and Rosenthal, H. (1984). The Polarization of American Politics. *The Journal of Politics*, 46(04): 1061–1079.

Pooley, Jefferson, and Michael J. Socolow (2013). The Myth of the War of the Worlds Panic. *Slate*, October 28. Retrieved online March 10, 2017, at http://www.slate.com/articles/arts/history/2013/10/orson_welles_war_of_the_worlds_panic_myth_the_infamous_radio_broadcast_did.html.

Portes, A., and Rumbaut, R. G. (2006). *Immigrant America: A Portrait*. University of California Press.

180 References

Portes, Alejandro, and Robert L. Bach (1980). Immigrant Earnings: Cuban and Mexican Immigrants in the United States. *International Migration Review*, 14: 315–341.

Preston, J. (2012). While Seeking Support, Obama Faces a Frustrated Hispanic Electorate. *Hispanic Trending*. Accessed on August 15, 2012, from http://www.hispanictrending. net/2012/06/while-seeking-support-obama-faces-afrustrated-hispanic-electorate.html.

Prior, M. (2013). Media and Political Polarization. *Annual Review of Political Science,* 16: 101–27.

Putnam, Robert (2000). *Bowling Alone*. New York: Simon & Schuster.

Putnam, Robert (2001). A Better Society in a Time of War, New York Times, October 19.

Putnam, Robert (2002). Bowling Together. *The American Prospect*, February 11.

Pyszczynski, T., Abdollahi, A., Solomon, S., Greenberg, J., Cohen, F., and Weise, D. (2006). Mortality Salience, Martyrdom, and Military Might: The Great Satan Versus the Axis of Evil. *Personality and Social Psychology Bulletin*, 32: 525–537.

Pyszczynski, Tom, A. Abdollahi, Sheldon Solomon, Jeff Greenberg, F. Cohen, and D. Weise (2006). Mortality Salience, Martyrdom, and Military Might: The Great Satan versus the Axis of Evil. *Personality and Social Psychology Bulletin*, 32: 525–537.

Pyszczynski, Tom, Jeff Greenberg, and Sheldon Solomon (2003). *In the Wake of 9/11: The Psychology of Terror*, Washington, DC: American Psychological Association.

Ragsdale, L. (1987). Presidential Speechmaking and the Public Audience: Individual Presidents and Group Attitudes. *Journal of Politics*, 49: 704–736.

Raphael, Steven, and Lucas Ronconi (2009). The Labor Market Impact of State-Level Immigration Legislation Targeted at Unauthorized Immigrants. Working Paper, Berkeley, CA: University of California, Berkeley.

Rasinski, Kenneth A., Jennifer Berktold, Tom W. Smith, and Bethany L. Albertson (2002). *America Recovers: A Follow-Up to a National Study of Public Response to the September 11th Terrorist Attacks*. Chicago, IL: National Opinion Research Center.

Redden, E. (2016). Trump Proposes Ideological Test for Entry to U.S. Inside Higher Ed. Accessed on November 11, 2016, from https://www.insidehighered.com/news/2016/08/16/trump-proposes-extreme-vetting-and-ideological-test-visas.

Reese, S, Rutigliano, L, Kideuk, H, and Jaekwan, J (2007). Mapping the Blogosphere: Professional and Citizen-Based Media in the Global News Arena. *Journalism*, 8(3): 235–261.

Reid, Lesley W., Harold E. Weiss, Robert M. Adelman, and Charles Jaret (2005). The Immigration-Crime Relationship: Evidence across US Metropolitan Areas. *Social Science Research*, 34: 757–80.

Republicans' Anti-Immigrant Race. (2015). *New York Times* (editorial), August 20.

Republican Party Platforms. (2016). Republican Party Platform. Online by Gerhard Peters and John T. Woolley, *The American Presidency Project*. http://www.presidency.ucsb.edu/papers_pdf/117718.pdf.

Republican Party Platforms. (2008). Republican Party Platform, September 1, 2008. Online by Gerhard Peters and John T. Woolley, *The American Presidency Project*. http://www.presidency.ucsb.edu/ws/?pid=78545.

References

Rich, Rank (2005). Two Top Guns Shoot Blanks. *New York Times*, June 19.

Riffe, D., Lacy, S., and Fico, F. (2005). *Analyzing Media Messages: Using Quantitative Content Analysis in Research*. Hillsdale, NJ: Erlbaum.

Riffkin, Rebecca (2015). Americans Name Terrorism as No. 1 U.S. Problem. *Gallup News Service*, December 14.

Rokeach, M. (1960). *The Open and Closed Mind*. New York: Basic Books.

Rosenfeld, M. J. (2002). Measure of Assimilation in the Marriage Market: Mexican Americans 1970–1990. *Journal of Marriage and Family*, 64: 152–62.

Rottinghaus. (2006). Rethinking Presidential Responsiveness: The Public Presidency and Rhetorical Congruency, 1953–2001. *Journal of Politics*, 68(3): 720–732.

Rucker, P. (2014). Hillary Clinton says She's a Huge Supporter of Immigration Reform. Politics. *Washington Post*. Accessed on November 16, 2016, from https://www.washingtonpost.com/news/post-politics/wp/2014/04/17/hillary-clinton-says-shes-a-huge-supporter-of-immigration-reform/.

Rumbaut, Rubén G. (2005). Turning Points in the Transition to Adulthood: Determinants of Educational Attainment, Incarceration, and Early Childbearing Among Children of Immigrants. *Ethnic and Racial Studies*, 28: 1041–1086.

Rumbaut, Rubén G. (2009). Undocumented Immigration and Rates of Crime and Imprisonment: Popular Myths and Empirical Realities. In *The Role of Local Police: Striking a Balance Between Immigration Enforcement and Civil Liberties* (119–39), edited by A. Khashu. Washington, DC: Police Foundation.

Rutledge, P. (1992). *The Vietnamese Experience in America*. Indiana University Press.

Saad, Lydia (2010). U.S. Fear of Terrorism Steady After Foiled Christmas Attack, *Gallup New Service*, January 13.

Saad, Lydia (2011). Majority in U.S. Say Bin Laden's Death Makes America Safer, *Gallup News Service*, May 4.

Sales, S. M. (1972). Economic Threat as a Determinant of Conversion Rates in Authoritarian and Nonauthoritarian Churches. *Journal of Personality and Social Psychology*, 23: 420–428.

Sales, S. M. (1973). Threat as a Factor in Authoritarianism. *Journal of Personality and Social Psychology*, 28: 44–57.

Sampson, Robert J., Jeffrey D. Morenoff, and Stephen Raudenbush (2005). Social Anatomy of Racial and Ethnic Disparities in Violence. *American Journal of Public Health* 95(2): 224–32.

Sampson, Robert J. (2008). Rethinking crime and immigration. *Contexts*, 7(1): 28–33.

Sampson, Robert J. (2006). Open Doors Don't Invite Criminals: Is Increased Immigration Behind the Drop in Crime? *New York Times*, March 11, p. A27.

Sander, Thomas H., and Robert Putnam (2002). Walking the Civic Talk After Sept. 11, *The Christian Science Monitor*, February 19.

Schafer, Chelsea E., and Greg M. Shaw (2009). Tolerance in the United States. *Public Opinion Quarterly*, 73(2): 404–431.

Schickler, E. (2000). Institutional change in the House of Representatives, 1867–1998: A Test of Partisan and Ideological Power Balance Models. *American Political Science Review*, 94(02): 269–288.

Schuck, Peter H. (1996). Alien Rumination. *Yale Law Journal*, 105: 1963–2012.

Schudson, Michael (2011). *The Sociology of News*. 2nd ed. New York: W. W. Norton.

Schultheis, E. (2016). President-elect Trump says how many Immigrants he'll Deport. CBS News. Accessed on November 13, 2016, from http://www.cbsnews.com/news/president-elect-trump-says-how-many-immigrants-hell-deport/.

Schüller, S., (2012). The Effects of 9/11 on Attitudes Toward Immigration and the Moderating Role of Education. *IZA Discussion Papers* 7052.

Segovia, Francine, and Renatta Defever (2010). American Public Opinion on Immigrants and Immigration Policy. *Public Opinion Quarterly*, 74(2): 375–394.

Sellin, Thorsten (1938). *Culture Conflict and Crime*. New York: Social Science Research

Sewell Jr, W. H. (1992). A Theory of Structure: Duality, Agency, and Transformation. *American Journal of Sociology*, 1–29.

Shane, Scott (2015). Homegrown Extremists Tied to Deadlier Toll Than Jihadists in U.S. Since 9/11. *New York Times*, June 24.

Sheingate, A. D. (2003). Political Entrepreneurship, Institutional Change, and American Political Development. *Studies in American Political Development*, 17(Fall): 185–203.

Shenon, P. (2003). New Asylum Policy Comes Under Fire. *New York Times*, March 19, A22.

Shlapentokh, Shiraev, and Woods (2005). *America: Sovereign Defender or Cowboy Nation?* Ashgate.

Shoemaker, Pamela, and Stephen Reese (2014). *Mediating the Message in the 21st Century: A Media Sociology Perspective*. 3rd ed. New York: Routledge.

Short, R., and Magana, L. (2002). Political Rhetoric, Immigration Attitudes, and Contemporary Prejudice: A Mexican American Dilemma. *The Journal of Social Psychology*, 142(6): 701–712.

Simon, R. J. (1996). Public and Political Opinion on the Admission of Refugees. *Refugees in America in the 1990s: A Reference Handbook*, 355.

Sjöberg, Lennart (2005). The Perceived Risk of Terrorism. *Risk Management: An International Journal*, 7: 43–61.

Skitka, Linda J., C. W. Bauman, and E. Mullen (2004). Political Tolerance and Coming to Psychological Closure Following the September 11, 2001, Terrorist Attacks: An Integrative Approach. *Personality and Social Psychology Bulletin*, 30(6): 743–756.

Skocpol, Theda (2002). Will 9/11 and the War on Terror Revitalize American Civic Democracy? *PS: Political Science and Politics*, 35(3): 537.

Skowronek, S. (1997). *The Politics Presidents Make: Leadership from John Adams to Bill Clinton*. Cambridge, MA: Belknap Press of Harvard University Press.

Slater, M. D. (2007). Reinforcing Spirals: The Mutual Influence of Media Selectivity and Media Effects and Their Impact on Individual Behavior and Social Identity. *Communication Theory*, 17(3): 281–303.

Slovic, Paul (2004). *The Perception of Risk*. London; Sterling, VA: Earthscan.

Smeltz, Dina, Ivo H. Daalder, Karl Friedhoff, and Craig Kafura (2015). America Divided: Political Partisanship and US Foreign Policy, *The Chicago Council on Global Affairs*, September 15. Retrieved online October 1, 2016, at https://www.thechicagocouncil.org/publication/america-divided-political-partisanship-and-us-foreign-policy.

References

Smith, C. A. (1983). The Audience of the "Rhetorical Presidency": An Analysis of President-Constituent Interactions. *Presidential Studies Quarterly*, 8: 613–622.

Smith, T. W., Rasinski, K., and Toce, M. (2001). *America Rebounds: A National Study of Public Response to the September 11th Terrorist Attacks, Preliminary Findings.* Chicago, IL: National Opinion Research Center.

Smith, Tom W., Kenneth A. Rasinski, and Marianna Toce (2001). *America Rebounds: A National Study of Public Response to the September 11th Terrorist Attacks, Preliminary Findings.* Chicago, IL: National Opinion Research Center.

Spalding, M. (1994). From Pluribus to Unum. *Policy Review*, 67: 35.

Spriggs, J. F., II. (1996). The Supreme Court and Federal Administrative Agencies. *American Journal of Political Science*, 40: 1122–51.

Spurlock, Morgan (2013). Immigration. CNN's *Inside Man*. Aired July 14, 10:00 pm EST.

Stanley, Alessandra (2011). As Word Spread About Bin Laden's Death, It Became a TV Moment, *New York Times*, May 3.

Stansfield, R., Akins, S., Rumbaut, R. G., and Hammer, R. B. (2013). Assessing the Effects of Recent Immigration on Serious Property Crime in Austin, Texas. *Sociological Perspectives*, 56(4): 647–672.

Stephens, G. R., and Wikstrom, N. (2007). *American Intergovernmental Relations: A Fragmented Federal Polity.* New York, NY: Oxford University Press.

Sterngold, J. (2001). Devastating Picture of Immigrants Dead in Arizona Desert, *New York Times*, May 26.

Stroud, N. J. (2011). *Niche News: The Politics of News Choice.* New York, NY: Oxford University Press.

Sullivan, Cheryl (2010). Biden vs. Cheney: Three Points of Dispute. *Christian Science Monitor*, February 14.

Sunstein, C. R. (2009). *Going to Extremes: How Like Minds Unite and Divide.* Oxford: Oxford University Press.

Sunstein, Cass (2004). Fear and Liberty. *Social Research*, 71(4): 976–996.

Suro, Roberto, and Jeffrey Passel. (2003). The Rise of the Second Generation: Changing Patterns of Hispanic Population Growth. *Pew Hispanic Center.* Washington, DC.

Swain, C. (2003). *Debating Immigration.* Cambridge University Press, 2007.

Swidler, A. (1986). Culture in Action: Symbols and Strategies. *American Sociological Review*, 51: 273–286.

Swidler, A. (2001). *Talk of Love: How Culture Matters.* Chicago: University of Chicago Press.

Taft, Donald R. (1936). Nationality and Crime. *American Sociological Review*, 1: 724–736.

Tajfel, H., and Turner, J. C. (1979). An Integrative Theory of Intergroup Conflict. In W. G. Austin and S. Worchel (Eds.). *The Social Psychology of Intergroup Relations.* Monterey, CA: Brooks/Cole.

Tajfel, Henri, and John Turner (1979). An Integrative Theory of Intergroup Conflict. In *The Social Psychology of Intergroup Relations*, eds. W. G. Austin and S. Worchel (Monterey, CA: Brooks/Cole, 1979), 33–48.

Talbert, J. C., Jones, B. D., and Baumgartner, F. R. (1995). Nonlegislative Hearings and Policy Change in Congress. *American Journal of Political Science*, 383–405.

Tarrow, S. (1992). Mentalities, Political Cultures, and Collective Action Frames: Constructing Meaning through Action. In *Frontiers of Social Movement Theory* (174–202), edited by A. D. Morris and C. McClurg Mueller. New Haven: Yale University Press.

Taxin, A. (2016). Politicians Decry Refugee Program after 2 Iraqi-born Men Arrested on Terrorism Charges. U.S. News & World Report. Accessed on November 17, 2016, from http://www.usnews.com/news/us/articles/2016–01–08/refugee-program-decried-after-iraqis-terror-related-arrests.

Taylor, Paul, Ana Gonzalez-Barrera, Jeffrey S. Passel, and Mark Hugo Lopez (2012). Recent Trends in Naturalization, 2000–2011, Pew Hispanic Center, November 14 . Retrieved online in May 2016, at http://www.pewhispanic.org/2012/11/14/ii-recent-trends-in-naturalization-2000–2011.

Ten Eyck, T. A., and Williment. M. (2003). The National Media and Things Genetic: Coverage in *The New York Times* (1971–2000) and *Washington Post*, (1977–2000). *Science Communication*, 25: 129–152.

The anti-immigrant binge (2015). *New York Times* (editorial), July 24.

The Deportation Party? (2015). *Wall Street Journal* (editorial), August 18.

The Great "Sanctuary City" Slander (2015). *New York Times* (editorial), October 16.

The Obama Legacy Project (2016). *Wall Street Journal* (editorial), January 13.

The Obama-Trump Dialectic (2015). *Wall Street Journal* (editorial), December 2015.

The Trump Effect, and How It Spreads (2015). *New York Times* (editorial), December 10.

Theriault, S. M. (2013). *The Gingrich Senators: The Roots of Partisan Warfare in Congress*. Oxford University Press.

Theriault, S. M., and Rohde, D. W. (2011). The Gingrich Senators and Party Polarization in the US Senate. *Journal of Politics*, 73(4): 1011–1024.

Tonry, Michael (Ed.) (1997). *Ethnicity, Crime and Immigration: Comparative and Cross-National Perspectives*. Chicago, IL: University of Chicago Press.

Traugott, Michael W., Ted Brader, Deborah Coral, Richard Curtin, David Featherman, Robert Groves, Martha Hill, James Jackson, Thomas Juster, Robert Kahn, Courtney Kennedy, Donald Kinder, Beth-Ellen Pennell, Matthew Shapiro, Mark Tessler, David Weir, and Robert Willis (2002). How Americans Responded: A Study of Public Reactions to 9/11/01. *PS: Political Science and Politics*, 35(3): 511–516.

Trejo, Stephen J. (1997). Why do Mexican Americans Earn Low Wages? *Journal of Political Economy*, 105: 1235–1268.

Tremewan, James (2009). Beliefs About the Economic Impact of Immigration. *TSE Working Papers Series*, March 24. Retrieved online in April 2016 at http://econpapers.repec.org/paper/tsewpaper/22141.htm.

Tulis, J. (1987). *The Rhetorical Presidency*. Princeton, NJ: Princeton University Press.

Turley, J. (2016). Trump's "Extreme Vetting" Is Harsh, But it Would Be Legal. *Washington Post*. Accessed on November 2, 2016, from https://www.washingtonpost.com/posteverything/wp/2016/08/16/trumps-extreme-vetting-is-harsh-but-it-would-be-legal/?utm_term=.76ce5b00df1b.

Trump's Fortress America. (2016). *Wall Street Journal* (editorial), September 2.

Tversky, Amos, and Daniel Kahneman (1974). Judgment under Uncertainty: Heuristics and Biases. *Science*, 185: 1124–1131.

U.S. Bureau of Justice Statistics, Department of Justice. (2015). Crime and Victimization, 2014. Retrieved from http://www.bjs.gov/ccntent/pub/pdf/cv14.pdf.

U.S. Commission on Immigration Reform. (1994). *Restoring Credibility*. Washington, DC: U.S. Commission on Immigration Reform.

United States Bureau of Labor Statistics. (2014). Foreign Born Represented 16.5 Percent of the U.S. Labor Force in 2014, up from 14.8 percent in 2005. *The Economics Daily*. Retrieved online in April 2016 http://www.bls.gov/opub/ted/2015/foreign-born-represented-17-percent-of-the-labor-force-in-2014-up-from-15-percent-in-2005.htm.

Valverde, M. (2016). Trump says Clinton Would Bring in 620,000 Refugees in Her First Term. Politifact TruthOMeter. Accessed on November 14, 2016, from http://www.politifact.com/truth-o-meter/statements/2016/sep/27/donald-trump/trump-says-clinton-would-bring-620000-refugees-her/.

Van Hook, Jennifer, Weiwei Zhang, Frank D. Bean, and Jeffrey S. Passel. (2006). Foreign-born Emigration: A New Approach and Estimates Based on Matched CPS Files. *Demography*, 43(2). Springer: 361–82.

Vavreck, L. (2009). *The Message Matters: The Economy and Presidential Campaigns*. Princeton, NJ: Princeton University Press.

Verkasalo, Markku, Robin Goodwin, and Irina Bezmenova (2006). Values Following a Major Terrorist Incident: Finnish Adolescent and Student Values Before and After September 11, 2001. *Journal of Applied Social Psychology*, 36(1): 144–160.

Von Hentig, Hans (1945). The First Generation and a Half: Notes on the Delinquency of the Native White of Mixed Parentage. *American Sociological Review*, 10: 792–798.

Wadsworth, T. (2010). Is Immigration Responsible for the Crime Drop? An Assessment of the Influence of Immigration on Changes in Violent Crime Between 1990 and 2000. *Social Science Quarterly*, 91(2): 531–553.

Waldman, P. (2016). Donald Trump's Deportation Double-Talk. *Washington Post*. Accessed on November 2, 2016, from https://www.washingtonpost.com/blogs/plum-line/wp/2016/09/05/donald-trumps-deportation-double-talk/?utm_term=.015b0e81ae44.

Wall Street Journal Editorial. (2000). They Always Get their Boy, *Wall Street Journal*, April 11.

Wall Street Journal Editorial. (2001). Citizen W., *Wall Street Journal*, July 11.

Warner, B. R., and Ryan, N. (2011). The Polarizing Influence of Fragmented Media: Lessons from Howard Dean. *Atlantic Journal of Communication*, 19(4): 201–215.

Warren, Robert, and Jeffrey S. Passel. 1987. A Count of the Uncountable: Estimates of Undocumented Aliens Counted in the 1980 United States Census. *Demography*, 24(3). Springer: 375–93.

Waters, Mary C. (2011). Debating Immigration: Are We Addressing the Right Issues? In Marcelo M. Suárez-Orozco, Vivian Louie and Roberto Suro (eds.), *Writing Immigration*. Oakland, CA: University of California Press.

186 *References*

Waters, Mary C., and Tomás R. Jiménez (2005). Assessing Immigrant Assimilation: New Empirical and Theoretical Challenges. *Annual Review of Sociology*, 31: 105–125.

Waters, Tony. (1999). *Crime and Immigrant Youth*. Thousand Oaks, CA: Sage.

Week, The. (2016). Hillary Clinton Mocks Donald Trump's "very tall," "beautiful" Wall. The Week. Accessed on November 16, 2016, from http://theweek.com/speedreads/611768/hillary-clinton-mocks-donald-trumps-tall-beautiful-wall.

Weise, David R., Thomas Arciszewski, Jean-François, Tom Pyszczynski, and Jeff Greenberg (2012). Terror Management and Attitudes Toward Immigrants Differential Effects of Mortality Salience for Low and High Right-Wing Authoritarians. *European Psychologist*, 17(1): 63–72.

Welch, R. (2000). Is Anybody Watching? The Audience for Televised Presidential Addresses. *Congress and the Presidency*, 27: 41–58.

Weller, C. (2006). The U.S. Economy in Review: 2006. *The Center for American Progress*. Accessed from https://www.americanprogress.org/issues/economy/news/2006/12/21/2420/the-u-s-economy-in-review-2006/.

Werner, E. (2014). Republicans Mull Response to Obama on Immigration. Politics, Huffington Post. Accessed on November 2, 2016, from http://www.huffingtonpost.com/huff-wires/20141114/us--immigration/.

Whitford, A., and Yates, J. (2009). *Presidential Rhetoric and the Public Agenda: Constructing the War on Drugs*. Baltimore, MD: Johns Hopkins University Press.

Williams, R. (2015). "Multicollinearity" University of Notre Dame. http://www3.nd.edu/~rwilliam/ Last revised January 13, 2015.

Williams, R. (2002). From the "Beloved Community" to "Family Values": Religious Language, Symbolic Repertories, and Democratic Culture. In *Social Movements: Identity, Culture, and the State* (247–65), edited by N. Whittier, D. Meyer, and B. Robnett. New York: Oxford University Press.

Winkler, C. (2006). *In the Name of Terrorism: Presidents on Political Violence in the Post-World War II Era*. Albany: State University of New York Press.

Woehrle, L., Coy, P. and Maney, G. (2008). Contesting Patriotism: Culture, Power and Strategy in the Peace. Rowman & Littlefield.

Wolf, M., and Holian, D. (2006). Polls, Elite Opinion, and the President: How Information and Issue Saliency Affect Approval. *Presidential Studies Quarterly*, 36(4): 584–605.

Wood, B. D. (2009). Presidential Saber Rattling and the Economy. *American Journal of Political Science*, 53(July): 695–709.

Wood, B. D. (2004). Presidential Rhetoric and Economic Leadership. *Presidential Studies Quarterly*, 34: 573–606.

Wood, B. D. (2007). *The Politics of Economic Leadership: The Causes and Consequences of Presidential Rhetoric*. Princeton, NJ: Princeton University Press.

Woods, Joshua (2007). What We Talk about When we Talk about Terrorism: Elite Press Coverage of Terrorism Risk from 1997 to 2005. *Harvard International Journal of Press/Politics*, 12(3): 3–20.

Woods, Joshua (2011a). Framing Terror: An Experimental Framing Effects Study of the Perceived Threat of Terrorism. *Critical Studies on Terrorism*, 4(2): 199–217.

Woods, Joshua (2011b). The 9/11 Effect: Toward a Social Science of the Terrorist Threat. *The Social Science Journal*, 48(1): 1–21.

Woods, Joshua (2012). *Freaking Out: A Decade of Living with Terrorism*. Lincoln: University of Nebraska Press.

Woods, Joshua, and Marciniak, A. (2017). The Effects of Perceived Threat, Political Orientation, and Framing on Public Reactions to Punitive Immigration Law Enforcement Practices. *Sociology of Race and Ethnicity*, 3(2): 202–217.

Woods, Joshua, Jason Manning, and Jacob Matz (2015). The Impression Management Tactics of an Immigration Think Tank. *Sociological Focus*, 48(4): 354–372.

Woods, Joshua, and Damien Arthur (2014). The Threat of Terrorism and the Changing Public Discourse on Immigration after September 11. *Sociological Spectrum*, 34(5): 421–441.

Woods, Robert. (2006). Tobacco's Tipping Point. *Policy Studies Journal*, 34(3): 419–436.

Woolley, J. and Peters, G. (2012). American Presidency Project Online by Gerhard Peters and John T. Woolley. *The American Presidency Project*. http://www.presidency.ucsb.edu/.

Wootson, C. (2016). Paul Ryan: Donald Trump Isn't Planning to Have a Roving "Deportation Force." *Washington Post*, The Fix. Accessed on November 14, 2016, from https://www.washingtonpost.com/news/the-fix/wp/2016/11/13/paul-ryan-donald-trump-isnt-planning-to-have-a-roving-deportation-force/.

Worsham, Jeff. (2006). Up in Smoke. *Policy Studies Journal*. 34(3): 437–452.

Yeager, Matthew G. (1997). Immigrants and Criminality: A Cross-National Review. *Criminal Justice Abstracts*, 29: 143–71.

Yen, Hope (2012). Minorities now Surpass Whites in US Births. *Spartanburg Herald*, May 17.

Yglesias, M. (2014). The Political Upside of Obama's Immigration Plan. Vox. Accessed on November 2, 2016, from http://www.vox.com/2014/11/17/7228539/immigration-politics-2016.

Yum, Young-Ok, and William Schenck-Hamlin (2005). Reactions to 9/11 as a Function of Terror Management and Perspective Taking. *Journal of Social Psychology*, 145(3): 265–286.

Zaller, J. (1992). *The Nature and Origins of Mass Opinion*. Cambridge, UK: Cambridge University Press.

Zats, Marjorie S., and Hilary Smith (2012). Immigration, Crime, and Victimization: Rhetoric and Reality. *Annual Review of Law and Social Science*, 8: 141–159.

Zarefsky, D. (2004). Presidential Rhetoric and the Power of Definition. *Presidential Studies Quarterly*, 34: 607–619.

Index

Note: Page references for figures are italicized

ABC News, 3, 31, 66, *67*, 127
Afghanistan, 100, 143
Alien and Sedition Acts, x–xii
Al Qaeda, 12, 31
American Community Survey (ACS), 5
anti-authoritarian tendencies, 28, 35–36, 118–19, 141, 143–44
anti-immigration groups, 14, 50, 66
Antiterrorism and Effective Death Penalty Act of 1996, 78
Arabs, 38–39, 41, 43, 49, 85, 93, 106, 112, *114*, 116, 144
Asian immigrants, 24, 85, *88*, *111*, *114*, 117
authoritarian tendencies, 28, 35–38, 51, 140, 142
authoritarian turn: in attitudes toward immigration, xvii, 27, 47, 63–66; as cultural elements in news, 48–49; and immigration policy, 99–104; in political culture, 50, 63, 66, 68, 124, 153
authorized immigrants, ix, 5, 17

Bell, Griffen, 56
bin Laden, Osama, 29, 38
Bipartisan Policy Center, 10

Boehner, John, 97
border crossings, 4, 10, 32, 34, 76
Border Patrol, 10, 34, *113*
border security, x, xiii, 1, 6, 9, 10, 33–34, 40, 50, 66, 81–82, 97–98, 100–3, *107*, *109–10*, 113, 115–17, 123, 129, 136, 141, 154
Brownback, Sam, 99, *110*
Bush administration, 9, 31, 33, 35, 42, 49–50, 73, 82, 89, 138. *See also* Bush, George W.
Bush, George W., xvii, 9, 31–33, 49, 68n2, 71, 74, 77, 79–81, 83, 86, 89, 94–95, 101–2, 118n1, 132, 141, 153. *See also* Bush administration
Bush, Herbert W., 134
Byrd, Robert C., 100–2, 110

Cantor, Eric, 97
Caribbean immigrants, 24, 56, 93, 117
Center for Immigration Studies, 6, 21, 127
Center for Migration Studies, 6
Central American immigrants, 4, 23, 79, 85, 93, 117, 128
Cheney, Dick, 31, 118n1

Index

Chinese Exclusion Act, xii–xiii, 49, 131
Chinese immigrants, xii–xiii
Clinton, Hillary, 120, 123–24, 131–32, 135–37, 140, 142, 154
Clinton, William Jefferson, ix, xvii, 71, 74, 76–78, 83, 86–88, 94–95, 96n7, 109, 153. *See also* Clinton administration
Clinton administration, 81, 87. *See also* Clinton, William Jefferson
CNN, 2–3, 66–67, 125–28
congressional immigration hearings, xviii, 97–117, 136; border security frames in, 97–98, 101–3, 107, 109–10, 113, 115–17; coding of, 106–7, 110; criminality frames in, 100, 103, 106, 108–9, 113, 116, 118n2; economic threat frames in, 100, 103, 106, 116; elected official testimony in, 103–4, 107–10, 114–15, 117; illegality frames in, 100, 103, 106, 108–10, 113–14, 116, 118n2; interest group testimony in, 104, 107–8, 111–12, 114–16, 118n2; non-elected bureaucrat testimony in, 108, 110, 113–16, 118n2; number of, 104–6, 108, 112; social identifiers in, 106–7, 111, 116; terrorism frames in, 100, 103, 106–8, 113–17, 118n2
Congressional Record, 52
Corbett, Tom, 98
counterterrorism strategies, xv, 9, 77, 152
criminality frame, 56, 59, *60*, 79, *86*, 87, 92, 94, 116, 118
cultural threat frame, 56–58, *60*, 65
culture of fear, 95, 143, 154
Current Population Survey (CPS), 5, 14
Customs and Border Patrol (CBP), 10, 34, *113*

Daschle, Tom, 100
Deferred Action for Childhood Arrivals (DACA), 133

Democratic Party, ix, 71, 76–78, 81–83, *91*, 93, 100–5, 115, 117, 118n1, 135, 141–43, 145n10, 154. *See also* Democrats
Democrats, 33, 51–52, 84, 119, 122–25, 128, 130, 141. *See also* Democratic Party
Denver Post, 55–56, 60, *61*, *67*
Department of Health and Human Services, 5
Department of Homeland Security, 5–6, 9–11, 30, 33–35, 44, 50, 81, 134. *See also* Immigration and Naturalization Services
DREAM Act (Development, Relief, and Education for Alien Minors), 134–35

echo chamber, 3, 124–28, 132
economic outcomes of immigration, 13–18, *17*, 24, 151
economic threat frame, 56, 59, *60*, 79, *86*, 87, 90
Enhanced Border Security and Visa Entry Reform Act of 2002, xi, 100–101, 107
ethnocentrism, 18
European/Canadian immigrants, 50–51, 58, 60, 62–64, 93
E-Verify, 17–18
Executive Order 9066, x–xi
Executive Order 13228—Establishing the Office of Homeland Security and the Homeland Security Council, 80

FBI (Federal Bureau of Investigation), 11, 32, 38, 76, 80, *113*, 142
Federation for American Immigration Reform, 6
Fox News, 3–4, 125–29

Gallup Organization, 29, 38–40, 74, 97, 121–22, 143
German immigrants, 19, 49
global warming, 126

Index

the Great Depression, ix, 35, 37, 149

Hart-Celler Act, xi
Hispanics, 82, 85, 88, 92–93, 106, *109*, 112, *114*, 117, 133, 139, 141, 145n10
Homeland Security Presidential Directive 2—Combating Terrorism Through Immigration Policies, 9, 32, 79
Houston Chronicle, 55, 60, *61*, 69n8

ICE (U.S. Immigration and Customs Enforcement), 17, 34
illegal immigrants. *See* immigrants, unauthorized
illegality frame, 56, 59, *60*, 79, *86*, 87, 89–90
Immigrant Reform and Control Act of 1986 (ICRA), xi, 5–6
immigrant threat narrative, xii, 49–50, 63–64, 68, 117. *See also* news frames
immigrants, English-language acquisition, 2, 19–21, 24, 27, 48, 56–57, 81, 152
immigrants, perceptions of: crime and, xiii, xviii, 2, 7–9, 23–24, 39, 40, 42–43, 49, 124; culture and, xiii–xiv, 2, 18–24, 35, 40, 47–49, 57, 72, 95; economy and, xiii, xvii, 2, 13–18, 27, 65, 151; jobs and, xii, 13–15, 42, 56, 123–24; national security and, xiii, xvii, 39, 50, 95, 128, 131–32; race and, xi, 21–23, 50–51, 124, 130, 152; terrorism and, xv, 2, 9–13, 28, 30, 41, 44, 122, 132, 151
immigrants, unauthorized ix, 123, 127, 138; citizenship and, xiii, 5, 19, 39, 53 107, 134–35, 140; deportation of, 14, 71 132, 138; numbers of, ix–x, 1–3, 5–6, 17, 23, 83, 123, 137, 151. *See also under* immigrants, perceptions of

Immigration and Naturalization Service (INS), 4, 9, 27, 32–34, 49–50, 52, 80, *107*, *113–14*. *See also* Department of Homeland Security
immigration policy, ix; authoritarian tendencies and, xii, 99–104, 117; border security and, 98, 102, 115–16; immigrant stereotypes and, 39, 41; links to terrorism and, x, 9, 28, 32, 77, 79–81, 83; 9/11 and, xvii, 9–10, 27–28, 32, 34, 73, 79, 83, 98, 117, 154; party control over, xvii, 100–2, 104–5; race and, xi, 38–39, 50, 83. *See also* congressional immigration hearings; *specific acts and executive orders*
immigration-terrorism nexus, 9–11, 59, 77, 131, 153
intergroup conflict theory, 18, 36
Iraq, 89, 126, 143
ISIS, 10–12

Japanese-Americans, xi, 49

Kennedy, Ted, 100, 110
King, Steve, 134

Latin American immigrants, 24, 83, 152
Latinos, xiii, 21, 49
legal immigrants. *See* authorized immigrants
Limbaugh, Rush, 127
Los Angeles Times, 69

Mariel boatlift, 15–16
Mexican border. *See* U.S.-Mexico border
Mexican immigrants, xiii, 18, 21, 43, 80, 130, 137, 140
Middle East, 23, 63, 69n5, 76, 85–86, 88, 93, 151
Migration Policy Institute, 6, 112
MSNBC, 2, 66, *67*, 127, 129
Muslims, 38–39, 41, 43, 49, 85, 93, 106, 112, *114*, 116, 144

National Bureau of Economic Research (NBER), 99
National Council of La Raza, 6, 91, 111
National Immigration Forum, 6
National Immigration Law Center, 6
National Public Radio, 66, *67*
nativist, 1, 18–19, 73
NBC News, 3, 66, *67*, 127
negative frames, xvii, xviii, 2, 47, 50, 53, 55, 57–62, 64–65, 72–75, 82, 84–87, 89–90, 92–94, 96, 99, 106–7, 110, 112–17; economic indicators as predictors of, 74, 90; geographical location as predictors of, 74–75, 90, 116
New America Foundation, 11–13
news frames, xvi–xvii, 2, 13, 31, 42–43, 48–51, 53–54, 64, 150. *See also* negative frames
news media, ix; with conservative slant, 47; immigration threat nexus and, 41, 47, 49, 75; with liberal slant, 47, 51, 54; portrayals of immigrants, xiii, 2, 16, 20, 22, 35, 43, 73, 137; portrayals of terrorism and immigration, xvii, 1–2, 12–13, 30–31, 44, 143–44; use of episodic frames, 18, 31. *See also* immigrant threat narrative; negative frames
New York Times, xvii, 7, 12, 30, 47, 51–56, 59–61, 64–68, 125, 129–32, 150, 153
9/11. *See* September 11, 2001
1980 Refugee Act, xi
1976 Immigration Act, xi
non-European immigrants, 50–51, 55, 58, 60, 62–64
NPR, 125, 147

Obama, Barack, xvii, 11, 31, 71, 74, 82–83, 86, 90, 94–95, 95–96n3, 98, 132–35, 138, 141–42, 144–45, 153
Obama administration. *See* Obama, Barack

Operation Wetback, xi
Orlando shooting, 11, *12*, 122

Pence, Mike, 119, 144n1
Pew Research Center, 5–6, 13, 20, 40, 52, 112, 120–25
Philadelphia Inquirer, 55, 60, *61*, *67*
presidential election of 2016, vi–x, xiii, xviii, 2, 71, 119, 121–24, 129–30, 132–33, 140–44. *See also* Clinton, Hillary; Pence, Mike; Trump, Donald
presidential rhetoric, xvii–xviii, 68, 71–73, 76, 83, 86–89, *91*, 92–95, 116–17, 132, 144, 153–54
psychometric paradigm, 30–32, 120
public perceptions of immigrants. *See* immigrants, perceptions of

radical Islamist frame, 31, 42, 122, 131–32, 151
Reagan, Ronald, 99, 125, 134
refugees, xiii, 5, 10–11, 14, 76, 79, 103, *107*, *109*, *111–12*, 119, 128, 139, 142, 151; Cuban, 14–16; Haitian, 96; Syrian, xviii, 9–11, 119, 124, 132, 141
Reid, Harry, 143
reliability, 57–58, 96, 106
Republican Party, ix, 2, 33, 71, 78, 81–83, 89, *91*, 93, 99–105, 114–16, 118n1, 131, 135, 139, 142–43, 154. *See also* Republicans
Republicans, 3, 10, 18, 51–52, 84, 97–98, 101–2, 117, 119, 122–25, 128, 130, 133–34, 140–41. *See also* Republican Party
residual method, 5–6
Roosevelt, Franklin Delano, x–xi, xiv
Roosevelt, Theodore, 140
Ryan, Paul, 139

San Jose Mercury News, 55, 60, *61*, *67*
September 11, 2001, ix–xi, xiv–xvii; anti-authoritarianism and, 35–36, 43; attitudes toward

immigration and, 39–41, 43–44; authoritarianism and, 36–38, 43–44; immigration policy and, 9–10, 24, 27, 32–34; media and, 44; post-9/11 terrorist attacks and, 11, *12*; terrorism threat perceptions and, 28–32, 44

Smith, Lamar, 56

social amplification framework, xiv–xvi, 148–50

social media, x, 44, 119, 125–26, 128, 144, 147, 150

South American immigrants, 85, 93, 117

southern U.S. border. *See* U.S.-Mexico border

stereotypes, xiv, 13, 31, 39, 48, 50, 120, 123, 136, 144, 149

structural intersectionality, 69

Tea Party, 52, 134

terrorism, threat of, ix–x, xv, xvii, 2, 10, 11, 23, 27, 28, 30, 121, 151; attitudes toward immigration and, 39–44, 49, 100, 119, 120, 124, 144; causes of, 30–32; civil liberties and, 35, 38, 39, 121, 122; institutionalizing and, 32–35; 9/11 and, 28–29, 37–38, 121, 152

terrorism threat frame, 13, 43, *60*, 82, *86*, 89–90, 93, 95, 115, 153

terrorist attacks, xviii, 11–13, 28–31, 33–34, 40, 42–43, 93, 120–21, 128, 144, 154

threat index, 58–62

Trump, Donald, xi–xii; authoritarian culture and, 140; the border wall and, 10, 71, 123, 132, 136–39,

144; deportation and, 39; estimate of immigrant population and, 2–4, 138; exaggerated statistics and, 139, 140, 142; Mexican immigrants and, xiii, 71, 73, 137–38; the Muslim ban and, xi–xii, 122, 131–32, 136, 139–43; the Syrian refugee crisis and, 10–11

undocumented immigrants. *See* unauthorized immigrants

USA Today, 55, 60–61, *67*

U.S. Census Bureau, 5–6, 18, 20–22, 106

U.S. Citizenship and Immigration Services (USCIS), 34, 134

U.S. Immigration and Customs Enforcement (ICE), 17, 34

U.S.-Mexico border, 10, 71, 73, 75, 132, 137. *See also* border crossing; border security

U.S. State Department, 10–11, *113*, 142

Victims of Immigration Crime Engagement (VOICE), 151

Wall Street Journal, xvii, 47, 51–56, 58, 60–61, 64–68, 129–32, 153

War of the Worlds, 147–150, 153

war on terror, x, xv, 32, 42, 49, 81

Washington Post, 30, 55, 60, *61*, *67*

weapons of mass destruction, 68n2, 78, 126

Welles, Orson, 147–149, 153

World Trade Center, 29, 65, 76–77, 129

xenophobia, 2, 27, 73, 144

About the Authors

Joshua Woods is associate professor of sociology in the Department of Sociology and Anthropology at West Virginia University. He received a PhD in sociology from Michigan State University. Josh's research has focused on perceived threats and social attitudes. His publications on this topic include a sole-authored book, *Freaking Out: A Decade of Living with Terrorism*; a co-edited book *America: Sovereign Defender or Cowboy Nation?*; and journal articles in *Sociology of Race and Ethnicity, Brown Journal of World Affairs, Critical Studies on Terrorism, Sociological Focus, Sociological Spectrum, Harvard International Journal of Press/Politics, Human Ecology Review*, and the *Social Science Journal*. He teaches courses in social psychology, media and society, and research methods.

C. Damien Arthur is assistant professor of public administration and policy at Marshall University, in the Department of Political Science and Public Administration. He completed a PhD in political science at West Virginia University and a Master's in public administration as well as an MTS in religion, culture, and personality at Boston University's School of Theology. Damien's research has focused upon leadership, primarily, presidential rhetorical leadership in relation to salient policies such as economics, institutional interaction, and immigration. He is author of *Economic Actors, Economic Behaviors, and Presidential Leadership: The Constrained Effects of Rhetoric*. He has published refereed journal articles in *Presidential Studies Quarterly, White House Studies*, and *Sociological Spectrum*. He is currently writing a comprehensive analysis of Senator Robert C. Byrd's leadership on the Appropriations Committee.

Lightning Source UK Ltd.
Milton Keynes UK
UKOW04n0916200917
309495UK00001B/14/P